Microsoft Access™ For Windows™

Step by Step

Margaret D. McGee
Judy Boyce
Microsoft Corporation

Microsoft PRESS

PUBLISHED BY
Microsoft Press
A Division of Microsoft Corporation
One Microsoft Way
Redmond, Washington 98052-6399

Copyright © 1993 by Microsoft Corporation

Library of Congress Cataloging-in-Publication Data
Microsoft access step by step / Microsoft Corporation.
     p.   cm.
  Includes index.
  ISBN 1-55615-482-8
  1. Data base management. 2. Microsoft Access. I. Microsoft
Corporation.
QA76.9.D3M56 1993
005.75'65--dc20   92-37698
                         CIP

Printed and bound in the United States of America.

1 2 3 4 5 6 7 8 9 MLML 8 7 6 5 4 3

Distributed to the book trade in Canada by Macmillan of Canada, a division of Canada Publishing Corporation.

Distributed to the book trade outside the United States and Canada by Penguin Books Ltd.

Penguin Books Ltd., Harmondsworth, Middlesex, England
Penguin Books Australia Ltd., Ringwood, Victoria, Australia
Penguin Books N.Z. Ltd., 182-190 Wairau Road, Auckland 10, New Zealand

British Cataloging-in-Publication Data available.

This book was produced using Microsoft Word.

Writers: Margaret D. McGee, Judy Boyce
Editors: Jean Farkas, editor; Claudia Mazzie-Ballheim, copy editor
Database and lesson development: Ruth Betza
Design: James St. George, designer; Donna Wallace, production lead

Contents

Lesson 11   **Creating User-Friendly Queries 151**

Lesson 12   **Using Action Queries to Manipulate Data 163**

Part 4 Customizing Your Forms

Lesson 13   **Using Controls to Show Text and Data 179**

Part 6   Customizing Your Reports

Part 7   Automating with Macros

Appendixes

About This Book

Microsoft Access™ is a database application for Microsoft® Windows™ that gives you unparalleled access to information. *Microsoft Access Step by Step* shows you how to take advantage of the power of Microsoft Access to find and manage the information you need.

You can use *Microsoft Access Step by Step* as a tutorial to learn Microsoft Access at your own pace and your own convenience, or you can use it in a classroom setting. As you go through the lessons, you'll get hands-on experience using the practice files on the accompanying disk. Instructions for copying the practice files to your computer's hard disk are given in "Getting Ready" later in this book.

Finding the Best Starting Point for You

This book is designed both for people who are learning Microsoft Access for the first time and for experienced users who want to learn about features they may not have tried out yet. In either case, *Microsoft Access Step by Step* will help you get the most out of Microsoft Access.

The modular design of this book offers you considerable flexibility in customizing your learning. You can go through the lessons in almost any order, skip lessons, and repeat lessons later to brush up on certain skills. Each lesson builds on concepts presented in previous lessons, so you may want to back up if you find that you don't understand the concepts and terminology used in a particular lesson. If the steps in one lesson require that you've completed the steps in an earlier lesson, you're told at the start of the lesson.

The following table recommends starting points depending on your Microsoft Access experience.

If you are	Follow these steps
New to Microsoft Access	Read "Getting Ready" later in this book. Next, work through Lessons 1 and 2 in order. Work through the other lessons in any order.
Experienced with some parts of Microsoft Access	Read "Getting Ready" later in this book. Then complete the lessons that best meet your needs.

Note   If you are new to Microsoft Windows, it would be a good idea to familiarize yourself with the basic elements of Windows before you start the lessons in this book. To review techniques such as how to use a mouse, open a menu, and select options from a menu or dialog box, consult the documentation that comes with Microsoft Windows, or see *Microsoft Windows 3.1 Step by Step*, published by Microsoft Press.

Using This Book As a Classroom Aid

If you're an instructor, you can use *Microsoft Access Step by Step* for teaching Microsoft Access to people who are new to the product and for teaching specific features of Microsoft Access to experienced users. You can choose from the lessons to tailor your classes to the needs of your students.

If you plan to teach the entire book, you should probably set aside three full days of classroom time to allow for discussion, questions, and any customized practice exercises you may create.

Cross-references to the Microsoft Access Documentation

You'll find references to *Microsoft Access Getting Started,* the *Microsoft Access User's Guide*, and online Help throughout this book. These references point you to more information about the task at hand.

- *Microsoft Access Getting Started* explains how to set up and start Microsoft Access. It also uses a series of brief, hands-on sessions with real-life examples to show you how to organize and work with data using Microsoft Access.

- *Microsoft Access User's Guide* is a comprehensive guide to creating and working with a Microsoft Access database. It provides in-depth information and examples to help you build and use a database.

- Online Help provides reference and how-to information for all Microsoft Access tasks. You'll learn more about using Help in "Getting Ready" later in this book.

Getting Ready

While completing the lessons in this book, you'll use the practice files on the accompanying disk to get hands-on practice with Microsoft Access. Follow the steps in "Installing the Step by Step Practice Files" to copy the practice files to your computer's hard disk. Then read through the rest of this section for a general introduction to working with Microsoft Access.

Installing the Step by Step Practice Files

Included with this book is a disk named "Microsoft Access Step by Step Practice Files." The following steps show you how to start Microsoft Windows and use File Manager to copy the PRACTICE directory on this disk with all of its files to the directory on your hard disk where you installed Microsoft Access. For details on installing Microsoft Access, see Chapter 2, "Microsoft Access Basics," in *Microsoft Access Getting Started.*

Start Windows

1 At the command prompt (such as C:\), type **win**

2 Press the ENTER key.

After you start Windows, the Program Manager window appears. You can start all your applications, including Microsoft Access, from Program Manager. (The appearance of your screen may be different from the following illustration, depending on your particular setup.)

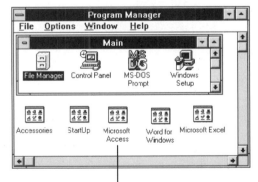

Microsoft Access group

The default installation of Microsoft Access creates a group named Microsoft Access. Double-clicking the Microsoft Access group icon opens the Microsoft Access group window, which contains the icons for Microsoft Access and its related applications.

Copy the practice files to your hard disk

1   Insert the "Microsoft Access Step by Step Practice Files" disk in drive A.

Note   These instructions assume that you are using drive A for the floppy disk and that you have installed Microsoft Access on drive C. If this is not the case, substitute the appropriate drive names.

Main

2   If the Main group isn't already open, open it by double-clicking its icon in the Program Manager window.

The Main window (Your Main window might have a different arrangement depending on your setup.)

File Manager

3   In the Main window, start File Manager by double-clicking its icon.

4   In the File Manager window, click the drive A icon.

Click here to view files on drive A.

5   If you have Windows version 3.0, double-click the A directory icon. This step is not necessary in Windows version 3.1.

6   Click the PRACTICE directory to select it.

Click here to select the PRACTICE directory.

7 From the File menu, choose Copy.

The Copy dialog box appears with PRACTICE in the From box.

8 In the To box, type the name of the directory on your hard disk in which you installed Microsoft Access; for example, **c:\access**

9 In Windows version 3.1, click the OK button or press ENTER. In Windows version 3.0, click the Copy button or press ENTER.

Now you have a subdirectory in your Microsoft Access directory named PRACTICE that contains the *Microsoft Access Step by Step* practice files.

10 To see the practice files, click the drive C icon, double-click the ACCESS directory, and then click the PRACTICE subdirectory.

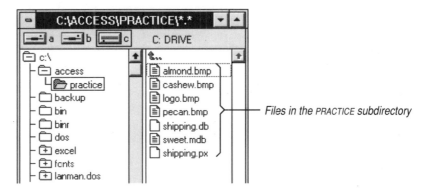

Files in the PRACTICE subdirectory

11 From the File menu, choose Exit to quit File Manager.

For more information about copying the PRACTICE directory using File Manager, see your Microsoft Windows documentation.

Starting Microsoft Access

After you install Microsoft Access and copy the practice files, you can start Microsoft Access.

Start Microsoft Access

Microsoft
Access

1 Double-click the Microsoft Access group icon.

Windows opens the Microsoft Access group.

Microsoft
Access

2 Double-click the Microsoft Access program icon.

The first time you start Microsoft Access after installing it, Microsoft Access displays the Welcome To Microsoft Access box. This box offers you choices on how to get started with Microsoft Access using Cue Cards, an online learning tool. You'll learn more about Cue Cards later in "Getting Ready."

3 If the Welcome To Microsoft Access box is displayed, choose the Close button to close it.

Microsoft Access displays the Microsoft Access startup window. From here, you can create a new database, open a database, or do basic database administration tasks.

What Is a Database?

A *database* is a collection of data that's related to a particular topic or purpose. For example, the database you'll use in this book, called the Sweet database, is a collection of data used to manage a fictional company named Sweet Lil's Chocolates. Sweet Lil's Chocolates sells boxes of gourmet chocolates by phone and mail order.

Microsoft Access is a relational database management system. In a relational database, you can organize data about different subjects into different tables, and then you can create relationships between the tables to bring related data together.

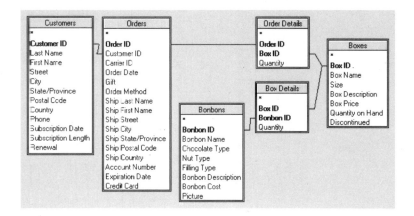

Tables in the Sweet database

In the Sweet database, for example, data about customers is stored in the Customers table and data about orders is stored in the Orders table. The two tables are related to each other, so that Microsoft Access can easily show customer information with related order information (such as a customer's name and phone number with the customer's orders). Later in this book, you'll learn how to create your own relational database, and you'll learn more about the advantages of organizing your data in this way.

Tip   As you go through the lessons, you'll work with all the tables in the Sweet database. For a handy reference of all the tables and their relationships, you might find it convenient to copy the preceding illustration and keep it beside your computer while you work.

The preceding illustration shows all the tables in the Sweet database and all the fields in each table. A *field* is a category of information that describes the subject of the table. When you look at the data in a table, each field is displayed as a column in the table.

Each field in the Boxes table contains data that describes a box of chocolates that Sweet Lil's sells.

Box ID	Box Name	Size	Box Description	Box Price	Quantity on Hand	Discontinued
ALLS	All Seasons	8	Blueberries, raspberries, and strawberries to enjoy all season, both bitter and sweet.	$14.00	700	No
ALPI	Alpine Collection	12	Straight from the high Cascades, alpine blueberries and strawberries in our best chocolate	$20.75	400	No
AUTU	Autumn Collection	16	Family-size box of Autumn favorites--Marzipan Maple, Oakleaf, Finch, and Swallow.	$43.00	200	No

Table: Boxes

Microsoft Access Step by Step

You often use the values in fields to pinpoint just the data you want to see. For example, if you want to see only the 12-ounce boxes, you tell Microsoft Access to show you the boxes with 12 in the Size field. Microsoft Access shows you those boxes and no others. You'll see how this works later in the book.

Using the Practice Files

The practice files include a database file named SWEET.MDB. It contains all the tables, forms, reports, and other database objects used to manage information at Sweet Lil's Chocolates. It's the only database file you'll use in the course of this book, and you'll use it in every lesson. This book refers to the SWEET.MDB database file as "the Sweet database."

The practice files also include:

- ALMOND.BMP, CASHEW.BMP, and PECAN.BMP. These are pictures of bonbons that you'll add to the database in Lesson 2, "Getting the Best View of Your Data."

- LOGO.BMP. This is a picture of Sweet Lil's corporate logo. You'll add this logo to forms in Lesson 14, "Using Pictures and Other Objects," and Lesson 21, "Customizing Your Work Environment."

- SHIPPING.DB and SHIPPING.PX. These are Paradox® files that you'll use in Lesson 7, "Attaching and Importing Data."

Open the Sweet database

1   If necessary, start Microsoft Access.

2   From the File menu, choose Open Database.

Microsoft Access displays the Open Database dialog box.

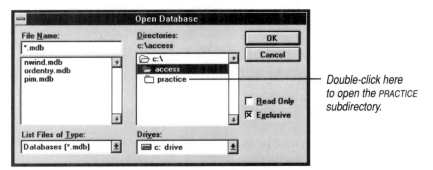

Double-click here to open the PRACTICE subdirectory.

3   In the Directories box, double-click the PRACTICE subdirectory to open it.

If you have no PRACTICE subdirectory, see "Installing the Step by Step Practice Files" earlier in this introduction.

4   In the File Name box, double-click SWEET.MDB.

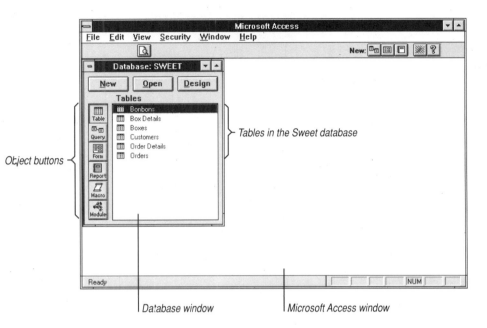

Microsoft Access displays the Database window for the Sweet database in the Microsoft Access window.

The Database window shows the tables that store data about Sweet Lil's business. From the Database window, you can open and work with any object in the database. To work with a table, you double-click the name of the table you want. To work with another type of object, you click the *object button* for the type of object you want. For example, to work with a form, you click the Form object button. Microsoft Access displays a list of forms in the database. Then you can double-click the name of the form you want to use.

Note   Microsoft Access databases are different from Paradox or dBASE® database files. In Paradox and dBASE, each table is a separate .DB or .DBF file, and other objects, such as forms and reports, are also stored in separate files. In Microsoft Access, your data and all the tools you need to use it are stored in the single database file.

Using Menus, Commands, and the Toolbar

You perform many operations in Microsoft Access by choosing a command from a menu or clicking a button on the toolbar.

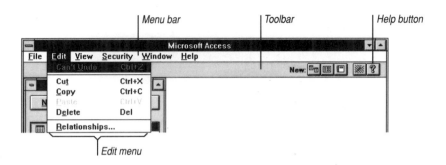

Menu bar   Toolbar   Help button

Edit menu

Menu names appear on the *menu bar*, across the top of the screen. To choose a command, click the menu name and then click the command on the list. The previous illustration shows the commands on the Edit menu in the Database window.

Some commands on menus have a *shortcut key* combination listed to the right of the command name. For example, the shortcut key for the Copy command on the Edit menu is CTRL+C. To use it, you hold down the CTRL key while you press the C key. Microsoft Access runs the Copy command, just as if you had chosen it from the Edit menu. Once you're familiar with the menus and commands, these shortcut keys can save you time.

Located below the menu bar is the *toolbar*. It contains buttons that are shortcuts for choosing commands and for working with Microsoft Access. For example, clicking the Help button is the same as pressing the F1 key to get Help.

The menus and list of commands on a menu and the tools on the toolbar can change depending on the type of information displayed in the active window. For example, if the active window shows the data in a table, the Edit menu contains more commands than if the active window is the Database window, and the toolbar contains more tools.

Tip   To get help on a window's toolbar or menu commands, press SHIFT+F1 when the window is active, and then click the toolbar or select the command you want help with.

If you don't see the toolbar on your screen, first choose Options from the View menu, and then check that Show Tool Bar under the General category is set to Yes. If it is set to Yes and you still don't see the toolbar, Microsoft Access may not be getting enough memory to show the toolbar. Exit Windows, restart your computer, and then start Microsoft Access without other applications running at the same time.

Using Cue Cards

Microsoft Access includes Cue Cards, an online learning tool that provides instructions to help you learn Microsoft Access while you build and use your own database. Cue Cards walk you through a task from start to finish. They provide graphical examples, guidance, and shortcuts to online reference material.

The following steps show you how to start and quit Cue Cards. You can follow them now if you want, or you can wait and try out Cue Cards later, after completing the lessons in this book.

Start Cue Cards

1 From the Help menu, choose Cue Cards.

Microsoft Access displays the main Cue Cards menu. Here you can choose what you want to do first. For an introduction to the parts of a database and how you can use them, choose the last option, entitled "I'm Not Sure."

2 When you finish using Cue Cards, quit Cue Cards by double-clicking the Control-menu box on the Cue Cards window.

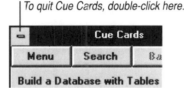

To quit Cue Cards, double-click here.

Getting Help

Help provides reference and how-to information for all Microsoft Access tasks. You can jump from one Help topic to related Help topics. You can also jump from Help to Cue Cards if you need guidance through each step of a task.

Get Help

▶ Press the F1 key.

When you press F1, Microsoft Access shows you Help for the active window, dialog box, or property. For example, if you press F1 in the Database window, Microsoft Access displays a list of topics about creating and using databases.

Searching for a Help Topic

This book and the Microsoft Access documentation contain references to Help for additional information about the task at hand. Sometimes the reference tells you to search Help for a keyword. For example, it might tell you to search Help for "opening tables." To follow the reference, you use the Search command on the Help menu.

Search Help

1 From the Help menu, choose Search. (If the Help window is already open, choose the Search button instead.)

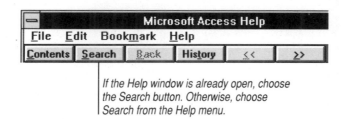

If the Help window is already open, choose the Search button. Otherwise, choose Search from the Help menu.

Microsoft Access displays the Search dialog box.

2 Type the keyword in the dialog box. For example, type **opening tables**

3 Choose the Show Topics button.

Type the keyword here...

```
┌──────────────────── Search ────────────────────┐
│ Type a word, or select one from the list.        ┌─────────────┐
│ Then choose Show Topics.                         │    Close    │
│                                                  └─────────────┘
│ opening tables                                   ┌─────────────┐
│  ┌────────────────────────────────────────┐     │ Show Topics │
│  │ opening tables                       ▲ │     └─────────────┘
│  │ OpenQuery                              │
│  │ OpenQueryDef                           │
│  │ OpenReport                             │
│  │ OpenTable                              │
│  │ operators: arithmetic                ▼ │
│  └────────────────────────────────────────┘
│
│ Select a topic, then choose Go To.              ┌─────────────┐
│                                                  │    Go To    │
│                                                  └─────────────┘
│  ┌────────────────────────────────────────┐
│  │ Create or Open a Table (Cue Cards)     │
│  │ Opening an Existing Table              │
│  │ OpenTable Action                       │
│  │ OpenTable Method                       │
│  │                                        │
│  └────────────────────────────────────────┘
└──────────────────────────────────────────────────┘
```

... and then choose the Show Topics button.

Help displays a list of topics associated with the keyword.

4 In the lower portion of the Search dialog box, double-click the topic you want to read. For example, double-click "Opening an Existing Table."

Microsoft Access displays the Help topic.

5 When you're finished looking at Help, close the Help window.

Double-click here to close the Help window.

```
┌────────────────── Microsoft Access Help ──────────────────┐
│  File    Edit    Bookmark    Help                          │
├────────────────────────────────────────────────────────────┤
│ Contents │ Search │ Back │ History │  <<  │  >>  │
└────────────────────────────────────────────────────────────┘
```

1 Data Basics

Adding Data with a Form

The most convenient place to keep the information you need is right at your desk. You might keep an accumulating stack of paper forms in a file folder next to the phone, as long as the stack doesn't get too big. But you have a problem if you try to keep *all* the information you need at your desk—pretty soon you can't find the desk!

You can use Microsoft Access to organize and store all kinds and quantities of information and have it available, with only a few clicks of your mouse. In this lesson, you'll find out how to open a Microsoft Access database, use a form to add new data, and move from record to record.

You will learn how to:

- Open a database.
- Open a form.
- Enter data.
- Select an option or a check box.
- Move from record to record.
- Open a table.
- Quit Microsoft Access.

Estimated lesson time: 20 minutes

What Is Data?

Data is anything you want to store and refer to again. In Microsoft Access, data can be text, numbers, dates, and pictures. For example, if you sell boxes of bonbons, you can store the names, pictures, and recipes of your bonbons, the prices and quantities of boxes, and the dates of sales.

In most cases, the easiest way to enter data is by using a *form.* Database forms resemble the paper forms we see in offices, find in junk mail, and lose from magazines. You type the data in the form, and Microsoft Access stores it in a table.

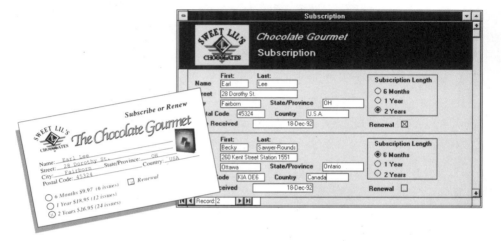

A *record* is a set of information that belongs together, such as all the information on one job application or magazine subscription card. A database can hold many records. The paper form and database form in the preceding illustration each show one record. A chocolate company might keep thousands of such records.

Start Microsoft Access

For information about starting Microsoft Access, see "Getting Ready" earlier in this book.

1   If you quit Microsoft Access at the end of "Getting Ready," or if you are beginning with this lesson, start Microsoft Access.

2   If the Microsoft Access window doesn't fill your screen, maximize the window.

Click here to maximize the Microsoft Access window.

Opening a Database

Sweet Lil's Chocolates, Inc., a fast-growing gourmet chocolate company, has switched to Microsoft Access to store data on its product lines and sales. To attract new customers, Sweet Lil's started a monthly newsletter called *Chocolate Gourmet*. After seeing how much time the database saved and how many errors it prevented, the Newsletter department wants to keep subscription information in the database too.

They've recruited you to be the first person to enter data using a new form called Subscriptions. The Sweet database contains the form you need. You'll open the database, open the Subscription form, and enter subscription data. The records you enter will be stored in the Customers table.

Open a database

1 From the File menu, choose Open Database.

Microsoft Access displays the Open Database dialog box.

2 In the Directories box, double-click the PRACTICE subdirectory to open it.

Double-click here.

The PRACTICE subdirectory is probably in your ACCESS directory. If you need help finding the PRACTICE subdirectory, see "Getting Ready" earlier in this book.

3   In the Filename box, double-click SWEET.MDB.

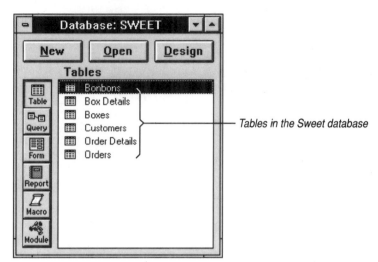

Tables in the Sweet database

Microsoft Access displays the Database window for the Sweet database. It shows the tables that store data about Sweet Lil's business. From the Database window, you can open and work with any object in the database.

Opening a Form

Now that you're in the Sweet database, you can open the Subscription form to enter the subscription information for a new customer.

Open a form

Form button

1   Click the Form button in the Database window.

Microsoft Access displays a list of the forms in the Sweet database.

2   Double-click the Subscription form.

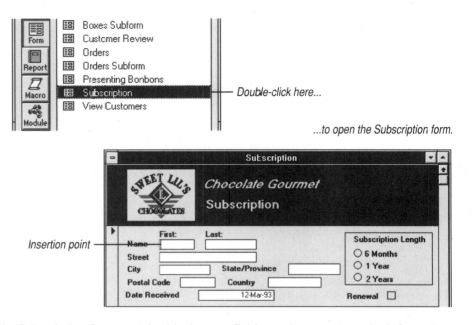

— Double-click here...

...to open the Subscription form.

Insertion point

The Subscription form contains blanks—or fields—where you type the information from the paper form. A *field* is an area on a form where you enter data, such as a space for a last name or an address.

The *insertion point* indicates where the information appears when you type. You can move the insertion point by clicking a different field or by pressing the TAB key. In general, forms are set up so that when you press TAB, the insertion point moves from left to right and from top to bottom.

Notice that Microsoft Access fills in the date in the Date Received field automatically so you don't have to type it.

Entering Data

You'll use the blank Subscription form on your screen to enter the subscription for a *Chocolate Gourmet* fan from Ohio. Here's what his paper subscription form looks like.

Add a name

1 Type **Earl** in the First Name field.

As soon as you start typing, Microsoft Access displays a new blank form below the one you're working in.

If you make a mistake, just press the BACKSPACE key, and then retype.

2 Press TAB to move the insertion point to the Last Name field (or click anywhere in the Last Name field).

You'll find pressing TAB convenient for moving to the next field when your hands are already on the keyboard.

3 Type **Lee** in the Last Name field.

Add an address

▶ Type the following address information, pressing TAB to move from field to field.

Street:	**28 Dorothy**
City:	**Fairborn**
State/Province:	**OH**
Postal Code:	**45324**
Country:	**USA**

You'll continue working on the form in just a minute.

Note From now on, you'll see instructions on how to move to the next field only if you need to do something other than press TAB. For a list of all the keys you can use while editing data in a form, press F1 to open Help, and then click the word Keyboard near the top of the Help window.

Selecting an Option Button or a Check Box

When you press TAB after typing **USA** in the Country field, Microsoft Access draws a dotted line around 6 months in the Subscription Length field instead of displaying the insertion point.

Subscription Length
○ ⌐6 Months⌐ ———— *This option has the focus.*
○ 1 Year
○ 2 Years

Subscription Length is an *option group.* Because an option group presents a set of options to select from, you don't have to type the data yourself — you just select an option. In this case, Earl Lee wants a 2-year subscription.

Select an option button

▶   Click the circle next to 2 Years. (Or press the DOWN ARROW key twice.)

Microsoft Access puts a dot in the button next to 2 Years, indicating that this option is selected.

Next, you'll fill out the Renewal field.

Select a check box

Renewal is a *check box.* When this kind of field is selected, you see an X in the box. Earl Lee's subscription is a renewal.

▶   Click the Renewal check box.

An X is displayed in the box.

Hint   To clear a selected check box, click it again. If you prefer to use the keyboard, you can press the SPACEBAR to select or clear a check box. Try it, and then be sure the check box is selected before continuing.

Moving from Record to Record

All the information in Earl Lee's subscription makes up one complete record. Now that you've entered Earl Lee's subscription, you're ready to start the next subscription.

Depending on the way a form is designed, you can see one or more than one record at a time while you use the form. If you can see the next record, you can move to it by clicking in it. Whether you can see the next record or not, you can move to it by pressing TAB from the last field in the current record (the record you're in now).

Save the record and move to the next record

▶ Click in the First Name field of the next record. (Or, in the Renewal field of the current record, press TAB.)

Microsoft Access saves Earl Lee's subscription information automatically when you go to a new record. You don't have to do anything else to save the first subscription.

Return to the previous record

Looking over your first entry, you notice that you didn't type **St.** in Earl Lee's street address. You'll return to the previous record to make the change.

1 Click after the y in Dorothy in the Street field of Earl Lee's record to return to the record. (Or press the PAGE UP key to go to the first field in the first record, and then press TAB to move to the Street field.)

If you move to a field by pressing TAB, Microsoft Access selects the entire value in the field. To change from the selection mode and place the insertion point at the end of the field, press F2. You can also press SHIFT+TAB to move backward through the fields.

2 Press SPACEBAR to insert a space after Dorothy, and then type **St.**

3 Click in the First Name field of the next record.

Microsoft Access saves your change to Earl Lee's record.

Note   While you were editing Earl Lee's record, you might have noticed that Microsoft Access put a pencil symbol in the area on the left side of the form. The pencil indicates that you've changed data in the current record, but your changes aren't saved yet. If you haven't changed data in the current record, Microsoft Access displays a triangle instead of a pencil. You can see how this works while you add the next record.

Now that you've got the hang of it, you're ready to enter the next subscription from the stack on your desk.

Add the first name

▶ Type **Becky** in the First Name field.

Notice that Becky's last name doesn't look as if it's going to fit in the Last Name field. If you were filling out a paper form, you'd have to squeeze the name in the space. But Microsoft Access forms can handle long names without a squeeze.

Add text to scrollable fields

1 Type **Sawyer-Roundstone** in the Last Name field.

As soon as you type one more letter than fits in the Last Name field, Microsoft Access scrolls the name so you can keep typing. The whole name is saved, even if you can't see it all at once.

2 Type **260 Kent Street Station 1551** in the Street field.

Finish entering the subscription

▶ Type the data below, pressing TAB to move from field to field.

City:	**Ottawa**
State/Province:	**Ontario**
Postal Code:	**K1A 0E6**
Country:	**Canada**
Subscription Length:	**6 months**
Renewal:	**No**

It's almost break time. Before you stop, proofread your entries. When you're finished proofreading, close the Subscription form.

Close the form

▶ Double-click the Control-menu box in the Subscription form's window. (Or from the File menu, choose Close.)

Be sure to double-click the form's Control-menu box, and not the Control-menu box for the Microsoft Access window.

Double-click the form's Control-menu box.

Opening a Table

The records you just added using the Subscription form were saved in the Customers table in the Sweet database. Take a look at your new records in the Customers table.

Display table names in the Database window

Table button

▶ Click the Table button in the Database window.

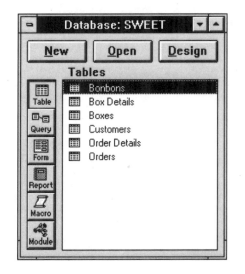

Microsoft Access displays the list of tables in the Sweet database.

Open the Customers table

▶ Double-click the Customers table.

Customer ID	Last Name	First Name	Street	City	State/Province
1	Hanson	Rita	304 King Edward Pl.	East Vancouver	British Columbia
2	Pence	Stephen	312 6th Ave.	Oakland	CA
3	Carter	Dale	14 S. Elm Dr.	Iselin	NJ
4	Jefferson	Walt	23 Tsawassen Blvd.	Tsawassen	British Columbia
5	Morales	M.	1001 West Pender	Vancouver	British Columbia
7	Wojack	Albert	923 West St.	Silver Spring	MD
8	Grant	Arlene	145, rue Châteauneuf	Charlesbourg	Québec
10	Murray	Harold	99 Murphy Way	Altadena	CA

Table: Customers

Microsoft Access opens the Customers table and shows you its records.

The two records you added are at the end of the list of customers. You can use the navigation buttons at the bottom of the form's window to move directly to the first, previous, next, or last record.

Move to the last record

▶ In the lower-left corner of the window, click the navigation button for the last record.

```
      16 Silverman          Frank
 |◄ ◄ Record: 1    ► ►|    ←|
```
Previous record   *Last record (Click here.)*
First record   *Next record*

Microsoft Access displays the last records in the table. The last two records are the ones you just added for Earl Lee and Becky Sawyer-Roundstone. Notice that Microsoft Access automatically assigned Earl and Becky customer ID numbers. You'll learn how to set up a table that automatically assigns ID numbers in Part Two, "Expanding a Database."

Tip   You can use the UP and DOWN ARROW keys, PAGE UP and PAGE DOWN, or the vertical scroll bar to move between records. But the fastest way to move in a large database is with the navigation buttons.

Quitting Microsoft Access

Since you're going on a break, it's best to quit Microsoft Access. That way, no one can damage your data while you're away. You can close the Customers table and quit Microsoft Access all in one step.

Quit Microsoft Access

▸ Double-click the Control-menu box in the Microsoft Access window.

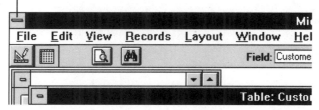

| Double-click the Control-menu box.

Before shutting down, Microsoft Access closes the Customers table (and any other database objects you might have open). If you made changes to the data in the Customers table before exiting, your changes are saved.

One Step Further

You're ready to fill out more subscriptions.

Enter two more subscriptions

1   Start Microsoft Access and open the Sweet database.

2   Open the Subscription form and add the subscriptions in the previous illustration.

Form button

Hint Click the Form button in the Database window to see the list of forms. Then select the Subscription form from the list.

When you're finished entering the records, close the Subscription form and quit Microsoft Access.

Lesson Summary

To	Do this	Button
Open a database	From the File menu, choose Open Database.	
Open a form	In the Database window, click the Form button, and then double-click the form you want to open.	
Select an option in an option group	Click the option, or press the DOWN ARROW key until the option is selected.	
Select or clear a check box	Click inside the box, or tab to the box and then press the SPACEBAR.	
Move from field to field	Click the field you want to move to. Or press TAB to move to the next field; press SHIFT+TAB to move to the previous field.	
Move to the previous record on a form	Press PAGE UP, or click the Previous Record button at the bottom of the form.	
Save data	Microsoft Access automatically saves your data. This usually happens when you move to another record or window, close the form, or exit Microsoft Access.	

Preview of the Next Lesson

In the next lesson, you'll use a form to look at records in two ways: one at a time arranged like a form, and several records at once, arranged like a table in row-and-column format. You'll copy data from one record to another and add a picture to a record.

Getting the Best View of Your Data

The best view of data isn't just one view—it depends on what you're doing at the time. When you add a new product, you might want to see all the details about that product at once. When you review a group of related products, you might prefer seeing all the products in a list. However the data is arranged, you need easy, convenient ways to add and edit data.

Microsoft Access forms have the flexibility to show you both kinds of views. In this lesson, you'll find out how to see different views of data using the same form, and you'll learn more techniques for adding and editing data on a form.

You will learn how to:

- Switch between Form view and Datasheet view of a form.
- Change the way a datasheet looks.
- Copy and move data.
- Select values from a list.
- Insert a picture in a record.

Estimated lesson time: 40 minutes

Understanding Views

A paper form shows one arrangement of your data. To see another arrangement, you have to use another form. A Microsoft Access form provides the flexibility of two views—Form view and Datasheet view. In Form view, the fields are arranged to show individual records to their best advantage. Datasheet view shows the same fields arranged in rows and columns, like a spreadsheet, so you can see multiple records at the same time.

One form...

...with different views

In Datasheet view, you can rearrange columns and resize columns and rows. In either view, Microsoft Access provides powerful editing features you can use to keep your data current.

Start the lesson

▶ Start Microsoft Access. If the Microsoft Access window doesn't fill your screen, maximize the window. Then open the Sweet database.

Switching Between Views of a Form

You've just been put in charge of Sweet Lil's new Fudge Mocha line. You'll use the Bonbons form to update existing records for Fudge Mocha bonbons and to add records for several new bonbons.

Open a form

1 Click the Form button in the Database window.

Microsoft Access displays a list of the forms in the Sweet database.

2 Double-click the Bonbons form.

Microsoft Access opens the Bonbons form and displays the record for Candlelight Ecstasy.

Form button

	Bonbons	
Bonbon Name: Candlelight Ecstasy	**Bonbon ID:** B01	

Description: Cashew in mocha cream covered with bittersweet chocolate, to keep lovers down to earth.

Chocolate Type: Bittersweet / Dark / Fudge / Milk

Filling Type: Mocha cream

Nut Type: Cashew

Cost: $0.30

Record: 1

Record in Form view

In Form view, the fields on the Bonbons form are arranged so you can see all the information about an individual bonbon at a glance. But for your current task, a row-and-column format would make it easier to compare fields from different Fudge Mochas.

Switch to Datasheet view

▶ Click the Datasheet view button on the toolbar.

Microsoft Access displays the records in the Bonbons form in a row-and-column layout.

Datasheet View button

Record in Datasheet view

Bonbon Name:	Bonbon ID:	Description:	Chocolate Type:	Fil
Candlelight Ecstasy	B01	Cashew in mocha c	Bittersweet	Moc
Bittersweet Blueberry	B02	Cascade Mountain	Bittersweet	Blue
Marzipan Oakleaf	B03	Marzipan shaped in	Bittersweet	Marz
Bittersweet Strawberry	B04	Olympic Wilderness	Bittersweet	Stra
Bittersweet Raspberry	B05	Orcas Island raspbe	Bittersweet	Rasp
Bittersweet Marmalade	B06	Marmalade covered	Bittersweet	Marn
Bittersweet Cherry	B07	Royal Anne cherry	Bittersweet	Cher
Hazelnut Bitters	B08	Classic hazelnut co	Bittersweet	None
Almond Supreme	D01	Whole almond han	Dark	None
Heart on a Sleeve	D02	Dark chocolate witl	Dark	Cher
Cashew Supreme	D03	Giant whole cashe	Dark	None
Almond Ambrosia	D04	Classic almond in a	Dark	Amai
Hazelnut Supreme	D06	Whole hazelnut hai	Dark	None
Classic Cherry	D07	Whole cherry in cla	Dark	Cher
Chocolate Kiwi	D08	Brazil nut surrounde	Dark	None
American Beauty	D09	Rich, dark chocola	Dark	None
Marzipan Delight	D11	Delicious marzipan	Dark	Marz
Walnut Fudge Mocha	F01	Sweet creamy moc	Fudge	Moc
Pistachio Fudge Mocha	F02	Sweet creamy moc	Fudge	Moc
Sweet Strawberry	M01	Olympic Wilderness	Milk	Stra
Macadamia Supreme	M02	Whole macadamia	Milk	None
Pistachio Supreme	M03	A cluster of pistach	Milk	None

Record: 1

Fudge Mochas

You can see that two of the bonbons in the new Fudge Mocha line — Walnut Fudge Mocha and Pistachio Fudge Mocha — are already in the database. These are the records you want to work with.

Move to a different record

▶ Click anywhere in the row for Walnut Fudge Mocha.

Marzipan Delight	D11
Walnut Fudge Mocha	F01
Pistachio Fudge Mocha	F02
Sweet Strawberry	M01

The triangle marks the current record.

Now the record for Walnut Fudge Mocha is the *current record*. If you switch back to Form view, that's the record you'll see on the form.

Switch views

1 Click the Form View button on the toolbar to switch to Form view.

Microsoft Access displays the record for Walnut Fudge Mocha in the form.

2 Click the Datasheet View button to return to Datasheet view.

Microsoft Access displays the form in Datasheet view. Walnut Fudge Mocha is still the current record.

Form View button

Datasheet View button

Microsoft Access Step by Step

Changing the Way a Datasheet Looks

The Bonbon Description field describes each bonbon in a sentence or two. You'll include these descriptions in Sweet Lil's catalog, so you want to make sure that the text is just right. With the datasheet laid out as it is now, you can see only part of each bonbon's description. To read an entire description, you'd have to use the arrow keys and the HOME and END keys to scroll through the text.

Description:
Sweet creamy moc
Sweet creamy moc

With rows that show only one line, you use the arrow keys and HOME and END to scroll through the text.

You'll change the datasheet's layout so you can read the entire description at once.

Description:
Sweet creamy mocha and walnut.
Sweet creamy mocha and pistachio.

When you make the rows high enough to show more than one line, the text wraps.

To change the height of rows in a datasheet, you use the *record selectors* on the left side of the records. You use the *field selector* at the top of a column to change the column's width.

Field selectors

Bonbon Name:	Bonbon ID:
Candlelight Ecstasy	B01
Bittersweet Blueberry	B02
Marzipan Oakleaf	B03

Record selectors

You'll start by changing the row height, so you can see all of a bonbon's description at once.

Change the height of rows in a datasheet

1   Position the pointer on the lower border of any record selector (on the left side of the record).

Candlelight Ecstasy
Bittersweet Blueberry

The pointer changes shape to show that you can resize the rows.

2 Drag the border down to make the rows higher. (*Dragging* an object means that you position the pointer over the object, hold down the mouse button while you move the mouse, and then release the mouse button when the object is where you want it to be.)

Microsoft Access resizes all the rows. (You can't resize just one row.)

3 If necessary, adjust the height of the rows until you can read the entire description for Bittersweet Blueberry.

Now that you've resized the rows, you'll adjust the width of some of the columns.

Change the width of a column in a datasheet

The column for the Bonbon ID field is wider than necessary. If you make the column narrower, you'll be able to see more of the other fields in the datasheet.

1 Position the pointer on the right border of the field selector for the Bonbon ID field.

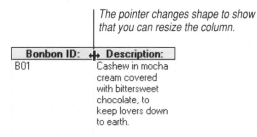

The pointer changes shape to show that you can resize the column.

2 Drag the border to the left to make the column narrower.

Next, you'll make the Cost field narrower.

3 Click in the scroll bar at the bottom of the form's window to see the rest of the fields.

Click here.

Microsoft Access scrolls the columns. (To scroll just one field at a time, click the arrows at either end of the scroll bar.)

4 Make the column for the Cost field narrower by dragging the right border of its field selector to the left.

Hide a column

The column for the Picture field doesn't show pictures for the bonbons in this view. (You can see pictures on forms in Form view, but not in Datasheet view.) Since the pictures aren't visible anyway, you might as well hide the Picture column.

▶ Drag the right border of the Picture column all the way to its left border.

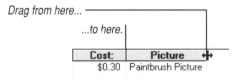

Microsoft Access hides the column.

Tip   To display hidden columns, choose the Show Columns command from the Layout menu. (If the Show Columns dialog box indicates the column is already showing, then it may not be completely hidden. Check to make sure you dragged its right border *all the way* to its left border.)

Notice that the Layout menu also contains a Hide Columns command. That command hides whatever column contains the insertion point when you choose the command. If you experiment with the Hide Columns command, be sure to use the Show Columns command to show any columns you've hidden (other than the Picture column) before continuing the lesson.

Freeze a column

Notice that when you scroll to the fields on the right side of the datasheet, you can't see the Bonbon Name field, so you can't tell which bonbon records you're viewing. It would be more convenient to be able to scroll horizontally through the fields with the Bonbon Name field anchored, or frozen, on the left. You can do that by freezing the column.

1   Scroll back to the left side of the form.

Click here.

2   Click in any row in the Bonbon Name column.

3   From the Layout menu, choose Freeze Columns.

Microsoft Access displays a bold line on the right border of the Bonbon Name column. Now the column is frozen.

4 Scroll horizontally to see the fields on the right side of the record, and then scroll back to the left side of the form.

This column doesn't scroll.   *All other columns scroll.*

Bonbons			
Bonbon Name:	**Filling Type:**	**Nut Type:**	**Cost:**
▶ Candlelight Ecstasy	Mocha cream	Cashew	$0.30
Bittersweet Blueberry	Blueberry	None	$0.25

Save the layout of a form's datasheet

You can save this convenient layout so the datasheet appears this way every time you use it.

▶ From the File menu, choose Save Form.

Scroll through a set of records

You're ready to work with the records in the Fudge Mocha line. But now that you've widened the rows in your datasheet, the records you want aren't visible. You can use either the vertical scroll bar or the PAGE DOWN key to scroll through the records.

1 Click below the scroll box in the vertical scroll bar. (Or press PAGE DOWN.)

— *Scroll box*

— *Click here.*

Microsoft Access scrolls down one page (window).

2 Continue to click below the scroll box until you see the Fudge Mochas in the list.

Notice that each time you click below the scroll box, the box moves down the scroll bar to show your relative position in the records. To scroll up or down just one record at a time, click the arrows at the top or bottom of the scroll bar.

Bonbons			
Bonbon Name:	**Bonbon ID:**	**Description:**	**Chocolate Type:**
▶ Walnut Fudge Mocha	F01	Sweet creamy mocha and walnut.	Fudge
Pistachio Fudge Mocha	F02	Sweet creamy mocha and pistachio.	Fudge
Sweet Strawberry	M01	Olympic Wilderness	Milk

Fudge Mochas

Tip   If you know the relative position of the records you're looking for, you can move to them very quickly by *dragging* the scroll box. For example, if you're looking for a record in the middle of the list, drag the scroll box to the middle of the vertical scroll bar. When you release the mouse button, Microsoft Access displays the records in the middle of the list.

Copying and Moving Data

You keep a database current and accurate by updating data in fields. Microsoft Access has convenient editing features that help you edit, move, copy, and delete data in fields. Not surprisingly, you'll find most editing features on the Edit menu.

When you edit in Microsoft Access, keep in mind a principle called *select and do*. If you want to copy, delete, or change something, you first *select* it, and then you *do* it by choosing the action you want from the menu or by using shortcut keys.

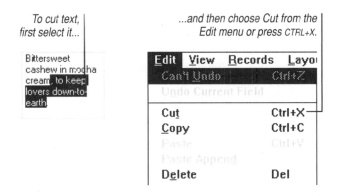

To cut text, first select it...

...and then choose Cut from the Edit menu or press CTRL+X.

When you cut or copy text or an object, Microsoft Access stores it in the Windows storage area called the *Clipboard*. When you paste, Microsoft Access pastes whatever is on the Clipboard at the current location of the insertion point. You can copy text from one field and then paste it into another field or into as many other fields as you need. That's because Windows keeps the Clipboard contents until you copy or cut something else.

Add text to a field

Market research tells you that chocolate fudge is a key ingredient for the success of your new line. You'll add the phrase "smothered in fudge" to the end of each bonbon's description.

1 In the Description field for the Walnut Fudge Mocha bonbon, click between the "t" in walnut and the period.

Microsoft Access places the insertion point where you click.

2 Press the SPACEBAR to insert a space, and then type **smothered in fudge**

Copy text from one field to another

Rather than type the phrase again, you can copy it to the Description field for the Pistachio Fudge Mocha bonbon.

1 Select the phrase "smothered in fudge," including the space in front of "smothered."

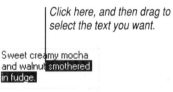

2 From the Edit menu, choose Copy. (Or press CTRL+C.)

Microsoft Access places a copy of the selected text on the Clipboard.

3 In the Description field for the Pistachio Fudge Mocha bonbon, position the insertion point between the "o" in pistachio and the period.

4 From the Edit menu, choose Paste. (Or press CTRL+V.)

Microsoft Access pastes the text from the Clipboard.

Note You use the same steps to move text, except you choose Cut instead of Copy from the Edit menu. Microsoft Access removes the text and places a copy of it on the Clipboard. Then you can paste the text where you want it.

Switch to Form view

Next, you'll enter records for Sweet Lil's three new fudge mochas — Pecan, Cashew, and Almond. You can add new records in either Datasheet view or Form view, but it's easier in Form view because you can see all the fields in a record at once.

Form View button

▶ Click the Form View button on the toolbar.

Microsoft Access displays the Bonbons form in Form view.

Begin a record

There's a new, blank record after the last record. You can use the navigation buttons to go to it quickly.

1 Click the navigation button for the last record, and then click the navigation button for the next record.

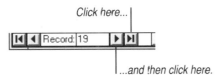

Click here...

...and then click here.

Microsoft Access displays the new record at the end of the records.

2 Type this data in the first two fields:

Bonbon Name: **Pecan Fudge Mocha**
Bonbon ID: **F03**

3 In the Description field, type **Creamy sweet mocha and nutty pecan**

The next part of the description, "smothered in fudge," is still on the Clipboard. Instead of typing it, you can paste it again.

4 Choose Paste from the Edit menu. (Or choose CTRL+V.)

5 Type a period at the end of the description.

Delete text

"Nutty" is redundant as an adjective for "pecan," so you'll delete it.

▶ Select the word "nutty" and the space after it, and then press the DEL key.

Tip To quickly select a word, double-click it.

Replace text

To match the other Fudge Mocha descriptions, you want this description to start with "Sweet creamy" rather than "Creamy sweet." You can replace the old text at the same time that you type the new text, without deleting it first.

1   Select "Creamy sweet" in the Description field.

2   Type **Sweet creamy**

Microsoft Access replaces the selected text with the text you type.

Now your description is correct.

Selecting Values from Lists

A *value* is an individual piece of data, such as a last name, an address, or an ID number. Selecting a value from a list is often quicker than typing the value yourself. But lists have another advantage besides speed—they help keep your data accurate. When you select a value from a list, you know it's spelled consistently and that it's a valid entry.

The Chocolate Type field on the Bonbons form is a special kind of field called a *list box*. List boxes display a list of values to select from. You can use either the mouse or the keyboard to select a value from the list.

The Nut Type and Filling Type fields are both *combo boxes*. With a combo box, you can either type the value yourself or select it from the list.

List boxes always display their lists.

You open a combo box to display its list.

Select a value in a list box

▶   In the Chocolate Type field, select Fudge. (Click Fudge to select it, or press TAB to move to the Chocolate Type field, and then type **f**.)

"Fudge" is the only value in the Chocolate Type list box that starts with f, so you can select Fudge by typing the first letter of the word. If the list box had more than one f value, you could type **f** to go to the first one and then use the DOWN ARROW key to move down the list.

Select a value in a combo box

You can either type the value you want in the Filling Type combo box, or you can select a value from the list. Often, it's easier and more accurate to select a value from the list.

1   Click the arrow in the Filling Type field to display the list. (Or press TAB to move to the Filling Type field, and then press F4.)

Filling Type:			— *Click here.*

Filling Type:

Nut Type:

Cost:

Record: 42

Amaretto
Blueberry
Cherry cream
Cherry, whole
Coconut
Marmalade
Marzipan
Mocha cream

This list shows you the fillings that Sweet Lil's uses.

2   Select Mocha cream from the list.

To select the value without using the mouse, type **mo**, the first two letters in Mocha. Because Mocha cream is the only value that starts with those two letters, Microsoft Access selects it. If you wanted to select Marmalade instead of Marzipan, you'd type **marm** (The list must be open for you to select the value by typing its first letters.)

3   Type **Pecan** in the Nut Type field or select it from the list.

Enter the bonbon cost

▶   Type **.25** in the Bonbon Cost field, and then press TAB to move to the last field on the form.

Notice that when you leave the Bonbon Cost field, Microsoft Access automatically formats the value to show that it's a currency value.

You're ready to add the last value to this record—the bonbon's picture.

Inserting a Picture in a Record

You can store most any kind of information in your database, including pictures, graphs, sounds, and other objects from other applications. An *OLE object* is any piece of information created with an application for Windows that supports *object linking and embedding* (OLE). Microsoft Access stores OLE objects in a field in a table. You can store a different OLE object in each record, just as you can store a different name or address in a text field for each record. You can display the objects in any form or report.

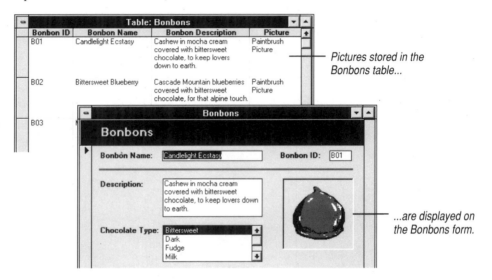

Pictures stored in the Bonbons table...

...are displayed on the Bonbons form.

The Picture field on the Bonbons form is a special type of field called an *object frame*. You use this type of field to add, edit, or view OLE objects in your tables.

Note   To do the steps in this section, you must be using Windows version 3.1 or later, because Windows 3.1 comes with a version of Paintbrush that supports OLE. The version of Paintbrush™ that comes with Windows version 3.0 does not support OLE. If you're using Windows 3.0, you can still add pictures you've created with Paintbrush to your database by copying and pasting the pictures between Paintbrush and your form. For more information, search Help for "copying OLE objects."

Add a picture to a record

The picture for Pecan Fudge Mocha is in a file called PECAN.BMP. You'll *insert* the picture in the record for Pecan Fudge Mocha.

1   With the Picture field selected, choose Insert Object from the Edit menu.

```
┌─────────────────────────────────────────────┐
│ ─            Insert Object                    │
│ Object Type:                                  │
│ ┌──────────────────────────────┐ ┌─────────┐ │
│ │Equation                    ▲ │ │   OK    │ │
│ │Microsoft Drawing             │ └─────────┘ │
│ │Microsoft Excel Chart         │ ┌─────────┐ │
│ │Microsoft Excel Macrosheet    │ │ Cancel  │ │
│ │Microsoft Excel Worksheet   ▼ │ └─────────┘ │
│ └──────────────────────────────┘ ┌─────────┐ │
│                                   │ File... │ │
│                                   └─────────┘ │
└─────────────────────────────────────────────┘
```

Microsoft Access displays the Insert Object dialog box.

2   Scroll down the list of object types and select Paintbrush Picture.

If you were going to draw the picture yourself, you'd choose the OK button now or double-click Paintbrush Picture, and Paintbrush would start with an empty drawing area for you to draw your picture. But since the picture already exists in a file, you'll tell Microsoft Access where to find it instead.

3   Choose the File button.

Microsoft Access displays the Insert Object From File dialog box. The PECAN.BMP file was copied to your PRACTICE directory when you copied the practice files to your hard disk.

You'll learn more about using OLE in Microsoft Access in Lesson 14,"Using Pictures and Other Objects."

4   If necessary, use the Directories list to switch to the PRACTICE directory, and then double-click PECAN.BMP.

```
┌────────────────────────────────────────────────────┐
│ ─                   Bonbons              ▼  ▲       │
│ ┌──────────────────────────────────────────┐ ▲     │
│ │ Bonbons                                   │       │
│ │                                           │       │
│ │ Bonbon Name: [Fecan Fudge Mocha]   Bonbon ID: [F03]│
│ │                                           │       │
│ │ Description:   Sweet creamy mocha and   ┌──────┐  │
│ │                pecan smothered in fudge.│      │  │
│ │                                         │      │  │
│ │                                         └──────┘  │
│ │                                           │       │
│ │ Chocolate Type: [Dark              ▲]     │       │
│ │                  Fudge                    │       │
│ │                  Milk                     │       │
│ │                  White             ▼]     │       │
│ └──────────────────────────────────────────┘       │
└────────────────────────────────────────────────────┘
```

Microsoft Access inserts the picture in the Picture field.

One Step Further

You're ready to add the other two fudge mocha bonbons to the database. Before you start, here's a tip for fast data entry: You can use the Ditto key, CTRL+' (single quote), as a speedy way to fill in fields with the same or similar values as in the previous record.

For example, the Description fields in the Fudge Mocha line are all alike except for the type of nut. You could copy and paste the description and then edit it, but using the Ditto key is faster. When you move to a field and then press CTRL+', Microsoft Access automatically fills in the value from the same field in the previous record. Then you can edit the value if necessary.

Add two more records

▶ Use the Bonbons form to add the records for Cashew Fudge Mocha and Almond Fudge Mocha to the database. The following tables show the data for the two records. Use the Ditto key to speed up your work.

Remember that to display a new, empty record, you click the navigation button for the last record and then click the button for the next record. The navigation buttons are in the lower-left corner of the window.

Field	Data
Bonbon Name	**Cashew Fudge Mocha**
Bonbon ID	**F04**
Description	**Sweet creamy mocha and cashew smothered in fudge.**
Chocolate Type	**Fudge**
Filling Type	**Mocha cream**
Nut Type	**Cashew**
Cost	**.24**
Picture	**CASHEW.BMP**

Field	Data
Bonbon Name	**Almond Fudge Mocha**
Bonbon ID	**F05**
Description	**Sweet creamy mocha and almond smothered in fudge.**
Chocolate Type	**Fudge**
Filling Type	**Mocha cream**
Nut Type	**Almond**
Cost	**.19**
Picture	**ALMOND.BMP**

Edit a picture

If you're using Windows version 3.1, you can edit a bonbon's picture directly from the Bonbons form.

The background of the picture for Almond Fudge Mocha doesn't match the other bonbon pictures, which all have light gray backgrounds. You'll fix the Almond Fudge Mocha picture to be like the others.

1 In the record for Almond Fudge Mocha, double-click the Picture field.

Microsoft Access starts Paintbrush and displays the picture in the Paintbrush window.

Paint roller tool

2 Change the background to light gray. (First, click the light gray color in the Palette at the bottom of the window, and then click the paint roller tool. With the paint roller tool selected, click the white background of the picture. If you make a mistake, choose the Undo command from the Edit menu.)

For help using Paintbrush, press F1, or see your Windows documentation.

3 When you're finished editing the picture, choose the Exit & Return To Microsoft Access command from the File menu. When Paintbrush asks if you want to update the picture, choose Yes.

Close the form

▶ When you're finished with the lesson, save and close the Bonbons form.

Lesson Summary

To	Do this	Button
Switch between Form view and Datasheet view	Click the Datasheet View button or the Form View button on the toolbar.	▦ ▦
Change the height of rows or the width of a column in a datasheet	Drag the border of any record selector to resize rows; drag the right border of the column's field selector to resize a column.	
Hide a column in a datasheet	Drag the right border of the column's field selector all the way to its left border.	
Show hidden columns in a datasheet	From the Layout menu, choose Show Columns.	
Freeze the leftmost column or columns in a datasheet	Select the column or columns, and then choose Freeze Columns from the Layout menu.	
Copy text from one field to another	Select the text; choose Copy from the Edit menu; place the insertion point where you want the text to be in the other field; and then choose Paste from the Edit menu.	
Move text from one field to another	Same as copying, but use the Cut command instead of the Copy command.	
Insert a picture in a record	Move to the field that will contain the picture, and then choose Insert Object from the Edit menu.	
Edit a Paintbrush picture in a field (Windows version 3.1 only)	Double-click the picture.	
Fill in a field with the value from the same field in the previous record	Move to the field you want to fill in, and then press CTRL+'.	

For more information on	See
Using a form to enter and edit data	Chapter 14, "Adding and Editing Data," in the *Microsoft Access User's Guide*.
Keyboard shortcuts for data entry	Open a form in Form or Datasheet view, press F1, and then click the word Keyboard.
Adding and editing OLE objects in your database	Chapter 13, "Using Pictures, Graphs, and Other Objects," in the *Microsoft Access User's Guide*.

Preview of the Next Lesson

In the next lesson, you'll use the Sweet Boxes form to add a new box of bonbons to the database. This form contains a subform that shows which bonbons are in each box.

Saving Time with Forms

When you fill out a paper form, it's easy to make a small mistake that wastes a lot of time later, when you're ready to use the information. A simple subtraction error can result in a frustrating hour checking figures; a forgotten bit of information can eat up time while you look for the missing information and record it correctly. What you need is a form that does calculations for you, looks up missing information, and warns you if the data you enter isn't correct.

Microsoft Access forms can do all this for you. In this lesson, you'll find out how to use forms that help you start with the right data — and stay with it.

You will learn how to:

- Use a form with a subform to add and change data.
- Use a validation message to help you enter the right data.
- Undo your edits.
- Use a command button to perform a complicated task.
- Delete a record.

Estimated lesson time: 20 minutes

Understanding Forms with Subforms

The form you'll use in this lesson — Boxes — is more complex than either the Subscription form or the Bonbons form that you used in the first two lessons. But with Microsoft Access forms, "more complex" doesn't necessarily mean "harder."

You'll learn how to create a form with a subform in Lesson 15, "Showing Related Records and Calculations on Forms."

The Boxes form contains a *subform* that displays the contents of each box of bonbons. That means you can look at information about the whole box on the main form at the same time you look at information about the bonbons in the box on the subform. You can scroll through the records in the subform, adding and deleting bonbons, until the box has the contents you want.

| The main form displays data about the box of bonbons. | The subform displays data about the bonbons in the box. |

The advantage of using a form with a subform is that you can work with data from two different tables at the same time. In the Boxes form, data you enter on the main form is stored in the Boxes table. Data you enter on the subform is stored in the Box Details table.

Start the lesson

▶ Start Microsoft Access. If the Microsoft Access window doesn't fill your screen, maximize the window. Then open the Sweet database.

Adding a Record to a Form with a Subform

You'll use the Boxes form to add a new box of bonbons called Winter Collection to Sweet Lil's line of products.

Open a form and go to the new record

Form button

1 Open the Boxes form. (If tables are currently listed in the Database window, be sure to click the Form button first. Otherwise, you'll open the Boxes table instead of the Boxes form.)

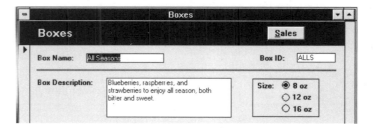

Microsoft Access displays the record for All Seasons — the first box in the Boxes table. You need to go to the new record at the end of the records.

2 Click the navigation button for the last record, and then click the navigation button for the next record.

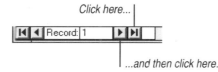

Click here...

...and then click here.

Microsoft Access displays the new record at the end of the records.

Enter data in the main form

1 Type the following data in the fields on the main form:

Box Name:	**Winter Collection**
Box ID:	**WINT**
Box Description:	**Nuts and berries coated with chocolate and fudge for those long winter evenings by the fire.**

2 Select 12 oz in the Size option group.

3 Press the TAB key to move to the subform.

Microsoft Access moves the insertion point to the first field in the subform. You'll add six different bonbons to the Winter Collection, each one containing either berries or nuts.

Enter a record in the subform

The first field in the subform will contain the Bonbon ID for the first bonbon in the Winter Collection box. The bonbon you want is Bittersweet Blueberry, but you're not sure of its ID number. The ID combo box can help you find the ID you want.

1   Open the list for the ID combo box.

Click here.

You'll learn how to create a combo box like this in Lesson 16, "Providing Choices in Combo Boxes."

The list shows two columns: IDs in the first column and the corresponding bonbon name in the second column. When you select a row, only the ID gets stored in the field. The names are there to help you make the right selection.

2   Select the row for Bittersweet Blueberry.

Microsoft Access puts the Bonbon ID, B02, in the ID field and fills in the Bonbon Name, Chocolate, Nut, Filling, and Cost fields automatically. Notice that this form was designed so that the fields you fill in are displayed in white, and all others have a gray background.

3   Press the TAB key to move to the next field.

Microsoft Access skips the fields that are already filled in and moves the insertion point to the Qty field.

4   Type **3** in the Qty field, and then press TAB.

Microsoft Access saves the first record in the subform and moves the insertion point to the first field in the second record.

Note   While you add the remaining bonbons to the subform, notice that the Box Cost field in the lower-left corner of the main form changes for each new record in the subform. How much a box costs Sweet Lil's depends on which bonbons are in the box. The Boxes form figures the box cost automatically while you're adding bonbons to the box.

Enter more subform records

1   Add these two bonbons to the Winter Collection.

ID		Qty
B05	Bittersweet Raspberry	**3**
D03	Cashew Supreme	**3**

The record for the Cashew Supreme bonbon fills up the subform, but you have two more bonbons to add to the box. Notice the vertical scroll bar on the right side of the subform. That means the subform can contain more records, and you can scroll up and down through the records to see them.

2 After filling in the quantity of the Cashew Supreme record, press TAB to go to the next record in the subform.

The subform scrolls to show another new, blank record.

3 Add these three bonbons to the Winter Collection.

ID		Qty
D07	Classic Cherry	3
F01	Walnut Fudge Mocha	3
F02	Pistachio Fudge Mocha	3

4 When you're finished adding the records, scroll up and down in the subform to check your work. Make sure each record is correct before going on.

Moving out of a subform

Now that you've added all the bonbons to the new box, you're ready to fill in the fields in the lower portion of the main form—Box Price and Quantity on Hand.

▶ Press CTRL+TAB to move to the next field on the main form.

Microsoft Access moves the insertion point out of the subform to Box Price, on the main form. You can also move to the Box Price field by clicking it, but when you're entering new records, it's often easier to keep your hands on the keyboard rather than move back and forth between the mouse and the keyboard.

Tip When you're using a form with a subform, you can think of the CTRL key as the "subform" key. Just as pressing TAB moves you to the next field within a subform or main form, pressing CTRL+TAB moves you from the subform to the next field in the main form. And just as pressing SHIFT+TAB moves you to the previous field within a subform or main form, pressing CTRL+SHIFT+TAB moves you from the subform to the previous field in the main form.

Entering the Right Data

You've already seen a number of ways that a Microsoft Access form can help you enter the right data. For example, the ID combo box in the subform helps you pick the right ID by showing you bonbon names as well as IDs. Once you pick a bonbon, Microsoft Access automatically fills in fields such as the Bonbon Name and Chocolate fields, saving you time and the possibility of data entry errors in those fields. And while you're adding bonbons to the box, Microsoft Access automatically figures the cost of the box and displays it in the Box Cost field, saving you the effort of making the calculation yourself.

A form can also help you enter the right data by displaying a message when you enter incorrect information.

Get help correcting wrong data

The note you have from Sweet Lil's Marketing department says to start the new box at the special introductory price of $7.50.

1   Type **7.50** in the Box Price field, and then press TAB.

Microsoft Access displays a validation message that tells you the value you entered is incorrect and gives you information on how to correct the problem.

```
┌─────────────────────────────────────────────────────────┐
│ ▬ │           Microsoft Access                          │
├─────────────────────────────────────────────────────────┤
│  ┌─┐   Box price too low. Check with the Marketing department for │
│  │!│   pricing information, and then enter a price that's at least box │
│  └─┘   cost times 2.                                     │
│                                                          │
│              ┌────────┐    ┌────────┐                    │
│              │   OK   │    │  Help  │                    │
│              └────────┘    └────────┘                    │
└─────────────────────────────────────────────────────────┘
```

Note   If the message doesn't appear, the problem may be in the Box Cost field. The Box Price field checks the value in the Box Cost field and displays its message if the price is less than twice the cost. The Box Cost field is calculated automatically from the records entered in the subform. If you don't see the message, check to make sure you entered the subform records correctly.

2   Press the OK button.

After calling the Marketing department, you find out that they made a mistake on their note and meant to start the box at $17.50.

3   Add a **1** before the 7 in the Box Price field, and then press TAB.

Microsoft Access accepts this price, adds a dollar sign, and moves the insertion point to the Quantity on Hand field.

4   Type **0** (zero) in the Quantity on Hand field.

This is a new box, so you don't have any in stock yet.

Note   Microsoft Access rejected the price of $7.50 because the Box Price field has a *validation rule* attached to it. Microsoft Access checks the value you enter in the field against the rule, and if the value breaks the rule, displays a message. You can't leave the field until you correct the invalid data.

But suppose you need to look up a value on a different form before you can correct the error. You have to leave the current form to correct the error, but Microsoft Access won't let you leave the form as long as the invalid data you entered is still there. In that case, choose the OK button when Microsoft Access displays the message, and then press the ESC key. Microsoft Access replaces your value with the value that the field started out with (in this example, the field was empty), and then treats the field as if you had never changed it. Now you can leave the field or form.

Undoing Your Edits

Have you ever wanted to take back something you said as soon as you said it? The same thing often happens when you update data on a form. With Microsoft Access forms, you *can* take it back. You can use the Undo button on the toolbar to undo your most recent action, and you can use the Undo commands on the Edit menu to undo other recent actions.

Make changes and then undo your most recent action

1 Replace "Nuts and berries" at the beginning of the description for the Winter Collection with **Berries and nuts**

2 Add **roaring** in front of "fire."

After looking over the changes, you decide that "roaring" doesn't sound quite right.

3 Click the Undo button on the toolbar.

Microsoft Access deletes "roaring," your most recent change.

Undo button

Undo all edits in the current field

After making numerous changes to the text in a field, you might decide that you prefer the original text.

▶ From the Edit menu, choose Undo Current Field.

Microsoft Access undoes all the edits you made to the field since moving the insertion point into the field.

Using a Command Button

Sometimes one task turns into many related tasks. For example, you might be looking at information about the contents of a product on one form and realize that you want to see sales information for the product, too. So you open a sales form and find the appropriate sales information. This related task can require a number of steps to complete.

A *command button* on a form condenses related tasks like these into a single step: pushing the command button. A command button can perform one action or a whole series of actions, depending on how the button's defined.

Now that you've added the Winter Collection box to the database, you'll use a command button to check on the sales of one of Sweet Lil's best sellers — the Autumn Collection.

Go to a specific record

The Autumn Collection is the third box in the Boxes table.

1   Type **3** in the Record Number box between the navigation buttons in the lower-left corner of the window.

> |◄◄| |◄| Record: 3 |►| |►►|
>
> └ Replace the current record number with 3.

2   Press the ENTER key.

Microsoft Access displays the record for the Autumn Collection — the third record in the table.

Use a command button to perform a task

The Boxes form shows the contents of the Autumn Collection box. You can use the Sales command button to see the sales for this box.

1   Click the Sales button at the top of the Boxes form.

Click the Sales button to open the Box Sales form... |

Boxes

Boxes   [Sales]

Box Name: Autumn Collection   **Box ID:** AUTU

Box Sales

Box Sales

Box Name: Autumn Collection   **Box ID:** AUTU

Size: ○ 8 oz
      ○ 12 oz
      ● 16 oz

Daily Sales

Order Date	Qty	Box Price	Ext Price
02-Nov-92	3	$43.00	$129.00
04-Nov-92	2	$43.00	$86.00
05-Nov-92	1	$43.00	$43.00
06-Nov-92	1	$43.00	$43.00

...and view the sales figures for the Autumn Collection.

Microsoft Access displays the Box Sales form. Like the Boxes form, the Box Sales form is a form with a subform. The main form shows the name of the box at the top and the total sales for the box at the bottom of the form. The subform shows daily sales for the box.

2   If you want, scroll through the records in the Daily Sales subform to see all the sales.

3   When you're finished looking at the sales of the Autumn Collection, double-click the Control-menu box in the Box Sales form to close it (or choose Close from the File menu).

Double-click here.

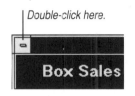

4   Close the Boxes form.

Deleting Records

In most databases, the only real constant is that data is constantly changing. You add records when you have new people or things to keep track of. You change records when the data changes. And you delete records when you no longer need to track the people or things that the records are about.

Sweet Lil's receives this note in the morning's mail:

Dear Sweet Lil's:

My son buys your chocolates frequently and loves them. In fact, he told me that he recently gave you my name to add to your customer list. I'm trying to lose some weight, so please don't add me to your list. No need to waste the catalog.

Thank you,

Francois Marcus

Go to the record you want to delete

Francois Marcus was just added to the Customers table last night. Using the View Customers form, you'll delete his record now.

1   Open the View Customers form.

2   Go to the last record.

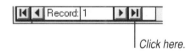

Click here.

If you followed the steps in Lesson 1, the four new customers you added to the database are at the end of the records, and Francois Marcus's record is right before theirs. If you didn't do Lesson 1, Francois Marcus's record is the last record.

3 If necessary, click the Previous Record button until you see Francois Marcus's record.

Click here.

Delete a record

To delete a record, you must first select it.

1 Click the record selector at the left edge of the form. (Or click in any field in the record, and then choose Select Record from the Edit menu.)

Click here.

Microsoft Access darkens the record selector to show you that the record is selected.

2 Press the DEL key. When Microsoft Access asks you to confirm the deletion, choose the OK button.

The record is deleted.

One Step Further

Now that Sweet Lil's has an Autumn Collection and a Winter Collection, you'll add one more season — Spring.

Add a new box

▶ Using the Boxes form, add a new box called Spring Collection. Use the following data for the new box:

Box Name:	**Spring Collection**
Box ID:	**SPRI**
Box Description:	**Hearts and flowers make the perfect gift for springtime lovers.**
Size:	**12 oz**

Contents:

ID		Qty
D02	Heart on a Sleeve	**3**
D09	American Beauty	**3**
M06	Lover's Heart	**3**
M10	Forget-Me-Not	**3**
W02	Calla Lily	**3**
W03	Broken Heart	**3**

Box Price: **$23.50**
Quantity on Hand: **0**

Delete a record in a subform

The flower bonbons are more popular this year than the heart bonbons.

▶ Delete the Lover's Heart bonbon from the Spring Collection, and then add 1 to the quantity of the American Beauty, Forget-Me-Not, and Calla Lily bonbons, so the box contains four of each flower bonbon.

Hint You use the same techniques to delete a record in a subform as you do in any other form. First select the record by clicking its record selector (on the left side of the subform, not the main form), or by clicking in the record and choosing Select Record from the Edit menu. Then press the DEL key.

Close the form

▶ When you're finished with the lesson, close the Boxes form.

Lesson Summary

To	Do this	Button
Move from a main form to a field on a subform	Click the field in the subform. Or from the last field on the main form before the subform, press TAB.	
Move from a subform to a field on a main form	Click the field in the main form. Or press CTRL+TAB to move to the next field on the main form; press CTRL+SHIFT+TAB to move to the previous field on the main form.	

Microsoft Access Step by Step

To	Do this	Button
Respond to a validation message (a message that says you entered the wrong data in a field)	Choose the OK button, and then correct the data in the field. To leave the form without correcting the data, press ESC.	
Undo your changes	Click the Undo button on the toolbar or use the Undo commands on the Edit menu.	
Go directly to a specific record	Type the record's number in the Record Number box between the navigation buttons at the bottom of the form.	
Delete a record	Select the record by clicking its record selector or by clicking in the record and choosing Select Record from the Edit menu. Then press the DEL key.	

For more information on	See
Adding and editing data on a form	Chapter 14, "Adding and Editing Data," in the *Microsoft Access User's Guide*. Or choose Cue Cards from the Help menu, and then choose "Work with Data."

Preview of the Next Lesson

In the next lesson, you'll learn how to zero in on the data that answers your questions. You'll find out how to filter records to get a set of related records, sort records, and find a record with a particular value in it.

Answering Questions

You ask the questions; Microsoft Access provides the answers. When you're interested in milk chocolates, you don't want to look at data about bittersweets. When you're interested in your Toronto customers, you don't want to see all your other customers.

While you're viewing data in forms, you can focus on the information you're interested in without wading through irrelevant data. In this lesson, you'll find out how to ask questions so that Microsoft Access displays only the data you want to see.

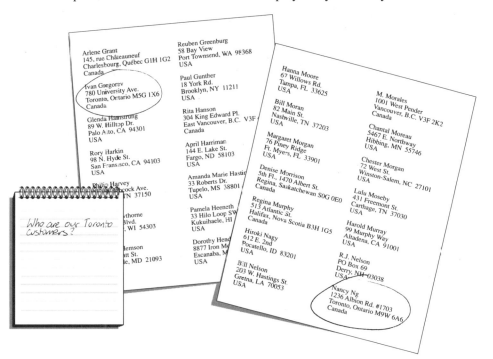

You will learn how to:

- Find a record with a particular value in it.
- Filter records to get a set of related records.
- Sort records.

Estimated lesson time: 35 minutes

Finding One Record or One Hundred Records

You'll find Microsoft Access more helpful than a filing cabinet or a pile of paper because you can find just the records you need, sorted the way you want them. Whether your database contains hundreds, thousands, or even millions of records, Microsoft Access finds just what you ask for and sorts the data just the way you want.

For quick searches, when you're looking for only one record, use the Find button on the toolbar. For example, you can find the record for the bonbon named Brazilian Supreme.

When you want to see a particular group of records, such as all the customers in Toronto, you create a *filter* to tell Microsoft Access which records you're interested in. When you create a filter, you give Microsoft Access a set of *criteria* that describes the records you want to see. Microsoft Access then displays the records in a form or in a form's datasheet.

Using a filter, you can also *sort* records in alphabetic or numeric order. For example, you could sort your customers alphabetically by last name.

Start the lesson

▸ Start Microsoft Access. If the Microsoft Access window doesn't fill your screen, maximize the window. Then open the Sweet database.

Finding a Record

This morning you found a slip of paper on your desk saying "Call N. Valerio—she's going to cancel her order if you don't get back to her immediately!" But the note doesn't have a phone number on it. You need to look up the number in the Sweet database.

A fast way to get this customer's record is to use the Find button on the toolbar.

Open a form

Form button

▶ Open the Customer Review form. (Remember, you click the Form button in the Database window to see the list of forms.)

Microsoft Access opens the form and displays the first record.

Find a record

1 Click in the Last Name field. You don't need to select the entire last name — just click anywhere in the field.

2 Click the Find button on the toolbar.

Find button

Microsoft Access displays the Find dialog box. The title bar of the Find dialog box shows the name of the field you're searching in—Last Name.

3   Type **Valerio** in the Find What box.

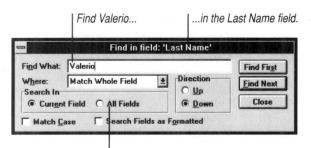

Find Valerio...   *...in the Last Name field.*

*You can also search in all
fields for the value you enter.*

Notice that you have the option of searching in all the fields for Valerio. Since you
know the value is in the Last Name field (the current field), you can make the
search go faster by searching only in the current field.

4   Choose the Find First button.

Microsoft Access displays the record for Nina Valerio. (If the Find dialog box
blocks your view of the form, you can move it out of the way by dragging its title
bar.)

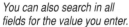

Record for Nina Valerio

This looks like the customer you need to call, but you'd better check just to make
sure there's not another customer with the same last name.

5   Choose the Find Next button.

Microsoft Access doesn't find another Valerio. It asks if you want to continue the
search from the beginning of the set of records.

6   Choose the No button.

Now you know that you have only one customer named Valerio, and you can go
ahead and give her a call.

7   Choose the Close button to close the Find dialog box.

Find a record even if you don't know much about it

As soon as you hang up the phone with Nina Valerio, you get a call from a clerk in Sweet Lil's Shipping department. He's having trouble reading the address on a shipping label. All he can make out is part of the street name, which starts with "Stew." He asks if you could find the name and address of the customer with this small amount of information.

1   In the Customer Review form, click in the field that contains the street address (the first line in the address).

You don't have to go back to the first record in the table — you can use the Find button from any customer's record.

Find button

2   Click the Find button on the toolbar.

Microsoft Access displays the Find dialog box. The Find What box still contains your last entry, Valerio.

3   Type **Stew** in the Find What box.

4   In the Where box, select Any Part of Field.

Because "Stew" is only part of the street name, you want to search for it no matter where it occurs in the field.

5   Choose the Find First button.

Microsoft Access finds an address with "Stewart" in the street address.

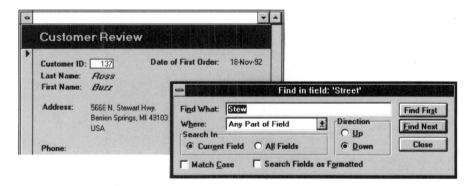

6   Choose the Find Next button.

Microsoft Access finds a second record with "stew" in the address. Notice that this "stew" doesn't have a capital S, since it appears in the middle of a word. You could make this search case-sensitive (that is, find only text with the same uppercase and lowercase letters you type) by selecting the Match Case check box. Then Microsoft Access would find only those records that contain "Stew" starting with a capital S. But in this case, you want to find all instances of "stew" regardless of case.

7 Choose the Find Next button again.

Microsoft Access asks if you want to continue the search from the beginning of the set of records. Because you started this search from the middle of the records, Microsoft Access hasn't searched the first records in the set yet.

8 Choose Yes to search the first records.

Microsoft Access doesn't find another "Stew," so you have two possible customers for the Shipping department.

9 Choose the Close button to close the Find dialog box, and then close the Customer Review form.

Filtering to Find a Group of Related Records

Suppose you're creating a promotional box of chocolates, and you want to include a bonbon that contains white chocolate. You'd like to review all the bonbons that contain white chocolate before making your choice.

Display the Filter window

1 Open the Bonbons form.

Microsoft Access opens the form and displays the first record in the Bonbons table. The Bonbons form is designed to display a single record of data. In this case, you want to look at all the bonbons that contain white chocolate at the same time, so you'll switch to the form's Datasheet view.

Datasheet View button

2 Click the Datasheet View button on the toolbar.

Bonbon Name:	Bonbon ID:	Description:	Chocolate Type:	Fillin
Candlelight Ecstasy	B01	Cashew in mocha c	Bittersweet	Mocha
Bittersweet Blueberry	B02	Cascade Mountain	Bittersweet	Blueberr
Marzipan Oakleaf	B03	Marzipan shaped in	Bittersweet	Marzipar
Bittersweet Strawberry	B04	Olympic Wilderness	Bittersweet	Strawbe
Bittersweet Raspberry	B05	Orcas Island raspbe	Bittersweet	Raspber
Bittersweet Marmalade	B06	Marmalade covered	Bittersweet	Marmala
Bittersweet Cherry	B07	Royal Anne cherry	Bittersweet	Cherry,
Hazelnut Bitters	B08	Classic hazelnut co	Bittersweet	None
Almond Supreme	D01	Whole almond han	Dark	None
Heart on a Sleeve	D02	Dark chocolate with	Dark	Cherry c

Record: 1

If you followed the steps in Lesson 2, "Getting the Best View of Your Data," your datasheet looks a little different from the preceding illustration. The appearance of the datasheet doesn't matter, though — you can still follow the steps given in this lesson to create a filter.

Notice that the form shows the type of chocolate each bonbon contains. For example, Candlelight Ecstasy has bittersweet chocolate.

*Edit Filter/Sort
button*

3 Click the Edit Filter/Sort button on the toolbar.

Microsoft Access opens the Filter window, where you describe the records you want to see. The upper portion of the window contains a *field list* of all the fields on the Bonbons form. The lower portion is the *filter grid*, where you set criteria for the records you want to see.

Choose fields and specify criteria

You want to see only the white chocolate bonbons, so you'll set criteria that will limit the records to only those bonbons. Start by choosing the field for which you want to set criteria. The type of chocolate is stored in the Chocolate Type field.

1 Drag the Chocolate Type field to the first cell in the Field row of the filter grid. (To drag the field, click it and hold down the mouse button while you move the mouse. Release the mouse button when the field is positioned over the cell.)

2 Move the insertion point to the Criteria cell below the Chocolate Type field.

3 Type **white** in the cell, and press the ENTER key.

Microsoft Access adds quotation marks after you press ENTER. However, if you type a text value that contains spaces or commas, you must enclose the value in quotation marks yourself.

Apply the filter and look at the results

Apply Filter/Sort button

▶ Click the Apply Filter/Sort button on the toolbar.

Bonbons			
Bonbon Name:	**Bonbon ID:**	**Description:**	**Chocolate Type:**
Marzipan Swallow	W01	Swallow-shaped m:	White
Calla Lily	W02	Elegant white choc	White
Broken Heart	W03	Two halves of a Ge	White
Brazilian Supreme	W06	A whole Brazil nut l	White

White chocolate bonbons

Microsoft Access searches for bonbons with white chocolate and displays these records in the datasheet.

Add more criteria

Since you have to keep the cost of this promotional box down, you'd like to see only the white chocolate bonbons that cost less than $0.30 apiece.

1 Click the Filter window to make it the active window.

The Filter window still displays the filter you created earlier to find the bonbons with white chocolate.

2 In the field list, scroll down until you see the Bonbon Cost field.

3 Drag the Bonbon Cost field from the field list to the cell in the Field row next to the Chocolate Type field.

4 In the Criteria cell for the Bonbon Cost field, type **<.30** and then press ENTER. (This tells Microsoft Access to select all the white chocolate bonbons that cost less than $0.30.)

Field:	Chocolate Type	Bonbon Cost
Sort:		
Criteria:	"white"	<0.3
or:		

5 Click the Apply Filter/Sort button on the toolbar.

Bonbons				
Bonbon Name:	**Bonbon ID:**	**Description:**	**Chocolate Type:**	**Filli**
Calla Lily	W02	Elegant white choc	White	None
Brazilian Supreme	W06	A whole Brazil nut l	White	None

Only two bonbons with white chocolate cost less than $0.30.

6 To see all the records again, click the Show All Records button.

Microsoft Access displays all the records in the datasheet, not just the records for bonbons with white chocolate.

➤ To learn more about other types of criteria, see "Specifying Criteria" in Chapter 15, "Finding and Sorting Data," in the *Microsoft Access User's Guide.*

Sorting Records

Suppose you want to introduce your new assistant to the different kinds of bonbons that Sweet Lil's makes. She knows the names of the bonbons, but you'd like her to learn more about their ingredients, too. To make the bonbons easier for her to find, you'll sort them in alphabetical order.

Sort records alphabetically

1 Click the Filter window to make it the active window.

The criteria for white chocolate bonbons that cost less than $0.30 is still in the Filter window.

2 From the Edit menu, choose Delete All.

Microsoft Access deletes all information from the filter grid.

3 Drag the Bonbon Name field from the field list to the first cell in the Field row.

4 Click the Sort cell below the Bonbon Name field, and then click the arrow in the cell to open the list.

5 Select Ascending from the list.

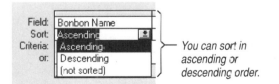

You can sort in ascending or descending order.

*Apply Filter/Sort
button*

6   Click the Apply Filter/Sort button to apply the filter.

Bonbons				
Bonbon Name:	**Bonbon ID:**	**Description:**	**Chocolate Type:**	
Almond Ambrosia	D04	Classic almond in a	Dark	Am
Almond Supreme	D01	Whole almond han	Dark	No
American Beauty	D09	Rich, dark chocola	Dark	No
Apple Amore	M07	Creamy milk chocol	Milk	No
Bittersweet Blueberry	B02	Cascade Mountain	Bittersweet	Blu
Bittersweet Cherry	B07	Royal Anne cherry	Bittersweet	Ch
Bittersweet Marmalade	B06	Marmalade covered	Bittersweet	Ma

The bonbons are in alphabetical order.

Sort records numerically

Your assistant wants to know which bonbons are the most expensive. Sort the records so that the datasheet displays the most expensive bonbons first.

1   Click the Filter window.

2   From the Edit menu, choose Delete All.

3   Drag the Bonbon Cost field from the field list to the first cell in the Field row.

4   Click the Sort cell below the Bonbon Cost field.

5   Select Descending from the list.

*Apply Filter/Sort
button*

6   Click the Apply Filter/Sort button to apply the filter.

7   Scroll to the right so that you can see the Cost column.

Bonbons			
Chocolate Type:	**Filling Type:**	**Nut Type:**	**Cost:**
Dark	Amaretto	Almond	$0.44
Bittersweet	Marzipan	None	$0.40
Milk	None	Macadamia	$0.40
Dark	Marzipan	None	$0.38
Milk	Marzipan	None	$0.37
Milk	Amaretto	Hazelnut	$0.36

*Records are sorted
in descending order
by cost.*

Microsoft Access displays the most expensive bonbon first and then lists the rest of the bonbons in descending order of cost.

8   Close the Bonbons form.

Microsoft Access doesn't save the filter with the form: The next time you open the Bonbons form, the records won't be filtered or sorted. In the lessons in Part Three, "Asking Questions and Getting Answers," you'll learn how to create and use a *query*. A query is like a saved filter. You can use it to always display records that meet certain criteria and are sorted in a particular order.

One Step Further

Now that you can use the Sweet database to answer questions, the questions are coming thick and fast.

What's the customer's name?

Find button

You want to return a call to a customer, but all you have is the phone number: (619) 555-0807. Use the Find button with the Customer Review form to quickly get the customer's name. Remember to click the field that contains the phone number before you click the Find button.

What kind of nut was it?

Here's a customer's letter:

Dear Sweet Lil's:

Please help us with a family bet. We enjoyed one of your delicious assortments, but we can't agree about the ingredients of one of the bonbons. The bonbon is milk chocolate with a cherry cream filling, but is the nut a hazelnut or an almond? We don't remember what the candy was called.

Sincerely,

Mona, Humphrey, Cici, and Fred Montori

Open the Bonbons form, and create a filter that shows you the bonbons with Milk in the Chocolate Type field and Cherry cream in the Filling Type field. When you're typing criteria, you'll need to put quotation marks around Cherry cream because it contains a space.

Bonbon Name:	Bonbon ID:	Description:	Chocolate Type:	Filling Type:	Nut Type:
Lover's Heart	M06	Heart-shaped milk	Milk	Cherry cream	None
Hazelnut Cherry	M14	Finest hazelnut st	Milk	Cherry cream	Hazelnut

Your filter should show only these two bonbons. The family members who bet on hazelnut win the pot.

*Datasheet View
button*

Tip   You can see all the records that match your filter's criteria at once by looking at the form in Datasheet view instead of in Form view. Just press the Datasheet View button on the toolbar.

Who are the new customers from Canada?

Sweet Lil's recently launched an expensive marketing promotion in Canada. It's time to decide whether to recommend the promotion for the United States.

Using the Customer Review form, create a filter that shows the Canadian customers who were added on or after 15-Dec-92, the first day of the promotion. Sort the records so you see the newest customers (those with the most recent Date of First Order) first.

Tip   You'll use these two fields in the filter: Country and Date of First Order. The expression for on or after 15-Dec-92 is **>=15-Dec-92**. After you enter the expression, Microsoft Access puts number signs (#) around the date, indicating that it is a date/time value.

Scroll across the datasheet to see the dates.

City, State/Prov	Country	Phone:	Date of First Ord
Bridgetown, Nova Scotia B0S 1C0	Canada	(902) 555-5302	29-Dec-92
Belleville, Ontario K8P 1H3	Canada	(613) 555-7408	28-Dec-92
Nepean, Ontario K2E 7J6	Canada	(613) 555-0017	26-Dec-92
Alberton, Prince Edward Island	Canada	(902) 555-2749	26-Dec-92

Customer Review

The records should be sorted in descending order by the date of the first order.

Lesson Summary

To	Do this	Button
Find a specific record	Click the Find button and fill in the dialog box.	
Create a filter	Open a form. Then click the Edit Filter/Sort button on the toolbar.	
Choose a field for a filter	Drag a field from the field list to a cell in the Field row of the filter grid.	
Set criteria for a filter	In the filter grid, type criteria in the Criteria cell below the field for which you want to set criteria.	

To	Do this	Button
Apply a filter	Click the Apply Filter/Sort button on the toolbar.	
Sort records in a filter	In the filter grid, select Ascending or Descending in the Sort cell below the field you want to sort on.	
Look at all records after you've applied a filter	Click the Show All Records button.	

For more information on	See
Filtering, sorting, and finding records	Chapter 7, "Finding the Data You Want," in *Microsoft Access Getting Started,* and Chapter 15, "Finding and Sorting Data," in the *Microsoft Access User's Guide.*

Preview of the Next Lesson

In the next lesson, you'll learn how to use reports to print information from your database. You'll print a sales report, and you'll create and print mailing labels.

Printing Reports and Mailing Labels

How many different ways do you use a customer's address or a product's name? The address might appear on an invoice and a mailing label. The product name might appear on the same invoice and on a sales report. Using Microsoft Access forms and reports, you can arrange and combine your data however you want. To present your data to its best advantage in print, use a report.

Reports can show all of the information in the database or just the information you want to highlight. Reports can also show other critical information, such as subtotals and totals. In this lesson, you'll open, preview, and print a sales report. Then you'll create a mailing label report and print your mailing labels.

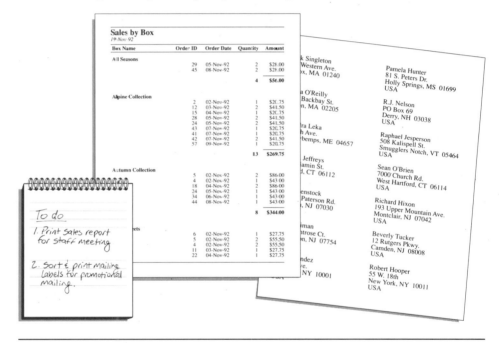

You will learn how to:

- Open and preview a report.
- Print a report.
- Create and print mailing labels.

Estimated lesson time: 25 minutes

What Is a Report?

Up to now, you've used forms to put information in your database and to edit and find that information. Now you'll use reports to print the results of your work.

You can use either a form or a report to print detailed information, such as lists of records. For example, you could use either a form or a report to print a list of all your customers. But a report is especially useful when you want to print summary information, such as subtotals and totals. Microsoft Access calculates these for you and prints them on your report.

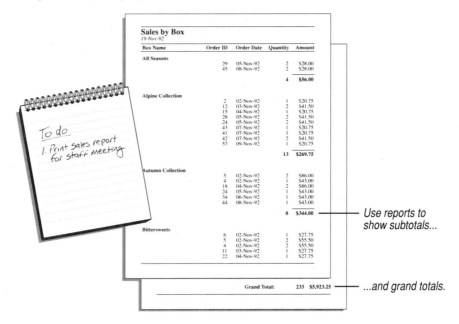

Use reports to show subtotals...

...and grand totals.

A report also gives you greater control than a form over exactly where the data prints on a page. For example, you can use a report to print records in snaking columns, like entries in a phone book. This type of layout is especially useful for printing mailing labels and phone lists.

Start the lesson

▶   Start Microsoft Access. If the Microsoft Access window doesn't fill your screen, maximize the window. Then open the Sweet database.

Previewing a Report

Sweet Lil's marketing staff is planning a mail-order campaign to stimulate sales for assortments of chocolates that aren't selling well. You can print a report on recent box sales that will help you pick which boxes to promote. You'll use the Sales by Box report to see how the assortments have been selling during a one-week period in November.

Opening a report is the same as opening a form or table: You display the list of reports in the Database window and then double-click the report you want. The report opens in *Print Preview* so you can see how it looks before printing it.

Preview a report

Report button

1   In the Database window, click the Report button.

2   Double-click the Sales by Box report.

Microsoft Access displays the first of two dialog boxes that ask you to enter the dates for the period you want the report to cover.

3   Type **2-Nov-92** as a starting date, and then press the ENTER key.

Microsoft Access recognizes a number of ways to enter dates. For example, you could have used 11/2/92, another United States format. The Canada (English) format is 2/11/92.

Note   To find out which country your computer is set up for, open the Windows Control Panel and double-click the International section, which will display the Country setting as well as the setting for the Date and other formats.

---

4   In the next dialog box, type **9-Nov-92** as an ending date, and then press ENTER.

Microsoft Access collects the appropriate data and opens the report in Print Preview.

The pointer changes to a magnifying glass.

Report: Sales by Box				

Sales by Box
12-Jan-93

Box Name	Order ID	Order Date	Quantity	Amount
All Seasons				
	29	05-Nov-92	2	$28.00
	45	08-Nov-92	2	$28.00
			4	**$56.00**

Alpine Collection

The report is magnified in Print Preview so that you can clearly read the data. The magnifying glass pointer means you can switch views: Zoom out to see how the data is laid out on the whole page, and zoom in to see the magnified view.

Look at a whole page at once

▶ Click anywhere on the report.

Microsoft Access shows you the whole page. The layout looks fine. Now you'll check to make sure you have the data you want.

Zoom in on the data

▶ Click anywhere on the report.

Now you're looking at the magnified view again.

Move around the page

▶ Use the vertical scroll bar to move up and down the page, and use the horizontal scroll bar to move from left to right.

	30	06-Nov-92	2	$55.50
	40	07-Nov-92	2	$55.50
	38	07-Nov-92	1	$27.75
	47	.08-Nov-92	1	$27.75

1

Page: 1

Scroll across to see the right side of the page.

Scroll down to see the bottom of the page.

The data looks right— sales for the week of November 2, 1992. Before printing the report, take a quick look at each page.

Move from page to page

Your report is five pages long. The last page includes the grand total for all the boxes.

▶   Use the navigation buttons at the bottom of the window to page through the report.

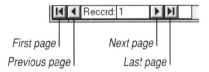

The report looks great — it's ready to print.

Printing a Report

When you print a report, you have the option of specifying a range of pages if you don't want to print the entire report, and you can specify how many copies you want to print. If you print more than one copy, you can have Microsoft Access collate the copies for you. You can also print the report to a file instead of to the printer so that you can print the file at a later date.

If you're set up to print, you can print the Sales by Box report now. For help setting up a printer, see Appendix A, "Installing and Setting Up Your Printer."

Print a report from Print Preview

| Print... |

Print button

1   Click the Print button on the toolbar.

Microsoft Access displays the Print dialog box. In this case, you want to print one copy of the whole report, so you don't need to change any of the settings in the Print dialog box.

2   Choose the OK button.

Microsoft Access prints the report.

3   Close the Sales by Box report.

Tip   As you've seen, when you double-click a report in the Database window, Microsoft Access opens it in Print Preview so you can check out how it will look on the page before you print it. To print a report without opening it first in Print Preview, select the report in the Database window, and then choose Print from the File menu.

Creating Mailing Labels

Based on your report, you decide to promote the two slowest-selling boxes by discounting them in a special mailing to all customers. You'll create mailing labels and print the labels sorted by postal code.

To create mailing labels, you use an *AccessWizard*. An AccessWizard is like a database expert who asks you questions about the form or report you want and then builds it for you according to your answers. You use *FormWizards* to build forms and *ReportWizards* to build reports. Your mailing labels will be a new report in the database.

Create mailing labels

Because you just printed the Sales by Box report, the Database window is still showing the list of reports.

New

New button

1 Choose the New button.

Microsoft Access displays the New Report dialog box.

2 In the Select A Table/Query box, click the arrow to display the list of tables and queries, and then select the Customers table.

The Customers table contains the names and addresses you want to print in the mailing labels.

3 Choose the ReportWizards button.

Select Customers from the list...

...and then choose the ReportWizards button.

This tells Microsoft Access that you want to have an AccessWizard create your report for you. Microsoft Access asks which AccessWizard you want to use.

4 Double-click the Mailing Label ReportWizard.

The AccessWizard displays the first in a series of dialog boxes that you'll use to define your mailing labels. In the first dialog box, you define the label's appearance.

Define the label's appearance

1 In the Available Fields box, double-click the First Name field.

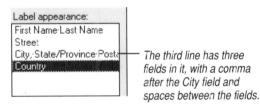

Double-click here...   *...to add the field to the label.*

Click here to remove a field.

Microsoft Access adds the field to the first line of your mailing label.

Space button

2 Click the Space button to put a space between first names and last names.

3 Double-click the Last Name field.

Microsoft Access adds the Last Name field to the first line of your mailing label.

Return button

4 Click the Return button to go to the second line of the mailing label.

5 Define the second, third, and fourth lines of the mailing label like this:

- Street field in the second line
- City, State/Province, and Postal Code fields in the third line, with appropriate punctuation between them
- Country field in the fourth line

Left Arrow button

If you make a mistake in a line of text, select the line and use the left arrow between the Available Fields box and the Label Appearance box to remove an item from the mailing label. When you're finished, the box for your mailing label's appearance looks like this.

Label appearance:
First Name·Last Name
Street
City,·State/Province·Posta
Country

The third line has three fields in it, with a comma after the City field and spaces between the fields.

6 Choose the Next button to move to the next dialog box.

Now that you've defined the mailing label's appearance, you'll tell Microsoft Access how to sort the printed labels.

Sort the labels

You want to sort the mailing labels by postal code so that all the labels with the same postal code are printed together.

1 In the Available Fields box, double-click the Postal Code field.

Microsoft Access adds Postal Code to the list of fields that define the sort order.

2 Choose the Next button.

Finally, you can tell Microsoft Access the exact size of your label stock.

Select the mailing label size

You can choose from a wide range of label sizes, listed in either English measurements (inches) or metric measurements. If you have label stock on hand, use the Avery stock number to help you select the label size you want.

1 Select the label size for Avery number 4144. (Choose EAL O4 if you're using metric measurements.)

2 Choose the Next button.

That's it! You've finished designing your mailing labels.

Preview your mailing labels

▶ Click the Print Preview button.

| Labels are sorted by postal code.

Microsoft Access shows you how the labels will print on the page. If you want, scroll through the labels.

Note If the top line of your text is cut off, it's probably because of the printer driver you're using. The label sizes selected in this lesson are for sprocket-feed stock that would be printed on a dot matrix printer.

Since you know that you'll be making frequent mailings to your customers, you can save this mailing label report so that it's available anytime you want customer labels.

Save and close the mailing label report

1   From the File menu, choose Save.

Microsoft Access displays the Save As dialog box.

2   Type **Customer Mailing Labels** in the Report Name box.

3   Choose the OK button.

4   Close the Customer Mailing Labels report.

Your new report appears in the list of reports in the Database window. Now whenever you need mailing labels for your customers, you can just print this report.

Note   When you saved the Customer Mailing Labels report, you saved the *definition* of the mailing labels but not the actual names and addresses that print on the labels. The data printed on the labels is stored in the Customers table. When Sweet Lil's gets a new customer, you add the customer's information to the Customers table. When a customer moves, you update the address in the Customers table. The next time you print the Customer Mailing Labels report, Microsoft Access automatically draws the most current data from the Customers table and prints a label for each customer.

One Step Further

The holiday season is usually Sweet Lil's busiest time. You can use the Sales by Box report to check out December sales.

How were sales in December?

Preview and then print the Sales by Box report, printing only the sales between 1-Dec-92 and 31-Dec-92. When you're finished, close the report.

Create a phone list

The Mailing Label ReportWizard makes it easy to create a wide variety of mailing labels, but you might find it useful for other types of reports, too — for example, a handy phone list you can keep beside your phone or in your briefcase.

1   Create a new report based on the Customers table. Using the Mailing Label ReportWizard, define your report so that when it's printed, the labels include the data shown in the following illustration. Sort the list by last name and select the label size for Avery number 5161. (Choose L7162 if you're using metric measurements.)

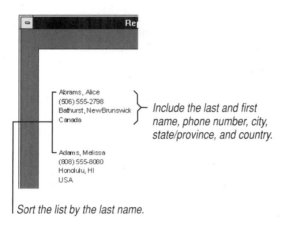

Abrams, Alice
(506) 555-2798
Bathurst, NewBrunswick
Canada

} *Include the last and first name, phone number, city, state/province, and country.*

Adams, Melissa
(808) 555-8080
Honolulu, HI
USA

| *Sort the list by the last name.*

Hint To create a new report, first display reports in the Database window, and then choose the New button.

For more information, see the lessons in Part 6: "Customizing Your Reports."

2 Display the report in Print Preview to see how it looks. When you're finished, save the report, name it Customer Phone List, and then close it.

Once you've created a report with an AccessWizard, you can make changes and adjustments in the design to customize the report's appearance.

Lesson Summary

To	Do this	Button
Open and preview a report	In the Database window, click the Report button, and then double-click the report you want.	Report
Go back and forth between a magnified view of a report in Print Preview and a view of the whole page	Click anywhere on the report.	
Move from page to page in a report in Print Preview	Use the navigation buttons at the bottom of the window.	
Print a report	In Print Preview, choose the Print button. To print a report directly from the Database window, select the report, and then choose Print from the File menu.	Print...

To	Do this	Button
Create mailing labels	In the Database window, click the Report button, and then choose the New button. Select the table or query that contains the data for the labels, and then click the ReportWizards button. Then select the Mailing Label ReportWizard.	

For more information on	See
Printing in Microsoft Access	Appendix A, "Installing and Setting Up Your Printer." Or, from the Print dialog box, press F1.

Preview of the Next Lesson

Now that you know how to get data into and out of a database, you're ready to start creating tables and forms of your own. In the next lesson, you'll learn how to create a new table and use its datasheet to add records to the table.

Part

2 Expanding a
Database

Adding a Table

When information is well organized, it's easy to find and manage. Photographs arranged in family albums, for example, are easier to find than those jumbled together in a box in the attic. In a Microsoft Access database, information is organized in tables. You can display the information in a wide variety of formats, but it's all stored in tables.

In this lesson, you'll find out how to create a table, define its fields, and add records in the table's datasheet.

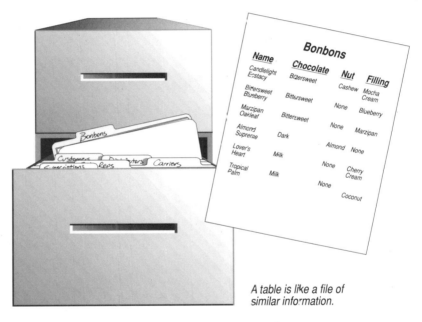

A table is like a file of similar information.

You will learn how to:

- Create a table.
- Add fields to the table.
- Set the table's primary key.
- Add records using the table's datasheet.
- Set field properties.

Estimated lesson time: 20 minutes

What Is a Table?

A database *table* is a collection of data with the same subject or topic. One table might contain data about customers, such as each customer's name, address, and phone number. Another table might contain data about bonbons, such as each bonbon's name, picture, and cost.

A Microsoft Access database is a collection of tables — or at least one table — that you use to store related information. The tables in the Sweet database, for example, all contain data relating to different parts of Sweet Lil's business.

You worked with fields when you added records using the Boxes form in Lesson 3. In this lesson, you'll learn how to define the fields in a table, and you'll see how fields and records are displayed in tables.

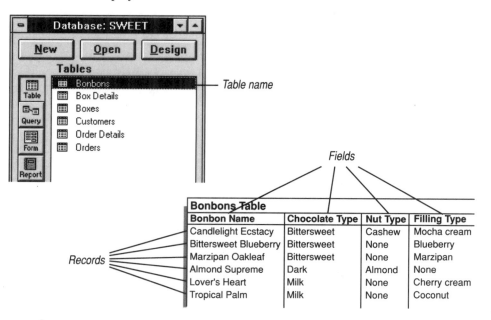

Each field appears as a column in the table and contains a category of information. For example, each field in the Bonbons table contains a different category of information that describes a bonbon, such as the name, chocolate type, or filling in the bonbon.

Each record appears as a row in the table and contains all the information about a particular person, item, or event (depending on the table's subject). Each record in the Bonbons table, for example, contains all the information about a particular bonbon. Each record in the Customers table contains all the information about a particular customer.

Start the lesson

▸ Start Microsoft Access. If the Microsoft Access window doesn't fill your screen, maximize the window. Then open the Sweet database.

Creating a Table

When you create a new table, you define how many fields the table has and what kind of data can be stored in each field. This tells Microsoft Access the basic structure of the table. Then, after naming and saving the table, you can add data to it.

Sweet Lil's Chocolates is growing fast. More and more customers who order chocolates on Sweet Lil's toll-free telephone line want their gift orders to arrive immediately, if not sooner. To meet their customer's needs, Sweet Lil's will begin using three shipping carriers instead of one, so that customers can choose air delivery if they wish. You'll add a table to the Sweet database to hold data on the three carriers. The Carriers table will contain three fields to identify each carrier's ID number, name, and method of delivery (surface or air).

Create a table

New button

▸ With tables listed in the Database window, choose the New button.

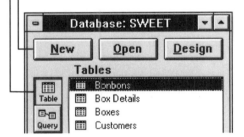

Microsoft Access opens a new table in Design view.

Adding Fields

You add a field to a table by typing the field name in the upper part of the table's Design view and selecting the field's *data type*. The data type tells Microsoft Access what kind of data to accept in the field.

Table's Design view

You add fields here. Each field must have a name and a data type. Descriptions are optional.

For details on all the data types, click the first box under Data Type and press F1.

The following table shows examples of fields with different data types and the data each could hold.

Field	Data type	Data you might enter
Last Name	Text	Houlihan
Box Price	Currency	$18.75
Picture	OLE Object	
Quantity on Hand	Number	500

Data types protect the accuracy of your data by restricting the type of information you can enter in a field. For example, you can't store a picture or a name in a field with the Currency data type.

Now, you're ready to add the first field to your new table. You'll use this field to store an ID number for each carrier.

Name a field

▶ Type **Carrier ID** in the first empty Field Name box.

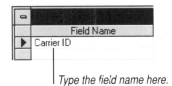

Type the field name here.

A field name can contain up to 64 characters, including spaces. It can include any punctuation mark except a period (.), an exclamation point (!), or brackets ([ ]).

Select a data type

You want each carrier to have a unique ID number. A simple code such as 1 for the first carrier, 2 for the second carrier, and 3 for the third carrier will work fine. Microsoft Access provides a data type called *Counter* that will assign the numbers for you automatically when you add each new carrier to the table. The Counter data type ensures that each new carrier you add has its own unique ID number.

1   Press the TAB key to move to the Data Type box.

By default, Microsoft Access gives the field the Text data type. The arrow in the box tells you that you can select the data type you want from a list.

2   Click the arrow to open the list, and then select Counter.

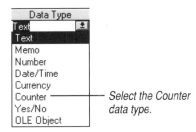

Select the Counter data type.

Notice that Microsoft Access displays properties for the field in the lower portion of the table's Design view. Later in this lesson, you'll learn how to set properties to further refine the definition of your fields.

Add a description

A description can help you remember the purpose of a field long after you define it. In addition, when you're adding data to the table, field descriptions can help you enter the right data. You'll see how that works later in this lesson, when you add records to the Carriers table.

1   Press TAB to move to the Description box.

2   Type **Number automatically assigned to new carrier** in the Description box, and then press TAB to move to the next field.

Add more fields

Next you'll add two additional fields: the Carrier Name field and the Delivery Method field. The Carrier Name field will store the names of the three carriers — Wild Fargo Carriers, Grey Goose Express, and Pegasus Overnight. These names are text, so you'll use the Text data type for this field.

1 Type **Carrier Name** in the second Field Name box.

Field Name	Data Type
Carrier ID	Counter
Carrier Name	

Add the second field here.

2 Press TAB to move to the Data Type box.

Microsoft Access automatically assigns the field the Text data type. This is the data type you want, so you don't need to change it.

3 In the Description box, type **Company name of carrier**, and then press TAB to move to the next field.

4 Type **Delivery Method** in the third Field Name box.

This field will store data indicating whether the carrier delivers by surface or by air.

5 Press TAB to move to the Data Type box, and then click the arrow to display the list of data types.

You can see that one of the data types is Yes/No. This looks like the right data type for the Delivery Method field, since this field can contain one of only two choices (carriers deliver either by surface or by air).

6 Select Yes/No as the data type for the Delivery Method field.

7 In the Description box, type **Yes for air; no for surface**

Table: Table1		
Field Name	Data Type	Description
Carrier ID	Counter	Number automatically assigned to new carrier
Carrier Name	Text	Company name of carrier
Delivery Method	Yes/No	Yes for air; no for surface

Get Help

Before you finish defining your table, you might want to make sure that the Yes/No data type is really the right choice for the Delivery Method field. To get more information about the data type, you can use Help.

1   Click in the Data Type box for the Delivery Method field, and then press the F1 key.

For more about using Help, see "Getting Ready" earlier in this book.

Microsoft Access displays Help about the data types. As you can see, the Yes/No data type is appropriate for fields that contain one of two values.

2   Close the Help window by double-clicking the Control-menu box.

| Double-click the Control-menu box.

⌐	**Microsoft Access Help**	▼	▲
File **Edit** **Bookmark** **Help**			
Contents	**Search**	**Back**	**History**	**<<**	**>>**		

Microsoft Access Help is *context-sensitive,* which means the context of your screen tells Microsoft Access which Help topic to display when you press F1. For example, if you press F1 with the insertion point in a Field Name box, Microsoft Access displays Help about field names. In many situations, you can get exactly the help you need by clicking at the appropriate place and then pressing F1.

Setting the Primary Key and Saving Your Table

Every table in your database should have a *primary key* — one or more fields whose values uniquely identify each record in the table. The primary key helps Microsoft Access search, find, and combine data as efficiently as possible.

A field with a Counter data type makes a perfect primary key. You know the field will contain a unique value for each record because Microsoft Access automatically enters sequential numbers in that field for each new record of data.

Set the primary key

1   Select the row that defines the Carrier ID field.

⌐			
	Field Name		
▶	Carrier ID		
	Carrier Name		

| Click here to select the row.

2   Click the Primary Key button on the toolbar.

Primary Key button

Microsoft Access puts a key symbol in the row selector for the Carrier ID field. This symbol tells you that the Carrier ID field is the table's primary key.

	Field Name
🔑▶	Carrier ID
	Carrier Name

Carrier ID is the table's primary key.

Your table definition is complete. You're ready to save the table and start adding records to it.

Save a table

1 From the File menu, choose Save.

Microsoft Access displays the Save As dialog box.

2 Type **Carriers** in the Table Name box, and then choose the OK button.

Microsoft Access saves the table. Now you can add the data for the three carriers.

*Properties
button*

Tip To change the primary key to a different field (or to no field), click the Properties button on the toolbar to display the table properties. You can delete the field name listed in the box for the Primary Key property, or you can change the setting to a different field or fields. For details, click in the Primary Key property box, and then press F1.

Adding Records in a Table's Datasheet

So far, you've been working with the Carriers table in Design view. To add or look at data in the table, you'll switch to the table's Datasheet view. You use the View buttons on the left side of the toolbar to switch back and forth between the two views.

File	**Edit**	**View**	**Window**	**Help**

Datasheet View button
Design View button

Switch to Datasheet view

▶ Click the Datasheet View button on the toolbar.

*Datasheet View
button*

You can add records to the table in Datasheet view.

```
 ┌─────────────────────────────────────────────┬───┬───┐
 │  ▬  ▐          Table: Carriers              │ ▼ │ ▲ │
 │     ┌─Carrier ID─┬─Carrier Name─┬─Delivery Method─┐
 │  ▶  │   Counter  │              │                 │
 │     │            │              │                 │
 │     │            │              │                 │
 │     │            │              │                 │
 │     │            │              │                 │
 ├──┬──┬──────────┬──┬──┬──────────────────────────┤
 │◄◄│◄ │Record: 1 │► │►►│                            │
 └──┴──┴──────────┴──┴──┴────────────────────────────┘
```

Start a record

Notice that Microsoft Access puts the word Counter in the Carrier ID field. That's to let you know that you don't have to fill in the field yourself; Microsoft Access will give each new record a number automatically.

1   Press TAB to move to the Carrier Name field.

2   Type **Wild Fargo Carriers**, and then press TAB to move to the Delivery Method field.

Delivery Method is a field with a Yes/No data type. When you defined the field, you gave it a description that said what Yes and No meant. Microsoft Access displays the field's description in the status bar, so you can see what value to enter.

```
 ┌────────────────────────────────────────────────────┬──┐
 │                                                     │ ▼│
 ├─┬───────────────────────────────────────────────┬──┼──┤
 │◄│                                               │ ►│  │
 ├─┴─────────────────────────┬──┬──┬──┬──┬─────┬───┴──┴──┤
 │ Yes for air; No for surface│  │  │  │  │ NUM │         │
 └────────────────────────────┴──┴──┴──┴──┴─────┴─────────┘
```

The status bar displays the field's description.

No is the default for the Delivery Method field. Wild Fargo Carriers uses surface as their delivery method, so you don't have to change the default value.

Save a record

▶   Press TAB to move to the next record.

When you move to the next record, Microsoft Access automatically saves the data in the first record. You don't have to do anything else to save the record. Notice that Microsoft Access gave Wild Fargo Carriers a carrier ID of 1.

Add more records

▶ Add these two records to the Carriers table:

Carrier Name: **Grey Goose Express**
Delivery Method: **Yes**

Carrier Name: **Pegasus Overnight**
Delivery Method: **Yes**

Setting Field Properties

Each field in a table has *properties* that you can use to control how Microsoft Access stores, handles, and displays data in the field. For example, to display numbers in a field as percentages, you would set the field's Format property to Percent.

Table: Order Details				
Order ID	Product ID	Unit Price	Quantity	Discount
10000	17	$27.00	4	0.00%
10001	25	$9.80	30	15.00%
10001	40	$12.80	40	0.00%

To display numbers as percentages...

Quantity	Number
Discount	Number

Field Properties

Field Size	Single
Format	Percent

...set the field's Format property to Percent.

Each data type has a different set of properties associated with it. Fields with the Text and Number data types, for example, have a property called FieldSize that sets the maximum size of data you can store in the field. Fields with the Yes/No data type, on the other hand, don't have a FieldSize property because the values stored in a Yes/No field have a fixed size.

All data types have a Caption property. You use the Caption property to display a column heading in Datasheet view that's different from the field name. Since the Delivery Method field will display Yes or No, you'd like its caption in Datasheet view to be Air Delivery instead of Delivery Method. You can give the field a custom caption by setting its Caption property.

Set a field property

Design View button

1 Click the Design View button on the toolbar to switch to Design view.

2 Click anywhere in the row for the Delivery Method field to display its field properties.

Table: Carriers	
Field Name	Data Type
Carrier ID	Counter
Carrier Name	Text
▶ Delivery Method	Yes/No

—— *Click in this row...*

Field Properties

Format	Yes/No
Caption	
Default Value	
Validation Rule	
Validation Text	

} *...to display the properties for the Delivery Method field.*

3   Type **Air Delivery** in the Caption property box.

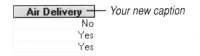

Format	Yes/No
Caption	Air Delivery
Default Value	
Validation Rule	
Validation Text	

—— *Caption property box*

Tip   For fast, detailed information on any property, just click in the property box, and press F1.

---

4   Switch to Datasheet view to see the new caption for the Delivery Method field. When Microsoft Access asks if you want to save the changes to the table, choose the OK button.

Air Delivery
No
Yes
Yes

—— *Your new caption*

Close the table

▶   From the File menu, choose Close.

Microsoft Access closes the Carriers table. Notice that this table now appears in the list of tables in the Database window.

One Step Further

Just when you thought you were finished with the Carriers table, you receive a note from Sylvia in the Shipping department.

SWEET LIL'S
CHOCOLATES

INTEROFFICE MEMO

Could you please add this information about our carriers to the database so we can look them up any time? Our contacts and their phones seem to change weekly, and we need a convenient place to keep them up-to-date.

Carrier	Contact Person	Contact Phone
Wild Fargo Carriers	Clyde Houlihan	(212) 555-7837
Grey Goose Express	Bella Lamont	(503) 555-9874
Pegasus Overnight	Morris Jantz	(206) 555-8988

Thanks,

Sylvia G.

Add fields to a table

▸ Add two fields called Contact Person and Contact Phone to the Carriers table. Give each field the Text data type. Set the FieldSize property of the Contact Phone field to 24.

Hint   To open the table in Design view, select it in the Database window, and then choose the Design button. Or double-click the table using the *right* mouse button (double-clicking with the left button opens the table in Datasheet view). You can add the new fields directly below the Delivery Method field.

Add more data

▸ Add the names and numbers from Sylvia's note to the Contact Person and Contact Phone fields. When you're finished, close the Carriers table.

Lesson Summary

To	Do this	Button
Create a table	Click the Table button in the Database window, and then choose the New button.	Table
Add a field to a table	In the first empty row of the table's Design view, type a field name in the Field Name box, and then select a data type in the Data Type box.	
Set properties for a field	Click the row that defines the field in the upper portion of the table's Design view, and then set the property in the lower portion of the window.	
Get Help on any field property	Click in the property box, and then press F1.	
Set a table's primary key	Select the row or rows in the table's Design view that define the field or fields you want to include in the primary key, and then click the Primary Key button on the toolbar.	
Add records in a table's datasheet	Open the table in Datasheet view. From the Database window, double-click the table. In the table's Design view, click the Datasheet View button on the toolbar. Then type the data in the fields.	
Modify a table's design	Select the table in the Database window, and then choose the Design button.	

For more information on	See
Deciding what tables belong in your database	Chapter 1, "Designing a Database," in the *Microsoft Access User's Guide*.
Adding fields and setting a table's primary key	Chapter 2, "Table Basics," in the *Microsoft Access User's Guide*.
Setting field properties	Chapter 3, "Changing and Customizing Tables," in the *Microsoft Access User's Guide*.

Preview of the Next Lesson

In the next lesson, you'll learn how to access data that's stored outside your Microsoft Access database in a different file format, and you'll learn how to import the data to make a new Microsoft Access table.

Attaching and Importing Data

Suppose you have sales data in a file that's not part of a Microsoft Access database. Can you use Microsoft Access to work with the data? The answer is probably *yes*. If the data is in a Microsoft Excel, Lotus® 1-2-3®, or text file, you can import it. If the data is in another database file format, such as a Paradox or Microsoft SQL Server file, you can import it, or you can attach it to your Microsoft Access database and use Microsoft Access to work with it.

In this lesson, you'll find out how to attach a table in a different database format to your Microsoft Access database and how to use Microsoft Access to work with data in the external table. You'll also learn how to import data into your Microsoft Access database and export data from Microsoft Access to a different file format.

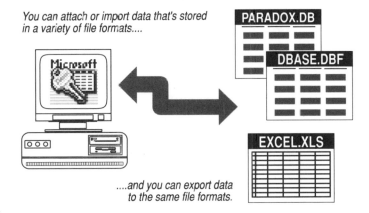

You can attach or import data that's stored in a variety of file formats....

PARADOX.DB

DBASE.DBF

EXCEL.XLS

....and you can export data to the same file formats.

You will learn how to:

- Attach an external table.
- Work with data in an attached table.
- Use a FormWizard to create a form for an attached table.
- Import data.
- Export data.

Estimated lesson time: 30 minutes

Using Data from Different Sources

When you *import* data into your Microsoft Access database, Microsoft Access copies the data from its source into a table in your database. You can import data from these file formats:

- A spreadsheet file, such as a Microsoft Excel or a Lotus 1-2-3 file.

- A text file, such as a file you might create with a word processing program or a text editor.

- A file in another database format, such as a FoxPro® file, a Paradox version 3.0 or 3.5 file, a dBASE III® or dBASE IV® file, a Btrieve® file (with an Xtrieve® dictionary file), a Microsoft SQL Server file, or another Microsoft Access database file.

If your file is a Microsoft Access, Paradox, dBASE, Btrieve, or Microsoft SQL Server database file, you have the choice of *attaching* the external table or importing it. An attached table isn't copied into your Microsoft Access database; the table stays in its original file format. You create a link between your Microsoft Access database and the external table. That way, you can use Microsoft Access to work with the data, and someone else can still use the table in its original application.

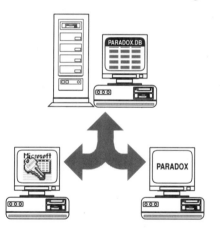

You can use Microsoft Access to work with data at the same time someone else uses another application to work with the same data.

In this lesson, you'll start by attaching a Paradox table to the Sweet database. Later, you'll import the data so that it's a Microsoft Access table.

Start the lesson

▶ Start Microsoft Access. If the Microsoft Access window doesn't fill your screen, maximize the window. Then open the Sweet database.

Attaching an External Table

If you attach an external table to your Microsoft Access database, you can view and update the data even if others are using it in the table's source application. You can create Microsoft Access forms and reports based on the external table. You can even use a query to combine external data with the data in your Microsoft Access tables. You'll learn more about using a query to combine data from different tables in Lesson 8, "Joining Tables to See Related Data."

As a small company, Sweet Lil's charged a flat shipping rate. Now that it has expanded nationwide and uses three carriers, you plan to base shipping charges to customers on the destination state or province and the selected carrier. A colleague in the Shipping department has a Paradox version 3.5 table that contains the data.

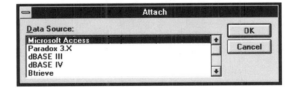

```
Viewing B:shipping table: Record 1 of 186          Main

B:SHIPPING—Carrier ID——Ship State/Province—Shipping Charge+
          1  |    1  |  AK             |     3.35 |
          2  |    1  |  AL             |     3.7  |
          3  |    1  |  AR             |     3.35 |
          4  |    1  |  AZ             |     3.35 |
          5  |    1  |  Alberta        |     3.35 |
          6  |    1  |  British Columbia |   3.35 |
```

The data you need is in a Paradox table.

Your colleague wants to continue using Paradox for the time being to keep track of his shipping data, so instead of importing the table into the Sweet database, you'll attach it. That way, your colleague can continue to use Paradox to work with the table while you work with it using Microsoft Access.

Attach an external table

1 From the File menu, choose Attach Table.

```
 ┌──────────────────── Attach ────────────────────┐
 │                                                  │
 │  Data Source:                       ┌────────┐  │
 │  ┌──────────────────────────────┐▲  │   OK   │  │
 │  │Microsoft Access              │   └────────┘  │
 │  │Paradox 3.X                   │   ┌────────┐  │
 │  │dBASE III                     │   │ Cancel │  │
 │  │dBASE IV                      │   └────────┘  │
 │  │Btrieve                       │▼              │
 │  └──────────────────────────────┘              │
 └──────────────────────────────────────────────────┘
```

Microsoft Access displays the Attach dialog box. You use it to tell Microsoft Access the external table's file format.

2 Double-click Paradox 3.X.

Microsoft Access displays the Select File dialog box, where you can choose the file you want to attach. The Paradox version 3.5 file SHIPPING.DB was copied to your PRACTICE directory when you copied the practice files to your hard disk.

3 If necessary, use the Directories list to open the PRACTICE directory.

4 In the File Name box, double-click SHIPPING.DB.

Microsoft Access attaches the table to your database and then displays a message to let you know that the table was successfully attached.

5 Choose the OK button to close the message box, and then choose the Close button to close the Select File dialog box.

Now the SHIPPING table appears in the Database window along with the other tables in the Sweet database.

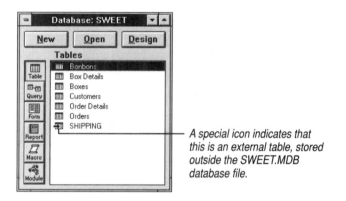

A special icon indicates that this is an external table, stored outside the SWEET.MDB database file.

Note In addition to SHIPPING.DB, a Paradox index file named SHIPPING.PX was copied to your PRACTICE directory when you copied the practice files to your hard disk. Paradox stores information about the table's primary key in this file. Microsoft Access needs the .PX file to open the attached table. If you delete or move the .PX file, you won't be able to open the attached table. For more information about attaching Paradox tables, see Chapter 4, "Importing, Exporting, and Attaching" in the *Microsoft Access User's Guide*.

Working with Data in an Attached Table

Once you attach an external table to your Microsoft Access database, you can use it much as you would a regular Microsoft Access table. You can't change the structure of an attached table (add, delete, or rearrange fields), but you can set field properties in the table's Design view to control the way Microsoft Access displays data from a field. You can also use field properties to give a field a default value or to check new data entered in a field to be sure it meets a rule you specify.

Open an attached table

▶ Double-click the SHIPPING table in the Database window.

Microsoft Access opens the table and displays its data.

Datasheet view of the SHIPPING table

Table: SHIPPING		
Carrier ID	**Ship State/Prov**	**Shipping Charge**
1	AK	3.35
1	AL	3.7
1	AR	3.35
1	AZ	3.35
1	Alberta	3.35
1	British Columbia	3.35
1	CA	3.35

Change a field property

You'd like to see the data in the Shipping Charge field displayed as currency. One of the Microsoft Access data types is Currency; maybe you can use it to display the data the way you want.

Design View button

1   Click the Design View button on the toolbar.

Microsoft Access displays a message to let you know that you can't modify some properties of an attached table. It asks if you want to open the table anyway.

2   Choose the OK button.

Microsoft Access displays the SHIPPING table in Design view.

3   Click the Data Type box for the Shipping Charge field.

Table: SHIPPING	
Field Name	**Data Type**
⚷ Carrier ID	Number
⚷ Ship State/Province	Text
▶ Shipping Charge	Number

Click here.

Microsoft Access displays the properties of the Shipping Charge field in the lower portion of the window. Notice that the Hint box beside the properties says that this property (DataType) can't be modified in attached tables. But you can still modify how Microsoft Access displays the data by setting the field's Format property.

4   Click the Format property box in the lower portion of the window.

Now the Hint box displays a hint about setting the Format property. If it were a property that you couldn't set in an attached table, the hint would let you know.

5   Set the Format property to Currency.

Field Size	Double
Format	Currency
Decimal Places	Auto

Click the arrow to display the list, and then select Currency.

Datasheet View button

6   Click the Datasheet View button on the toolbar. When Microsoft Access says that switching to Datasheet view requires you to save the changes in the table, choose the OK button.

Table: SHIPPING		
Carrier ID	**Ship State/Prov**	**Shipping Charge**
1	AK	$3.35
1	AL	$3.70
1	AR	$3.35
1	AZ	$3.35

Data formatted as currency.

Now the data is formatted the way you want.

7   Close the SHIPPING table.

Using a FormWizard to Create a Form Based on a Table

A table's datasheet is a convenient way to work with all the records in the table at the same time, but in some cases you might prefer using a form. For example, you can filter the records while you're using a form to view a subset of records, but not while you're using a table. Microsoft Access provides a fast way to create a form based on a table — use a FormWizard.

All three of Sweet Lil's carriers have raised their shipping charge to Alaska. You want to filter the records in the SHIPPING table so that you're looking at just the records for Alaska. To create the appropriate filter, you need a Shipping form.

SHIPPING		
Carrier ID	**Ship State/Province**	**Shipping Charge**
1	AK	$3.35
2	AK	$4.36
3	AK	$7.51

Using a form, you can filter records to see only the shipping charges to Alaska.

You can create this form quickly with a FormWizard.

Create a form

You use the same techniques to create a new form as you use to create any other Microsoft Access object.

1   Click the Form button in the Database window.

2   Choose the New button.

Form button

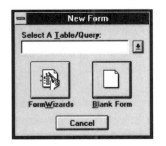

Microsoft Access displays the New Form dialog box.

3   In the Select A Table/Query box, click the arrow to display the list of tables and queries, and then select the SHIPPING table.

4   Choose the FormWizards button.

Microsoft Access displays the first FormWizard dialog box, which asks which AccessWizard you want to use.

5   Double-click the Tabular FormWizard.

A tabular form arranges the fields for each record in a row and displays as many rows (records) as will fit in the Form window.

6   Add all the fields in the SHIPPING table to the form, and then click the Next button.

7   Choose the Standard look for the form, and then click the Next button.

8   Accept "SHIPPING" as the title of the form, and then choose the Open button.

Microsoft Access creates a tabular form based on the SHIPPING table and opens it for you. You can use this form to work with the data in the attached Paradox table just as you'd use it to work with data in a Microsoft Access table.

Create a filter

You want to see three records — the shipping charges for each of the three carriers to Alaska.

1   Click the Edit Filter/Sort button on the toolbar.

2   Drag the Ship State/Province field from the field list to the first Field box in the lower portion of the Filter window.

3   Type **AK** in the Criteria box.

Edit Filter/Sort button

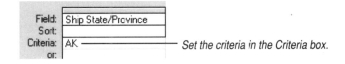

Set the criteria in the Criteria box.

*Apply Filter/Sort
button*

4 Click the Apply Filter/Sort button on the toolbar.

SHIPPING		
SHIPPING		
Carrier ID	**Ship State/Province**	**Shipping Charge**
1	AK	$3.35
2	AK	$4.36
3	AK	$7.51

> Shipping charges
> to Alaska.

*For details about
creating filters, see
Lesson 4,
"Answering
Questions."*

Microsoft Access shows you the records you want.

Change data

Each carrier has raised the shipping charge to Alaska by one dollar. You can use your
form to change the data in the attached SHIPPING table.

1 In each of the three records, increase the amount in the Shipping Charge field by
one dollar.

After you change the value in a field and leave the record, Microsoft Access saves
your change to the attached Paradox version 3.5 table.

2 When you're finished using your form, choose Save from the File menu to save it.

3 Name your form Shipping, and then close the form.

Now the Shipping form is part of the Sweet database.

Tip There's an even faster way to change a group of records: Use an *action query*.
With an action query, you can make the same change to many records in just one step.
For details, see Lesson 12, "Using Action Queries to Manipulate Data."

One Step Further

Your colleague in the Shipping department has decided to use Microsoft Access
instead of Paradox to manage his shipping data. This means you don't need to keep
the Paradox file of shipping charges anymore; you can import it so that it's part of the
Sweet database.

Import a table

▶ Use the Import command on the File menu to import the SHIPPING table.

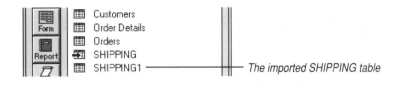

The imported SHIPPING table

Hint Choose Paradox 3.X in the Import dialog box, and then choose
SHIPPING.DB in the Select File dialog box.

Since your attached table is named SHIPPING, Microsoft Access gives the
imported table the name SHIPPING1. (You can't have two tables in a database
with the same name.)

Delete an attachment to an external table

Now that the data is stored in a Microsoft Access table, you don't need the attached
SHIPPING table.

▶ Select the attached SHIPPING table, and then press the DEL key.

Click here, and then
press the DEL key.

Microsoft Access deletes the attachment to the external Paradox table. (The
Paradox files are still in your PRACTICE directory; only the attachment to them is
deleted.)

Rename a table

▶ Use the Rename command on the File menu to rename the SHIPPING1 table
"Shipping."

Hint Select the SHIPPING1 table in the Database window, and then choose the
Rename command from the File menu.

Change field properties and set the primary key of an imported table

Now that the Shipping table is part of your Microsoft Access database, you can
customize the table's design. Open the Shipping table in Design view, and make the
following changes to the table's design.

1 Change the FieldSize property of the Carrier ID field from Double to Long
Integer. This limits values in the field to whole numbers. In addition, it enables
you to create a relationship between the Carriers table and the Shipping table.
You'll do that in Lesson 9, "Relating Tables."

2 Change the data type of the Shipping Charges field from Number to Currency.

3 Set the table's primary key to both the Carrier ID and the Ship State/Province fields.

Primary Key button

Hint You need to select the rows for both fields. To do that, drag through the row selector for each field. Or select the row for Carrier ID, and then hold down the SHIFT key while you select the row for Ship State/Province. When both rows are selected, click the Primary Key button on the toolbar.

---

4 Save your changes to the table's design. When Microsoft Access warns you that the field size of some fields have been changed to a shorter size and that some data might be lost, choose the OK button. You won't lose data in this case because the data in the fields is smaller than the new size limits.

Note You might wonder why you used two fields (Carrier ID and Ship State/Province) to make a primary key for the Shipping table. These two fields make a good primary key because taken together, their two values are unique for each record in the table. To see how this works, look at the table in Datasheet view. Each carrier ID appears in the table 59 times — once for every state and province. And each state or province appears in the table three times — once for every carrier. But the combination of a specific carrier ID and a specific state or province — 1 and AK, for example — appears in the table only once.

Export a table to a Microsoft Excel file

Suppose you want to use Microsoft Excel to analyze the data in the Boxes table. You can export the table to a Microsoft Excel file.

▶ Use the Export command on the File menu to export the Boxes table to a Microsoft Excel file. Name the exported file BOXES.XLS. If you have Microsoft Excel installed on your computer, open the BOXES.XLS file in Microsoft Excel to look at the exported data.

Lesson Summary

To	Do this	Button
Attach an external table to a Microsoft Access database	In the Database window, choose Attach Table from the File menu.	
Change field properties of an attached table	In the table's Design view, click the property you want to change. (The Hint text will let you know if it's a property you can't change.)	
Use a FormWizard to create a form based on a table	Click the Form button in the Database window, and then click the New button.	Form

To	Do this	Button
Import a table	In the Database window, choose Import from the File menu.	
Delete an attachment to an external table	In the Database window, select the attached table, and then press the DEL key. Microsoft Access deletes only the attachment, not the external table.	
Rename a table	Select the table in the Database window, and then choose Rename from the File menu.	
Export a table	In the Database window, choose Export from the File menu.	

For more information on	See
Importing, exporting, and attaching tables	Chapter 4, "Importing, Exporting, and Attaching" in the *Microsoft Access User's Guide*.
Setting a table's primary key	Chapter 2, "Table Basics" in the *Microsoft Access User's Guide*.

Preview of the Next Lesson

In the next lesson, you'll learn how to join the Carriers and Shipping tables so that you can see data from both tables in the same datasheet or in the same form.

Joining Tables to See Related Data

A simple list of product names becomes more interesting when you add the products' sales figures. That's because data becomes interesting when you put it together with other, related data. Using Microsoft Access, you can join tables that contain related data and then work with the related data together in a datasheet, form, or report. In this lesson, you'll find out how to create a query that contains fields from different tables. You'll join two tables, and then you'll create a new form based on the query.

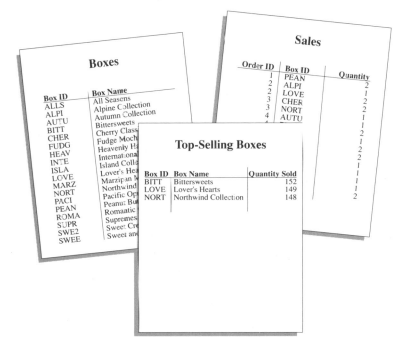

You will learn how to:

- Create a query that shows related data together.
- Add fields to a query.
- View a query's datasheet.
- Join tables in a query.
- Create a form based on a query.

Estimated lesson time: 20 minutes

What Is a Query?

A *query* defines a group of records you want to work with. You can think of a query as a request for a particular collection of data, such as "Show me the names and phone numbers for our carriers with their shipping charges." The answer to the request — the records that meet the definition — is called a *dynaset*. The records in a dynaset can include fields from one or more tables.

Dynaset of the Shipping Charges query

Select Query: Shipping Charges			
Carrier Name	**Contact Phone**	**Ship State/Province**	**Shipping Charge**
Wild Fargo Carriers	(555) 546-7837	AK	$4.35
Wild Fargo Carriers	(555) 546-7837	AL	$3.70
Wild Fargo Carriers	(555) 546-7837	Alberta	$3.35
Wild Fargo Carriers	(555) 546-7837	AR	$3.35
Wild Fargo Carriers	(555) 546-7837	AZ	$3.35
Wild Fargo Carriers	(555) 546-7837	British Columbia	$3.35

The query shows data from the Carriers table...

...with data from the Shipping table.

Table: Carriers			
Carrier ID	**Carrier Name**	**Contact Person**	**Contact Phone**
1	Wild Fargo Carriers	Clyde Houlihan	(555) 546-7837
2	Grey Goose Express	Bella Lamont	(555) 532-9874
3	Pegasus Overnight	Morris Jantz	(555) 513-8988

Table: Shipping		
Carrier ID	**Ship State/Province**	**Shipping Charge**
1	AK	$4.35
1	AL	$3.70
1	Alberta	$3.35
1	AR	$3.35
1	AZ	$3.35
1	British Columbia	$3.35

You use queries in much the same ways as you use tables. You can open a query and view its dynaset in a datasheet. You can base a form or a report on a query. You can even update the data in a query's dynaset and have the changes saved back to the table where the data is stored.

In fact, you may find that you use queries to work with data more often than tables. That's because you can use a query to sort data or to view a meaningful subset of all the data in your database. You can look at only the customers in your region, for example, instead of wading through all the customers in the Customers table, and you can see information about their purchases at the same time.

You might wonder why you need to create queries at all, if you end up using them just like tables. Why not simply include all the data you need in a table? The answer holds the secret to the great power of a relational database. When you create a separate table for each subject of data — customers, for example, or products — the result is a system that provides extraordinary flexibility in how you can bring related data together.

You can create one query that shows which customers bought which products, another query that shows which products sold best in Europe, and another that shows postal codes sorted according to product sales. You don't have to store the product information three times for the three different queries — each piece of information is stored once, in its table. How you use it is up to you.

Start the lesson

▶   In this lesson, you'll create a query that includes fields from the Carriers table created in Lesson 6, and the Shipping table, imported in Lesson 7. If you don't have these two tables, see Lessons 6 and 7 for instructions on adding them to the Sweet database. Then you can complete the exercises in this lesson.

Creating a Query That Shows Related Data Together

In Lesson 7, you created a form to work with the data in the Shipping table. The form shows all the fields in the Shipping table, but it doesn't necessarily show all the information you want when you're looking at shipping charges. For example, you might want to see the carrier's company name on the form as well as its ID number. But the Company Name field is in the Carriers table. How do you display it on the same form with fields from the Shipping table?

The Shipping form is based on one table, the Shipping table.

Shipping		

Shipping

Carrier ID	Ship State/Province	Shipping Charge
1	AK	$4.35
1	AL	$3.70
1	Alberta	$3.35

If you base the form on a query instead, you can include data from the Shipping table and the Carriers table, and you can still use the form to update data in the Shipping table.

Shipping Charges		

Shipping Charges

Carrier Name	Carrier ID	Ship State/Province
Wild Fargo Carriers	1	AK
Wild Fargo Carriers	1	AL
Wild Fargo Carriers	1	Alberta

Data from the Carriers table	*Data from the Shipping table*

You'll create a query that includes all the fields you want from both tables, and then create a new form based on the query.

Create a query

1 Click the Query button in the Database window.

Microsoft Access displays the list of queries in the Sweet database.

Query button

2 Choose the New button.

```
┌──────────────────────────────────────────────┐
│ ─            Add Table                        │
├──────────────────────────────────────────────┤
│  Table/Query:                                 │
│  ┌─────────────────────────┬─┐  ┌──────────┐  │
│  │ Bonbons                 │↑│  │   Add    │  │
│  │ Bonbons by Box          │ │  └──────────┘  │
│  │ Bonbons List            │ │  ┌──────────┐  │
│  │ Box Details             │ │  │  Close   │  │
│  │ Box List                │ │  └──────────┘  │
│  │ Box Sales Subform       │ │                │
│  │ Boxes                   │ │                │
│  │ Boxes Sold              │ │                │
│  │ Boxes Subform           │ │                │
│  │ Carriers                │↓│                │
│  └─────────────────────────┴─┘                │
└──────────────────────────────────────────────┘
```

The tables and queries in the Sweet database

Microsoft Access opens the Query window and displays the Add Table dialog box, where you select the tables and queries you want to include in your query. You want to see data from the Carriers table and the Shipping table.

3   Double-click the Carriers table to add it to the query, then scroll down the list, and double-click the Shipping table.

Microsoft Access adds the two tables to your query and displays the field lists for the tables in the upper portion of the Query window.

4   Choose the Close button to close the Add Table dialog box.

Note   Microsoft Access lists queries as well as tables in the Add Table dialog box. This means you can include fields from other queries in your query as well as table fields. In most cases, though, you'll probably want to add table fields to your query. For a diagram that shows which tables are in the Sweet database and what fields are in each table, see "Getting Ready" earlier in this book.

Adding Fields to a Query

As you can see, the Query window looks a lot like a form's Filter window. The top part of the window contains the field lists for the tables that are included in the query. The bottom part contains the QBE (Query by Example) grid, where you define which fields and records you want to see.

Field lists for tables included in the query

Use the QBE grid to specify which fields and records to
include in the query and how the records should be sorted.

You want to see the Carrier Name field from the Carriers table and all the fields from
the Shipping table. You'll add these fields to the QBE grid.

Add a field

▶ Drag the Carrier Name field from the Carriers field list to the first cell in the Field
row of the QBE grid. (To drag the field, click it and hold down the mouse button
while you move the mouse.)

Microsoft Access displays the field name in the Field cell.

Add all the fields in a field list to the QBE grid

You want to include all the fields from the Shipping table in your query. Microsoft Access provides a fast way to do this.

1 Double-click the title bar of the Shipping field list.

Microsoft Access selects all the fields.

2 Click inside the field list and hold down the mouse button. Drag the fields to the second Field cell in the QBE grid.

When you release the mouse button, Microsoft Access adds all the fields from the Shipping table to the query.

All the Shipping fields are added to the QBE grid.

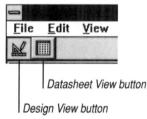

Field:	Carrier Name	Carrier ID	Ship State/Province	Shipping Charge
Sort:				
Show:	⊠	⊠	⊠	⊠
Criteria:				
or:				

Now you can look at the results of your query.

Viewing a Query's Datasheet

Like a table, a query has two views — Design view and Datasheet view. You can switch back and forth between the views by clicking the view buttons on the toolbar.

File	Edit	View
✒	▦	

Datasheet View button

Design View button

View the query's datasheet

Datasheet View button

1   Click the Datasheet View button on the toolbar.

Select Query: Query1			
Carrier Name	**Carrier ID**	**Ship State/Prov**	**Shipping Charge**
Wild Fargo Carriers	1	AK	$4.35
Grey Goose Expres	1	AK	$4.35
Pegasus Overnight	1	AK	$4.35
Wild Fargo Carriers	1	AL	$3.70
Grey Goose Expres	1	AL	$3.70
Pegasus Overnight	1	AL	$3.70

The query shows data from the Carriers table...

...and the Shipping table.

Microsoft Access displays the query in Datasheet view. Just as in a table's Datasheet view, it displays the query's records in row-and-column format. The query's records include one field from the Carriers table (Carrier Name) and three fields from the Shipping table (Carrier ID, Ship State/Province, and Shipping Charge).

2   Take a close look at the data in the query — especially the Carrier Name and Carrier ID data.

There's a problem in your query. Carrier ID number 1 belongs to Wild Fargo Carriers; carrier ID number 2 belongs to Grey Goose Express, and carrier ID number 3 belongs to Pegasus Overnight. But your query shows all three carriers with ID number 1.

Select Query:	
Carrier Name	**Carrier ID**
Wild Fargo Carriers	1
Grey Goose Express	1
Pegasus Overnight	1

All three carriers shouldn't have the same ID number. What's the problem?

3   Scroll down the records. You'll see that Microsoft Access has associated all three carrier names with all three carrier ID numbers.

The problem is that Microsoft Access doesn't know how to connect the carrier names from the Carriers table with the correct records in the Shipping table. To fix this problem, you'll *join* the two tables in the query. How you join the tables tells Microsoft Access how to associate the data.

Joining Tables

To associate data in different tables correctly, Microsoft Access uses matching values in equivalent fields in the two tables. You tell Microsoft Access which fields contain the matching values by drawing a *join line* between the two fields. In most cases, the primary key from one table is joined to a field in the other table that contains the matching values.

For example, the primary key in the Carriers table is the Carrier ID field: It contains a unique value for each carrier. The Shipping table also contains a Carrier ID field: It identifies which carrier has the shipping charge for the record.

Table: Carriers			
Carrier ID	**Carrier Name**	**Contact Person**	**Contact Phone**
1	Wild Fargo Carriers	Clyde Houlihan	(555) 546-7837
2	Grey Goose Express	Bella Lamont	(555) 532-9874
3	Pegasus Overnight	Morris Jantz	(555) 513-8988

Microsoft Access uses the carrier ID to match values in the two tables...

Table: Shipping		
Carrier ID	**Ship State/Province**	**Shipping Charge**
1	Yukon Territory	$10.50
2	AK	$5.36
2	AL	$5.21

Select Query: Query1			
Carrier Name	**Carrier ID**	**Ship State/Province**	**Shipping Charge**
Wild Fargo Carriers	1	Yukon Territory	$10.50
Grey Goose Express	2	AK	$5.36
Grey Goose Express	2	AL	$5.21

...and show you the related data in the datasheet.

When you join the Carrier ID field in the Carriers table to the Carrier ID field in the Shipping table, you're telling Microsoft Access to use the values in these two fields to associate the data correctly.

Join two tables in a query

Design View button

1 Click the Design View button on the toolbar to switch back to Design view.

2 Drag the Carrier ID field from the Carriers field list to the Carrier ID field in the Shipping field list.

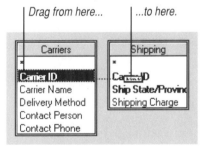

Drag from here...   *...to here.*

3 If you want, drag the Shipping field list away from the Carriers field list to see the join line more easily. (To drag the field list, click the title bar and hold down the mouse button while you move the mouse.)

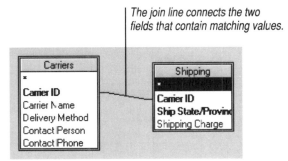

The join line connects the two fields that contain matching values.

View the datasheet

Datasheet View button

▶ Click the Datasheet View button on the toolbar, and then scroll down the records until the value in the Carrier ID field changes from 1 to 2.

Carrier Name	Carrier ID	Ship State/Prov	Shipping Charge
Wild Fargo Carriers	1	WI	$3.55
Wild Fargo Carriers	1	WV	$4.05
Wild Fargo Carriers	1	WY	$3.55
Wild Fargo Carriers	1	Yukon Territory	$10.50
Grey Goose Express	2	AK	$5.36
Grey Goose Express	2	AL	$5.21
Grey Goose Express	2	Alberta	$4.36

Select Query: Query1

Now Microsoft Access knows how to associate the data in the two tables correctly.

Note When you add tables from the Sweet database to a query, in many cases Microsoft Access automatically creates join lines between the tables. For example, if you add the Customers and Orders tables to a query, a join line appears between the two tables automatically. That's because there's a relationship defined between the tables. You'll find out how to define relationships in Lesson 9, "Relating Tables."

Save and name your query

1 From the File menu, choose Save Query.

Microsoft Access displays the Save As dialog box.

2 Name the query Shipping Charges, and choose the OK button.

3 Close the query.

4 To see your query in the Database window, scroll down the alphabetical list of queries.

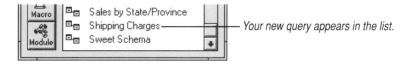

Your new query appears in the list.

Your query is saved in the Sweet database. You can open it anytime by double-clicking the query in the Database window. When you open the Shipping Charges query, Microsoft Access gets the most current data stored in the Carriers and Shipping tables and brings it together in the query's dynaset.

Note   You can create a query that combines data from more than one source by including attached tables, such as dBASE or Paradox tables, in the query. For example, suppose you didn't import the Shipping table at the end of Lesson 7 but instead maintained the attachment to the external Paradox file. You could still have used the external table in your query just as you used the imported table in this lesson.

One Step Further

When you're working with the data from the Shipping table, you might want to call a carrier to confirm a change in shipping charges. You'll add the Contact Phone field from the Carriers table to your query. Then you'll delete the Carrier ID field and create a new form based on the query.

Add a field to a query

1   Open the Shipping Charges query in Design view.

Hint   Select the query in the Database window, and then choose the Design button.

2   Add the Contact Phone field between the Carrier Name and Carrier ID fields.

Hint   If you drag a field to the QBE grid and drop it on a field that's already in the grid, the new field is inserted to the left of that field. You can also rearrange fields that are already in the grid. Just click the field selector to select it, then click again, and drag the field where you want it.

Delete a field from a query

Now that you can see the carrier name and phone number in your query's dynaset, you don't need to see the carrier ID number.

1   Click the field selector for the Carrier ID field, and then press the DEL key.

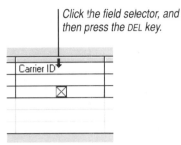

*Click the field selector, and
then press the DEL key.*

2   Save your changes.

Create a form based on a query

You could create your new form using the same technique you already used to create the Shipping form—click the Form button in the Database window, and then choose the New button. But in this case, you'll use two shortcuts to create a quick form based on the Shipping Charges query.

*New Form
button*

1   With the Shipping Charges query open, click the New Form button on the right side of the toolbar.

Microsoft Access displays the New Form dialog box, with Shipping Charges already selected in the Select A Table/Query box.

2   Click the FormWizards button.

3   Create a tabular form that includes all the fields in the Shipping Charges query.

Here's a tip to create a quick form. When the FormWizard asks you which fields to include on the form, click the Fast Forward button at the bottom of the dialog box. Microsoft Access adds all the fields to the form and builds a form with the default style.

*Click here to quickly create a
form that includes all the fields.*

4   Open your form to see how it looks. When you're finished looking at the form, save it and name it Shipping Charges. Then close the query.

Lesson Summary

To	Do this	Button
Create a query	Click the Query button in the Database window, and then choose the New button.	[Query button]
Add a table or query to a query	Double-click the table or query in the Add Table dialog box. If you need to add a table after you have closed the Add Table dialog box, choose Add Table from the Query menu.	
Add a field to a query	Drag the field from the field list in the upper portion of the Query window to an empty Field cell in the lower portion of the Query window. To insert a field between two existing fields, drop it on the field to the right.	
View a query's datasheet	Double-click the query in the Database window. Or, in the query's Design view, click the Datasheet View button on the toolbar.	[Datasheet View button]
Join tables in a query	The two tables must contain fields with matching values that Microsoft Access can use to relate the data. Drag the matching field from one field list and drop it on the matching field in the other field list.	
Delete a field from a query	Click the field's field selector in the QBE grid to select it, and then press the DEL key.	

For more information on	See
Creating queries	Chapter 5, "Query Basics," in the *Microsoft Access User's Guide*.
Joining tables in a query	Chapter 6, "Designing Select Queries," in the *Microsoft Access User's Guide*.

Preview of the Next Lesson

In the next lesson, you'll learn how to create relationships between tables so they're automatically joined in queries. You'll also learn more about designing tables for a relational database.

Relating Tables

Some encounters are temporary; others last a lifetime. You might have a few things in common with the person sitting next to you on an airplane, for example, but that doesn't mean you'll ever see the person again. In contrast, you probably have daily contact with a co-worker, a friend, a parent, or a child. It's similar with relationships between tables. If you want to see related information from two tables again and again, you can create a permanent relationship between them. That helps Microsoft Access automatically associate the information in the two tables whenever you use them together in a query, form, or report.

In this lesson, you'll learn how to create a relationship between two tables. You'll also learn how to evaluate relationships and to structure your tables so that they're related correctly.

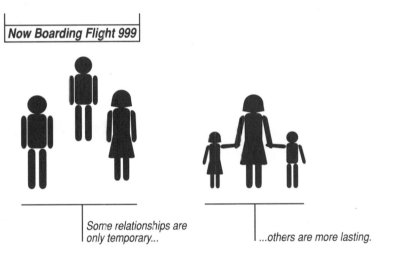

Some relationships are only temporary...

...others are more lasting.

You will learn how to:

- Create a relationship between two tables.
- Relate tables that contain multiple-field primary keys.
- Detect a many-to-many relationship and use a linking table.

Estimated lesson time: 40 minutes

Understanding Relationships

Once you create tables in your database and set each table's primary key, you can create relationships between the tables. A *relationship* is similar to a join in a query: Microsoft Access uses both of these to associate the data in two tables correctly. The difference is that a join exists only for a particular query. In contrast, a relationship can help Microsoft Access associate the data in any new query, form, or report that includes the two related tables.

You can create two types of relationships in Microsoft Access: a *one-to-many* relationship or a *one-to-one* relationship. One-to-many relationships are by far the most common. In this type of relationship, *one* record in one table can have *many* related records in the other table. For example, one customer can place one or more orders. So one record in a Customers table (called the *primary* table in the relationship) can have many matching records in an Orders table (the *related* table).

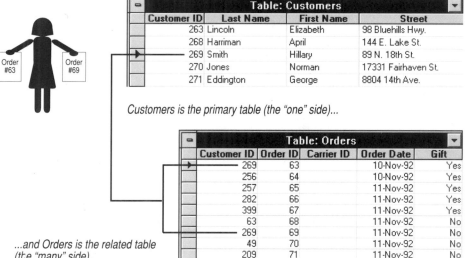

Customers is the primary table (the "one" side)...

...and Orders is the related table (the "many" side).

In a one-to-one relationship, on the other hand, one record in the primary table can have only one matching record in the related table. This type of relationship is less common than the one-to-many relationship. One reason you might use a one-to-one relationship would be when you want to separate information about employees into public and restricted data. For example, you might put public information, such as names and job titles, in one table and restricted information, such as salary information, in another table. These two tables would have a one-to-one relationship because each record in the public table would have only one matching record in the restricted table.

Note You can also have relationships between your tables that help ensure that the data in the relationship makes sense — for example, that you don't have orders in the Orders table with no matching customer in the Customers table. For details, see "Referential Integrity Rules" in Chapter 3, "Changing and Customizing Tables," in the *Microsoft Access User's Guide*.

Start the lesson

▶ In this lesson, you'll create a relationship between the Carriers table created in Lesson 6 and the Shipping table imported in Lesson 7. If you don't have these two tables, see Lessons 6 and 7 for instructions on adding them to the Sweet database. Then you can complete the exercises in this lesson.

Creating a Relationship Between Two Tables

Before you can create a relationship between two tables, the tables must contain matching fields. You relate the primary key field in the primary table (on the "one" side of the relationship) to a matching field in the related table. The matching field is sometimes called a *foreign key*.

In the relationship between the Carriers and Shipping tables in the Sweet database, the Carrier ID field is the matching field.

Carrier ID is the primary key of the Carriers table...

	Table: Carriers				
Carrier ID	**Carrier Name**	**Delivery Method**	**Contact Person**	**Contact Phone**
1	Wild Fargo Carriers	No	Clyde Houlihan	(555)546-7837
2	Grey Goose Expres	Yes	Bella Lamont	(555) 532-9874
3	Pegasus Overnight	No	Morris Jantz	(555) 513-8988

...and the matching field in the Shipping table.

	Table: Shipping	
Carrier ID	**Ship State/Province**	**Shipping Charge**
1	AK	$4.35
1	AL	$3.70
1	Alberta	$3.35
1	AR	$3.35
1	AZ	$3.35

This is a one-to-many relationship. One carrier can have many different shipping charges, depending on the destination of the package, so the Carriers table is the primary table in the relationship. When you create the relationship between these two tables, you'll relate Carrier ID in the Carriers table to Carrier ID in the Shipping table.

Before creating a relationship, figure out which table is the primary table (the table on the "one" side of the relationship) and which is the related table. If the related table doesn't contain a field with data that matches the data in the primary key field in the primary table, add the field to the related table so that you can create the relationship.

Tip   After you create a relationship between two tables, you can't modify or delete the primary key of either table without deleting the relationship first. For that reason, it's a good idea to test out a relationship between two tables before you actually create it. Add a few records to each of the tables, and then create some queries that join the tables. (You did this in Lesson 8 when you created the Shipping Charges query, for example.) When you're confident that each table has the right primary key and that the tables are structured so that you get the data you want from them, go ahead and create the relationship between the tables.

Create a relationship between two tables

1   Select the Carriers table in the Database window.

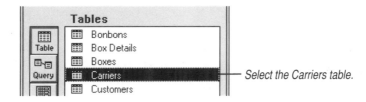

2   From the Edit menu, choose Relationships.

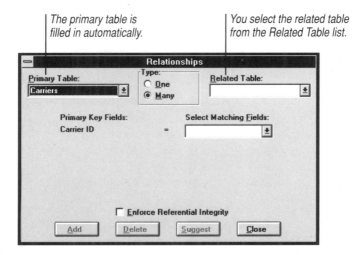

Microsoft Access displays the Relationships dialog box. The Carriers table is already selected for the Primary Table option, and the Type option is already set for a one-to-many relationship. You don't need to change either option.

3   Select the Shipping table from the Related Table list.

Once you've selected the matching table, you can select the matching field yourself, or you can have Microsoft Access suggest a field for you.

4   Choose the Suggest button.

Microsoft Access looks for a field in the Shipping table with the same characteristics as the primary key field in the Carriers table. It suggests the Carrier ID field in the Shipping table, which is the matching field you want.

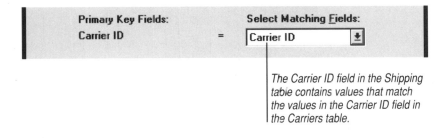

The Carrier ID field in the Shipping table contains values that match the values in the Carrier ID field in the Carriers table.

5   Choose the Add button to add the relationship between the Carriers and Shipping tables to the Sweet database.

6   Choose the Close button.

Note   Matching fields don't necessarily have to have the same name as the primary key fields they're related to. But they do have to contain matching data. In addition, they must have the same data type (with one exception), and if they have the Number data type, they must have the same field size.

The exception occurs when the primary key of the primary table has the Counter data type. In that case, the matching field in the related table can have either the Counter or Number data type (with its FieldSize property set to Long Integer). For example, the Carrier ID field in the Carriers table has the Counter data type. The Carrier ID field in the Shipping table has the Number data type, with its FieldSize property set to Long Integer.

Relating Tables with Multiple-Field Primary Keys

A table's primary key can consist of one or more fields. If a table with a multiple-field primary key is the primary table in a relationship, you must relate *all* the fields in its primary key to matching fields in the related table. To see why, take a look at the Shipping and Orders tables in the Sweet database. These two tables have a one-to-many relationship, with Shipping as the primary table.

Carrier 3 has one shipping charge to Illinois...

Table: Shipping		
Carrier ID	**Ship State/Province**	**Shipping Charge**
3	IL	$8.11
3	IN	$8.36
3	KS	$8.01
3	KY	$9.11
3	LA	$9.11

...and can ship many orders to Illinois...

Table: Orders			
Carrier ID	**Ship State/Province**	**Order ID**	**Order Date**
3	IL	402	29-Dec-92
1	Nova Scotia	404	29-Dec-92
2	NM	405	29-Dec-92
3	IL	406	29-Dec-92
2	KY	407	29-Dec-92
1	TX	408	29-Dec-92
3	NJ	409	29-Dec-92

...but each order has only one carrier and one destination.

The primary key for the Shipping table consists of two fields: Carrier ID and Ship State/Province. Before Microsoft Access can correctly relate a shipping charge to an order, it must be able to find matching data for *both* fields. That's because a shipping charge is based both on the carrier that the customer chooses and the destination of the order.

Relate a multiple-field primary key to matching fields

You'll create a relationship between the Shipping and Orders tables so that Microsoft Access can automatically look up an order's shipping charge.

1   Select the Shipping table in the Database window.

2   From the Edit menu, choose Relationships.

Microsoft Access displays the Relationships dialog box with the primary table, Shipping, already selected for you. Microsoft Access also lists the two fields that make up the primary key for the Shipping table.

3   In the Related Table list, select the Orders table.

Tip   If Microsoft Access says that you can't relate the tables, close the Relationships dialog box, and then check the design of your Shipping table. Its primary key should consist of *both* the Carrier ID field and the Ship State/Province field. The Carrier ID field should have the Number data type, and its FieldSize property should be set to Long Integer. The Ship State/Province field should have the Text data type. For help defining the table, see Lesson 7, "Attaching and Importing Data."

---

4   In the Matching Fields lists, match the Carrier ID field in the Shipping table to the Carrier ID field in the Orders table, and match the Ship State/Province field in the Shipping table to the Ship State/Province field in the Orders table.

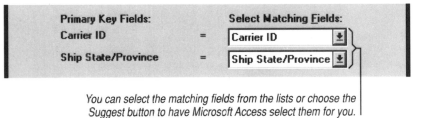

You can select the matching fields from the lists or choose the Suggest button to have Microsoft Access select them for you.

5   Choose the Add button to create the relationship, and then choose the Close button to close the Relationships dialog box.

Now Microsoft Access can use the values in the Carrier ID and Ship State/Province fields in the Orders table to find the appropriate shipping charge for an order.

See how your relationships work

You've created one relationship between the Carriers and Shipping tables and another relationship between the Shipping and Orders tables. You can see how the relationships work by creating a query that includes all three tables.

Query button

1   In the Database window, click the Query button to display the list of queries, and then choose the New button.

Microsoft Access displays the Add Table dialog box.

2   Add the Carriers, Orders, and Shipping tables to the query, and then close the Add Table dialog box.

3 Rearrange the field lists so that you can see the join lines between them.

To make the upper portion of the Query window bigger...

...drag this bar down.

To make the entire Query window bigger, drag its bottom border down.

As you can see, Microsoft Access uses the relationships you created to automatically join the tables in the query.

4 Add these fields to your query in this order:

- From the Orders table, the Order ID field

- From the Carriers table, the Carrier Name field

- From the Shipping table, the Shipping Charge field

5 Click the Datasheet View button on the toolbar to see the query's dynaset.

Datasheet View button

Order ID	Carrier Name	Shipping Charge
412	Wild Fargo Carriers	$3.35
408	Wild Fargo Carriers	$3.35
413	Grey Goose Express	$4.86
407	Grey Goose Express	$5.96
405	Grey Goose Express	$4.86

This shipping charge for order 405 is $4.86.

Microsoft Access displays the related data from all three tables.

6 Close the query.

You won't use this query again, so you don't need to save it.

Detecting Many-to-Many Relationships and Using Linking Tables

When you evaluate a relationship between two tables, it's important to look at the relationship from both sides. You might think at first that you have a one-to-many relationship when you actually have a *many-to-many* relationship. A many-to-many relationship occurs when one record in *either* table can have more than one matching record in the other table. In those cases, you need a third table that links the two tables before you can create the relationships.

The Boxes and Bonbons tables in the Sweet database are a good example. At first glance, you might think that boxes and bonbons have a one-to-many relationship, since one box can contain many different bonbons. But take a look at the relationship from the other side — the bonbons' side. One bonbon can appear in more than one box.

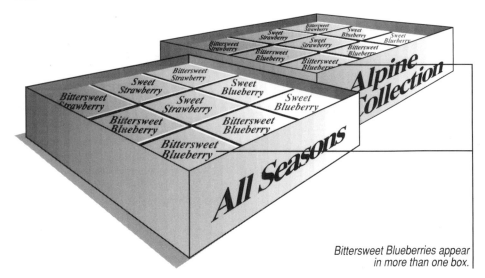

Bittersweet Blueberries appear in more than one box.

You'd have a problem if you tried to create a relationship between the Boxes table and the Bonbons table. Which is the primary table in the relationship?

Suppose you made Boxes the primary table in the relationship. You'd add a Box ID field to the Bonbons table to hold the matching values. But in the record for the Bittersweet Blueberry bonbon, you'd have to enter box IDs for both the All Seasons and Alpine Collection boxes, since the Bittersweet Blueberry bonbon appears in both boxes. If you do that, Microsoft Access can't relate the Bittersweet Blueberry record with the right boxes — you can have only one value in each matching field. The same thing happens if you try putting a Bonbon ID field in the Boxes table.

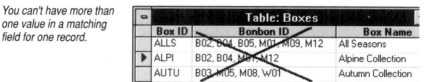

Table: Bonbons		
Bonbon ID	**Box ID**	**Bonbon Name**
B01	SWEE, ROMA, NORT	Candlelight Ecstasy
B02	ALLS, BITT, SWEE, ALPI	Bittersweet Blueberry
B03	MARZ, AUTU	Marzipan Oakleaf

You can't have more than one value in a matching field for one record.

Table: Boxes		
Box ID	**Bonbon ID**	**Box Name**
ALLS	B02, B04, B05, M01, M09, M12	All Seasons
▶ ALPI	B02, B04, M01, M12	Alpine Collection
AUTU	B03, M05, M08, W01	Autumn Collection

The solution is to create a linking table. In the Sweet database, the linking table is called Box Details. The primary key of the Box Details table consists of Box ID and Bonbon ID—the primary keys of the two tables you're trying to relate. It also contains a Quantity field, which tells you how many of each bonbon are in a box.

Table: Box Details		
Box ID	**Bonbon ID**	**Quantity**
ALLS	B02	2
ALLS	B04	2
ALLS	B05	2
ALLS	M01	2
ALLS	M09	2
ALLS	M12	2
ALPI	B02	4
ALPI	B04	5

The value in this field tells how many Bittersweet Blueberry bonbons are in the All Seasons collection.

One box has a record in the table for each kind of bonbon it contains.

One bonbon has a record in the table for each kind of box it's in.

The Boxes table has a one-to-many relationship with the Box Details table, and so does the Bonbons table. The Box Details table serves as a linking table between the two tables involved in the many-to-many relationship.

Tip   When you create a linking table, don't add fields to it that really belong in one of the two related tables. For example, you might be tempted to add the Box Name field to the Box Details table. But that field is already in the Boxes table; it shouldn't be repeated. The only fields that belong in the Box Details table are those needed to define the link (Box ID and Bonbon ID) and any field whose data describes the relationship between the records in the other two tables. The Quantity field qualifies because its data relates to *both* of the other tables — it tells how many of each bonbon are in each box.

One Step Further

It takes practice to be able to evaluate relationships between tables correctly. In this "One Step Further," you'll analyze the relationships between three sets of tables and tell how you'd relate the tables.

You can find answers to these problems in Appendix B, "Solutions to Database Design Problems."

Which employee took this order?

Customers call Sweet Lil's to place orders for boxes of bonbons. The Sweet database includes an Orders table that contains a record for each order, with information such as when the order was placed, where it should be shipped, and how the customer paid for it. Suppose you decide to add an Employees table to the database that includes a record for each employee, with information such as the employee's name, phone number, and date of hire.

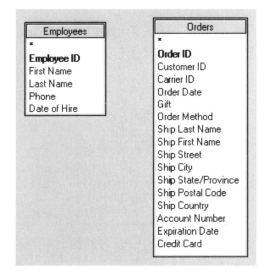

How would you relate these tables?

How would you relate the Employees and Orders tables so that you can easily find out the name of the employee who took an order? What fields do you need in each table to create the relationship? (Sketch out the relationship on a separate piece of paper before you look in Appendix B for the solution.)

Hint First, evaluate the relationship to determine which is the primary table in the relationship (the table on the "one" side of a one-to-many relationship) and which is the related table. You'll need a field in the related table that matches the primary key field in the primary table.

What products appear on an order?

In addition to the Orders table, the Sweet database includes a Boxes table that contains a record for each box in the product line, with information such as the box name, size, description, and price. How would you relate the Orders and Boxes tables so that you can easily find the name of all the boxes on an order?

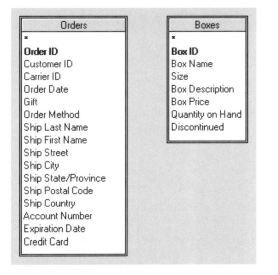

How would you relate these tables?

Hint   Be sure to analyze the relationship between the Orders and Boxes tables from both sides. An order could include more than one kind of box, and a box could appear on more than one order. Because these two tables are in a many-to-many relationship, you need to add a linking table between them.

Which movie will we watch tonight?

Suppose you have a large collection of movies on videocassette and laser disk. You create a database to help you decide which movie to watch tonight. It includes a Movies table that contains a record for each movie in your collection. Since you often choose a movie based on who's in it, your database also includes an Actors table with a record for each of your favorite actors.

How would you relate these tables?

You want to be able to look up a movie and see which of your favorite actors (if any) appears in it. You also want to be able to look up an actor and see if you have any of that actor's movies. How do you relate the two tables?

No hints this time — you're on your own!

Lesson Summary

To	Do this
Create a relationship between two tables	In the Database window, choose Relationships from the Edit menu.
Use a linking table in a many-to-many relationship	Create the linking table, and include in it the primary key fields from the two tables in the many-to-many relationship. Each of the tables in the many-to-many relationship has a one-to-many relationship with the linking table.

For more information on	See
Deciding what tables belong in your database	Chapter 1, "Designing a Database," in the *Microsoft Access User's Guide*.
Setting relationships between tables	Chapter 3, "Changing and Customizing Tables," in the *Microsoft Access User's Guide*.

Preview of the Next Lesson

Congratulations! In the lessons in Part 2, you learned how to create, join, and relate tables in your database. In the next lesson, you'll learn more about creating and using queries. You'll find out how to limit the records you see to those that meet criteria you set, and you'll also learn how to show totals and other calculations in a query.

Asking Questions and Getting Answers

Selecting the Records You Want

If your business changes from day to day, you'll frequently want to look at your data from different angles. At the end of the month, you'll want to find out how many orders you received for that month. When analyzing sales, you'll want to find out how many customers ordered gifts during the holiday season. Before calling your customers for a marketing campaign, you'll want to print out a list of the customers' names and phone numbers.

Using Microsoft Access queries, you can quickly pinpoint the records that you need. In this lesson, you'll create a variety of queries that select the data you want. You'll also calculate total values using a query, and you'll use a query to answer a "what if" question.

Which customers from California ordered gift boxes during December?

Customer	State/Province	Gift	Order Date
Adams, Cathy	CA	Yes	23-Dec-92
Fogerty, Sam	CA	Yes	09-Dec-92
Harkin, Rory	CA	Yes	03-Dec-92
Kennedy, Brian	CA	Yes	10-Dec-92
Kimball, Mary	CA	Yes	23-Dec-92
Kimball, Mary	CA	Yes	02-Dec-92
Kumar, Andrew	CA	Yes	19-Dec-92
Lopez, Maria	CA	Yes	10-Dec-92

You will learn how to:

- Create a query.
- Set criteria to get a set of related records.
- Sort data in a query.
- Hide a field.
- Find a range of values.
- Add another table to your query.
- Summarize data using a query.
- Change a field name in the datasheet.
- Show calculations in a field.

Estimated lesson time: 40 minutes

What is Graphical QBE?

*For more information
on queries, see
Lesson 8, "Joining
Tables to See
Related Data."*

In the Query window, you design a query using a feature called *graphical query by
example (QBE)*. With graphical QBE, you create queries by dragging fields from the
upper portion of the Query window to the QBE grid. You place the fields in the QBE
grid in the order you want them to appear in the datasheet. In this way, you use the
QBE grid to show Microsoft Access an example of what you want the results of your
query to look like.

After choosing fields, you use the QBE grid to zero in on the records you want.

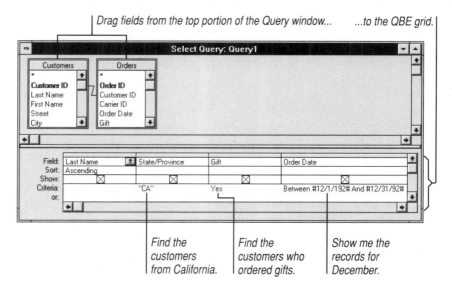

Drag fields from the top portion of the Query window...   ...to the QBE grid.

*Find the
customers
from California.*

*Find the
customers who
ordered gifts.*

*Show me the
records for
December.*

Another advantage of graphical QBE is that it makes it easy to build on a query.
Often, one question leads to another, and you find that you want to keep changing a
query. For example, you can start by finding all your customers from California. Then
by making small changes to the QBE grid, you can find all the California customers
who ordered gifts and finally all the California customers who ordered gifts in
December. And you can keep going, refining the query until you get it just right.

Start the lesson

▶ Start Microsoft Access. If the Microsoft Access window doesn't fill your screen,
    maximize the window. Then open the Sweet database.

Creating a Query

You're in charge of a telephone survey of Sweet Lil's customers in your sales region. Your region is New York state, so you'll use a query to get a list of the names and phone numbers of the New York customers.

You can base a query on either a table or another query. All the queries you create in this lesson are based on tables.

Create the query

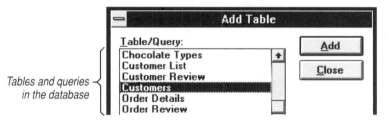

Query button

1   Click the Query button in the Database window.

2   Click the New button.

Microsoft Access opens the Query window and displays the Add Table dialog box. You use this dialog box to select the tables (or queries) you want in your query.

3   Scroll down in the Table/Query box until you see the Customers table.

4   Double-click the Customers table, and then choose the Close button.

In the top portion of the Query window, Microsoft Access displays a field list for the Customers table. The field list shows all the fields in the table. You use this list to select the fields you want to display in your query.

5 Drag the Customer ID field from the field list to the first cell in the Field row of the QBE grid.

Drag the Customer ID field from the field list...

...to the first cell in the QBE grid.

6 Drag the Last Name, First Name, State/Province, and Phone fields to the QBE grid. When you finish, the QBE grid has five fields.

7 From the File menu, choose Save.

8 In the Save As dialog box, type the name **NY Customers** and choose the OK button.

The name of the query appears in the title bar of the query.

Setting Criteria for the Records You Want

If you run the query now, you'll see records for all customers in the Customers table. But you're interested only in the customers from New York, so you'll set *criteria* to tell Microsoft Access to select only the records for New York customers.

For more information, see Appendix C, "Using Expressions."

When you set criteria for a query, you use an *expression*, a type of formula that specifies which records Microsoft Access should retrieve. For example, to find fields with a value greater than 5, you'd use the expression **>5**.

Specify criteria

1   In the QBE grid, click the Criteria cell below the State/Province field.

2   Type **NY** and press the ENTER key.

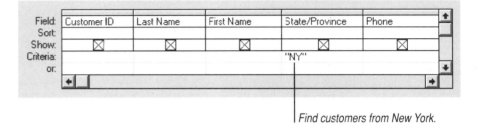

Find customers from New York.

Microsoft Access places quotation marks around NY after you press ENTER. If you type text that contains spaces or commas, you must enclose the text in quotation marks yourself. For example, if you're specifying criteria for a City field and you want to see records for Los Angeles, type **"Los Angeles"** in the Criteria cell.

Run your query

Datasheet View button

▶   To check the results of this query, click the Datasheet View button on the toolbar.

	Select Query: NY Customers			
Customer ID	**Last Name**	**First Name**	**State/Province**	**Phone**
12	Herron	Tom	NY	(212) 555-3944
13	Hernandez	Jim	NY	(212) 555-4893
16	Silverman	Frank	NY	(914) 555-2480
22	James	Carol	NY	(212) 555-2904

Microsoft Access displays the customers from New York state and their phone numbers.

Add more criteria

Now you have a list of customers in your sales region. But you want to call only your most recent customers, customers with customer IDs greater than 200. To find these customers, you'll add more criteria to the query.

Design View button

1   Click the Design View button on the toolbar to switch to Design view.

2   In the Criteria cell below the Customer ID field, type **>200**

By adding this criteria, you're now telling Microsoft Access: "Find customers who have customer IDs over 200 and who live in New York."

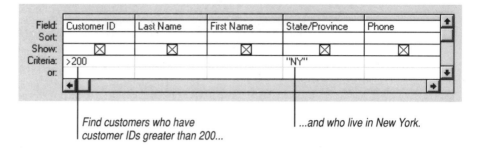

Find customers who have customer IDs greater than 200...   ...and who live in New York.

For more information on operators, see Appendix C, "Using Expressions."

Note The > (greater than) sign is an operator. Other operators you can use in expressions are < (less than), >= (greater than or equal to), and <= (less than or equal to).

Datasheet View button

3 Click the Datasheet View button to see the customers you're going to call.

Select Query: NY Customers				
Customer ID	Last Name	First Name	State/Province	Phone
249	Gunther	Paul	NY	(212) 555-4934
257	Petri	Laura	NY	(716) 555-0684
280	Kahn	Juliet	NY	(212) 555-9424
292	Singh	Rama	NY	(212) 555-4927

Sorting in a Query

For more sorting examples, see Lesson 4, "Answering Questions."

To make it easier to find a phone number for a specific customer, you can list the customers in alphabetical order. You'll change the NY Customers query so it sorts your customers by last name. If you've already created a filter in Lesson 4, you'll see that sorting in a query is the same as sorting in a filter.

Sort records alphabetically

1 Switch to Design view. (Click the Design View button on the toolbar.)

2 Click the Sort cell below the Last Name field.

Design View button

3 Select Ascending from the list.

Since this is a field that contains text data, Microsoft Access sorts from A through Z. For a field containing numbers, Microsoft Access sorts from 1 through 9. (If you select Descending, Microsoft Access sorts from Z through A or 9 through 1.)

Datasheet View button

4 Switch to the datasheet to see the names in alphabetical order. (Click the Datasheet View button on the toolbar.)

Select Query: NY Customers				
Customer ID	**Last Name**	**First Name**	**State/Province**	**Phone**
310	Brownlee	Jason	NY	(914) 555-0931
249	Gunther	Paul	NY	(212) 555-4934
298	Hendricks	Louise	NY	(516) 555-2067
280	Kahn	Juliet	NY	(212) 555-9424

Last names sorted A through Z

Hiding a Field

In the NY Customers query, you don't really need to see the State/Province field in the datasheet. The State/Province field always contains NY, and you already know that your customers are in New York. This field has to be included in Design view of the query, because you use it to set criteria. But you don't need to see this field in the datasheet. You'll use the Show box in the QBE grid to hide this field so it doesn't appear in the datasheet.

Hide a field

1   Switch to Design view.

2   In the Show row below the State/Province field, click the Show box so that the X disappears.

Field:	Customer D	Last Name	First Name	State/Province	
Sort:		Ascending			
Show:	☒	☒	☒	☐	
Criteria:				"NY"	
or:					

Click the Show box.

This tells Microsoft Access to use any criteria or sort information for this field, but not to show the field in the datasheet.

3   Switch to Datasheet view.

Select Query: NY Customers			
Customer ID	**Last Name**	**First Name**	**Phone**
310	Brownlee	Jason	(914) 555-0931
249	Gunther	Paul	(212) 555-4934
298	Hendricks	Louise	(516) 555-2067
280	Kahn	Juliet	(212) 555-9424

The State/Province field is no longer displayed.

4   From the File menu, choose Save Query and then close the query.

Finding a Range of Values

Lillian Farber, the president of the company, is analyzing the company's orders for each month. She's asked you to give her a list of all orders that were placed in November. She wants to know the order IDs, the customers' names, and the dates of the orders.

Create the query

New

New button

1   Click the New button in the Database window. (If queries aren't listed in the Database window, click the Query button first.)

2   Add the Orders table to the query, and then close the Add Table dialog box.

3   Add the Order ID, Customer ID, and Order Date fields to the QBE grid.

Field:	Order ID	Customer ID	Order Date	
Sort:				
Show:	☒	☒	☒	☐
Criteria:				
or:				

Specify criteria and check the results

You use an expression to select records during the month of November. This expression includes the **Between...And** operator.

1   In the Criteria cell below the Order Date field, type **Between 1-Nov-92 And 30-Nov-92** and then press ENTER.

Tip   Because this is a long expression, you may want to widen the Order Date field in the QBE grid so you can see the entire expression after you've typed it. To widen the field, click the right border of the field selector for the Order Date field and drag the border to the right.

Click and drag the border to widen the field.

Field:	Order ID	Customer ID	Order Date	
Sort:				
Show:	☒	☒	☒	
Criteria:			Between #11/1/92# And #11/30/92#	
or:				

Find orders for November.

Notice that Microsoft Access changes the format of the date and encloses each date in number signs (#). Microsoft Access uses the Date format for your country. The format shown above is the United States format. The Canada (English) format is **Between 1/11/92 And 30/11/92**.

Note   To find out which country your computer is set up for, open the Windows Control Panel and double-click the International section, which will display the Country setting as well as the Date and other formats.

---

2   Switch to Datasheet view to see the orders for November.

Order ID	Customer ID	Order Date
1	237	02-Nov-92
2	386	02-Nov-92
3	158	02-Nov-92
4	332	02-Nov-92

Select Query: Query1

3   Save the query, and name it Order Information.

Adding Another Table to Your Query

What's wrong with the query you just created? It's accurate—it shows you the data you want—but it's not very usable. You wanted to display the customer for each order, so you used the Customer ID field, the only customer field that's available in the Orders table. But what you really want is the customer's name, not just an ID number.

To get customer names, you need the Customers table, which contains the Last Name and First Name fields. You'll add the Customers table to your query and replace the Customer ID field with the Last Name and First Name fields.

Add the Customers table

1   Switch to Design view.

2   From the Query menu, choose Add Table.

Microsoft Access displays the Add Table dialog box.

For more about related tables, see Lesson 8, "Joining Tables to See Related Data."

3   Double-click the Customers table, and then choose the Close button.

Microsoft Access adds the Customers table to your query. Notice the line between the Customer ID fields in the two field lists. Microsoft Access uses this *join line* to relate the data in the two tables correctly.

Delete a field

You'll delete the Customer ID field from the QBE grid so that you can replace it with the Last Name and First Name fields from the Customers table.

1 Select the Customer ID field.

Click here to select.

2 Press the DEL key to delete the field from the query.

Add fields to replace the deleted field

1 From the Customers table, drag the Last Name field to the QBE grid, placing it over the Order Date field.

Drag from here...

...to here.

When you release the mouse button, the Order Date field moves to the right, making room for the Last Name field.

2   From the Customers table, drag the First Name field to the QBE grid, placing it over the Order Date field. When you finish, the QBE grid has four fields.

Field:	Order ID	Last Name	First Name	Order Date
Sort:				
Show:	☒	☒	☒	☒
Criteria:				Between #11/1/92# A
or:				

3   Take a look at the datasheet.

Select Query: Order Information			
Order ID	**Last Name**	**First Name**	**Order Date**
1 O'Brien		Sean	02-Nov-92
2 Burchard		Kristi	02-Nov-92
3 Chatterjee		Bednar	02-Nov-92
4 Rahman		Farhana	02-Nov-92

Now you can see customer names instead of customer ID numbers.

Find all customers whose last names begin with Z

You've just hung up the phone after talking with a customer. She told you her name, but you remember only that it started with a Z. You need to find her order ID right away, so you'll look for last names that start with Z.

For more details, search Help for "wildcard characters."

To look for these names, use this expression: Z*. The asterisk (*) is a wildcard character that stands for any number of characters.

1   Switch to Design view.

2   In the Criteria cell below the Last Name field, type **Z*** and press ENTER.

Field:	Order ID	Last Name	First Name	Order Date
Sort:				
Show:	☒	☒	☒	☒
Criteria:		Like "Z*"		Between #11/1/92# A
or:				

Microsoft Access changes your criteria to Like "Z*"

3   Switch to Datasheet view to see the customers whose last names begin with Z and who placed orders in November.

4   Save the query.

Summarizing Data

The Order Information query showed you a list of orders by customer. Often, you'll want more than just a list of orders; you'll also want to know the total number of orders placed by country or the total value of all boxes within one order. You can use Microsoft Access queries to perform these calculations for you.

When you design your query, you specify which fields to use for grouping records and which fields to use for totals (calculations). For example, you can calculate the total number of bonbons (the type of calculation) within each box (the group).

Select Query: Query1	
Box Name	**Number of Bonbons**
All Seasons	12
Alpine Collection	18
Autumn Collection	24
Bittersweets	24
Cherry Classics	12

For each box...   *...find the total number of bonbons.*

You'll create a new query by modifying the Order Information query. The new query will find the total number of orders by country.

Modify the query

1   Switch to Design view of the Order Information query.

2   From the File menu, choose Save As. Then name the query Total Orders by Country.

3   Delete the Last Name, First Name, and Order Date fields from the query.

4   In the QBE grid, add the Country field from the Customers table to the left of the Order ID field.

Field:	Country	Order ID	
Sort:			
Show:	☒	☒	
Criteria:			
or:			

Calculate totals in your query

Totals button

1   Click the Totals button on the toolbar.

Field:	Country	Order ID		
Total:	Group By	Group By		
Sort:				
Show:	☒	☒		
Criteria:				
or:				

Total row ───Total:

Microsoft Access displays the Total row in the QBE grid and fills in each box with "Group By."

2 Click the Total cell below the Order ID field, and then click the arrow. From the drop-down list, select Count.

Field:	Country	Order ID		
Total:	Group By	Group By		
Sort:		Group By		
Show:	☒	Sum		
Criteria:		Avg		
or:		Min		
		Max		
		Count		
		StDev		
		Var		

Click here.

Since there is one order ID for each order, you are counting the number of orders. You're grouping by country, so the count will be the count of orders for each country.

3 Switch to Datasheet view.

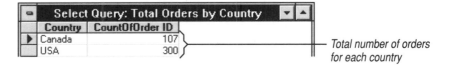

Select Query: Total Orders by Country	
Country	**CountOfOrder ID**
Canada	107
USA	300

Total number of orders for each country

The datasheet shows the total number of orders for each country. Microsoft Access gives this column a name: CountOfOrder ID.

Totaling by country and city

You'd like to investigate further. You want to know how many orders you've received from each state or province within each country.

1 Switch to Design view.

2 Add the State/Province field from the Customers table to the QBE grid. Place the field between the County and Order ID fields.

Field:	Country	State/Province	Order ID	
Total:	Group By	Group By	Count	
Sort:				
Show:	☒	☒	☒	
Criteria:				
or:				

3 Switch to Datasheet view.

Select Query: Total Orders by Country			
Country	**State/Province**	**Total Orders**	
Canada	Alberta	7	
Canada	British Columbia	8	
Canada	Manitoba	6	
Canada	New Brunswick	3	
Canada	Newfoundland	3	
Canada	Nova Scotia	14	
Canada	Ontario	27	
Canada	Prince Edward Island	2	
Canada	Québec	21	
Canada	Saskatchewan	9	
Canada	Yukon Territory	7	
USA	AK	2	
USA	AL	1	

Microsoft Access groups first by country (because this is the first Group By field in the QBE grid) and then by state or province. The totals are calculated for each state or province within each country.

Changing a Name in the Datasheet

In the previous query, the datasheet column heading CountOfOrder ID is a generic name assigned by Microsoft Access. You can easily change this name so that the datasheet shows a more meaningful name, such as Total Orders.

Change a field name

1 Switch to Design view.

2 In the QBE grid, place the insertion point immediately to the left of the Order ID field name, and then click the mouse button. Type **Total Orders:** to the left of the field name. (Be sure to include the colon.)

This name will be displayed as a column heading.

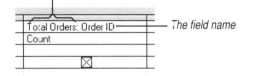

The field name

3   Look at the new heading in Datasheet view.

Country	State/Province	Total Orders
Canada	Alberta	7
Canada	British Columbia	8
Canada	Manitoba	6
Canada	New Brunswick	3

Select Query: Total Orders by Country

4   Save the query, and then close it.

Showing Calculations in a Field

When you're running a business, one of your most common questions is "What if?" Sweet Lil's is no exception. The chocolates are selling so well that the sales manager wants to know "What if I raise prices on our boxes by 5 percent?"

Since the tables in the Sweet database don't contain a field that shows prices raised by 5 percent, you'll use a query with a calculated field to answer this question.

Create the query

1   Create a new query, and add the Boxes table.

2   Add the Box Name and Box Price fields to the QBE grid.

Field:	Box Name	Box Price	
Sort:			
Show:	⊠	⊠	
Criteria:			
or:			

The query you've just created will display the current price for each box.

3   Look at the query in Datasheet view.

4   Save the query, and name it Raise Prices.

Add a calculated field

Now you'll add a calculated field that will show what prices would be if you raised them by 5 percent.

1   In Design view, place the insertion point in the empty Field cell to the right of the Box Price cell.

For more details on using expressions in calculated fields, see Appendix C, "Using Expressions."

2   Type **[Box Price]*1.05** and press ENTER. You include square brackets around Box Price because this field name contains a space. (Multiplying by 1.05 is the same as raising the price by 5 percent.)

Tip   You can widen the datasheet column to make room for the expression. Or you can press SHIFT+F2 to open the Zoom box and then enter the expression in the Zoom box.

Microsoft Access adds Expr1 as the field name.

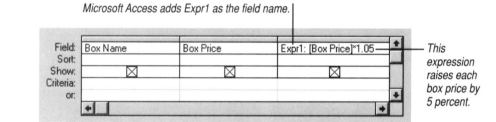

This expression raises each box price by 5 percent.

After you press ENTER, Microsoft Access adds a name for the field: Expr1. This is the name that will appear as the heading for this row in the datasheet.

Change the name of the calculated field and check the results

Since the heading Expr1 is a generic name that doesn't describe your data very well, you can change the name for this field to "New Price."

1   Select the name Expr1 in the Field cell. Do not select the colon (:) following the name.

2   Type **New Price** over Expr1.

3   Switch to Datasheet view to see the new prices.

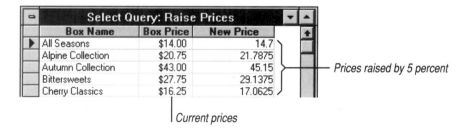

Prices raised by 5 percent

Current prices

For more information on expressions, see Appendix C, "Using Expressions."

Tip The new prices don't have the Currency format you see in the Box Price field. But you can use the **CCur** function to display these values as currency. To try it out, return to Design view and click the cell with the New Price expression. Then press SHIFT+F2 to open the Zoom box. In the Zoom box replace New Price: [Box Price]*1.05 with **New Price: CCur([Box Price]*1.05)**. (Be sure to include the parentheses.) Choose the OK button, and then switch to Datasheet view to see the results.

4 Save and close the query.

One Step Further

Now that you've created so many queries, you can get the answers to even more questions.

Note The queries you'll create in these exercises are all based on tables. Before choosing the tables, you may want to look at the Sweet database diagram in "Getting Ready" at the beginning of this book.

Finding the right box for a gift

You're trying to decide which box to order for your mother. You want to get a box larger than the 8-ounce size, but you have to keep the price under $30.00.

Create a new query using the Boxes table. The datasheet should look something this.

Select Query: Box for Mother		
Box Name	**Size**	**Box Price**
Alpine Collection	12	$20.75
Bittersweets	16	$27.75
Fudge Mocha Fantasy	12	$18.00
Peanut Butter Delights	12	$19.00
Sweet Creams	12	$23.00
Sweet and Bitter	16	$27.75

Larger than 8 ounces | Less than $30.00

Hint Remember that > is the operator for greater than and < means less than. In the expression you use to find boxes with prices less than $30.00, do not include a dollar sign ($).

Which boxes should we use for the big promotion?

Sweet Lil's is planning a large-scale promotion to push medium-priced assortments of bonbons ("Quality Everyone Can Afford"). You want to advertise only boxes that have prices between $17.00 and $25.00 and inventories of 200 or more (more than 200 on hand). You'd like to list the boxes in alphabetical order.

Create a new query that will select the boxes you want. Name the query "Mid-Priced Boxes." The datasheet for the query should look like the following illustration.

Select Query: Mid-Priced Boxes		
Box Name	**Box Price**	**Quantity on Hand**
▶ Alpine Collection	$20.75	400
Fudge Mocha Fantasy	$18.00	400
Lover's Hearts	$17.50	300
Pacific Opulence	$21.00	500
Peanut Butter Delights	$19.00	900
Supremes	$18.25	400

—— *More than 200 boxes on hand*

| *Boxes in alphabetical order* | *Prices between $17.00 and $25.00*

Hint   Use the Boxes table. In the expression you use to find boxes with prices between $17.00 and $25.00, do not include a dollar sign ($).

Lesson Summary

To	Do this	Button
Create a query	In the Database window, click the Query button and then choose the New button.	🔲 Query
Set criteria	In the QBE grid, enter criteria in the Criteria cell for any fields in the query.	
Sort the records in a query	In the QBE grid, select Ascending or Descending in the Sort cell for the field you want to sort.	
Find a range of data	In the QBE grid, enter criteria using the **Between...And** operator.	
Add another table to your query	From the Query menu, choose Add Table, and then double-click the table you want to add.	
Create totals	Click the Totals button on the toolbar. Then choose a total function (such as **Sum** or **Count**) in the Total cell for the field you want to calculate.	Σ

To	Do this	Button
Give a field a custom name	In the QBE grid, type a name followed by a colon immediately before the field name. The new name you type will appear as the column heading in the datasheet.	
Showing calculations in a field	In the Field cell, add an expression that calculates a value.	

For more information on	See	
Creating queries	Chapter 5, "Query Basics," and Chapter 6, "Designing Select Queries," in the *Microsoft Access User's Guide*.	
Creating expressions	Appendix C, "Expressions" in the *Microsoft Access User's Guide*.	

Preview of the Next Lesson

In the next lesson, you'll learn how to make queries easier to use. You'll create a query that displays a dialog box prompting you for criteria. When you run the query, you'll type criteria in the dialog box, and Microsoft Access will display the datasheet.

Creating User-Friendly Queries

How often do you ask the same types of questions about your data? A customer might call to ask for information about your 12-ounce boxes of candy, and later another customer might ask for information about the 8-ounce boxes. You could create several Microsoft Access queries to answer these questions. But there's a shortcut—to save time, you can create a *parameter query*. A parameter query prompts you for criteria each time you run the query, so you can use the same query over and over again to answer different but related questions.

In this lesson, you'll find out how to create parameter queries. Then you'll create a report based on a parameter query.

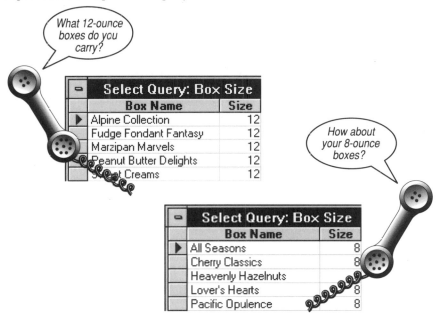

You will learn how to:

- Create a parameter query.

- Use parameters to find a range of records.

- Base a report on a parameter query.

Estimated lesson time: 20 minutes

What Is a Parameter Query?

A parameter query asks you to enter one or more parameters—or criteria—when you run the query. For example, a parameter query might ask you to enter a beginning and ending date. Microsoft Access runs the query using your parameters as criteria and then displays the datasheet. Typically, you create a parameter query when you expect to run a query frequently, but you'll be using different criteria each time you run it.

*When you run the query, Microsoft
Access asks you for the criteria...*

```
┌──────────────────────────────────────────┐
│ ━    │      Enter Parameter Value         │
├──────────────────────────────────────────┤
│ Enter size of box in ounces - 8, 12, or 16│
│ ┌──────────────────────────────────────┐ │
│ │12                                    │ │
│ └──────────────────────────────────────┘ │
│                                            │
│    ┌──────────┐      ┌──────────┐         │
│    │    OK    │      │  Cancel  │         │
│    └──────────┘      └──────────┘         │
└──────────────────────────────────────────┘
```

━	Select Query: Box Size	
	Box Name	**Size**
▶	Alpine Collection	12
	Fudge Fondant Fantasy	12
	Marzipan Marvels	12
	Peanut Butter Delights	12
	Sweet Creams	12

...and then displays the datasheet.

Parameter queries save time, and they're easy to use. Because the query displays dialog boxes that prompt you for criteria, you don't have to change the design of your query every time you want to use different criteria.

Parameter queries are especially helpful as the basis for reports. For example, suppose you run a sales report at the end of every week. You can create a parameter query that prompts you for the dates you're interested in. You use the parameter query as the basis of your report so that Microsoft Access prompts you for the dates you want included in the report automatically.

Start the lesson

▶ Start Microsoft Access. If the Microsoft Access window doesn't fill your screen, maximize the window. Then open the Sweet database.

Creating a Parameter Query

You're designing new boxes of bonbons, and you want to feature a different type of chocolate in each box. Today you might want to run the query to see a list of dark chocolate bonbons; tomorrow you might want to take a look at milk chocolates. You'll design a parameter query that asks you which type of chocolate you're interested in.

Create the query

1 With queries listed in the Database window, click the New button.

Microsoft Access displays the Query window and the Add Table dialog box.

2 Add the Bonbons table to the query, and close the Add Table dialog box.

3 Add the Bonbon Name, Chocolate Type, Bonbon Cost, and Bonbon Description fields to the QBE grid.

Tip   Instead of dragging the fields, you can double-click them in the field list to quickly move them to the QBE grid.

---

4 In the Sort cell below the Bonbon Name field, select Ascending to have Microsoft Access display the bonbons in alphabetical order.

Field:	Bonbon Name	Chocolate Type	Bonbon Cost	Bonbon Description	
Sort:	Ascending				
Show:	Ascending	☒	☒	☒	
Criteria:	Descending				
or:	(not sorted)				

5 Save the query, and name it Bonbon Information.

Now that you've created a query and added fields, you're ready to specify criteria. To do this, you do not type an expression in the Criteria row of the QBE grid, as you have done in other queries. Instead, you type the prompt that you want to appear in the dialog box when you run the query. Then you define the data type of the value that should be entered in the dialog box.

Set criteria with a parameter

▶ In the Criteria cell below the Chocolate Type field, type **[Enter chocolate type]**
This is the prompt that appears in the dialog box when you run the query.

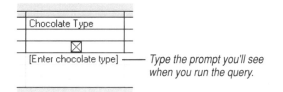

Chocolate Type

[Enter chocolate type] ——— *Type the prompt you'll see when you run the query.*

You can use a longer prompt if you think it would be more helpful. For example, you could have typed **[What type of chocolate are you interested in?]** Be sure to enclose the prompt in square brackets.

Define the parameter's data type

Before running the query, you'll define the data type of the Chocolate Type field (the field for which you're entering a parameter). Microsoft Access needs this information to run the query.

1 From the Query menu, choose Parameters.

Microsoft Access displays the Query Parameters dialog box.

2 In the Parameter cell, type **Enter chocolate type** (the prompt you just typed in the Criteria cell but without the brackets).

Query Parameters	
Parameter	Data Type
Enter chocolate type	Text

3 Press the TAB key to go to the Data Type cell.

Note that the default data type is Text. This is the correct data type for the Chocolate Type field.

4 Choose the OK button on the Query Parameters dialog box.

Run the query

Datasheet View button

1 Click the Datasheet View button.

Enter Parameter Value
Enter chocolate type
Bittersweet
OK   Cancel

Microsoft Access displays the Enter Parameter Value dialog box.

2 Type **Bittersweet** and choose the OK button.

Select Query: Bonbon Information				
Bonbon Name	**Chocolate Type**	**Bonbon Cost**	**Bonbon Description**	
▶ Bittersweet Blueberry	Bittersweet	$0.25	Cascade Mountain blueber	
Bittersweet Cherry	Bittersweet	$0.26	Royal Anne cherry covered	
Bittersweet Marmalade	Bittersweet	$0.17	Marmalade covered with b	
Bittersweet Raspberry	Bittersweet	$0.25	Orcas Island raspberry cov	
Bittersweet Strawberry	Bittersweet	$0.23	Olympic Wilderness strawb	

Microsoft Access runs the query and displays the records for bittersweet bonbons.

3 Save the query.

4 Switch back to Design view and run the query again, specifying another chocolate type, such as dark or milk chocolate.

Using Parameters to Find a Range of Records

When you're running the Bonbon Information query, you might want to limit the bonbons to a specific cost range. To do this, you'll add two new parameters to the Bonbon Information query. These parameters will specify the lowest and the highest cost of bonbons that will appear in the datasheet.

Add a range of parameters

To add a range of parameters, you'll use the **Between...And** operator. Before displaying the datasheet, Microsoft Access will need two parameters: the lowest cost and the highest cost.

Design View button

1 Click the Design View button on the toolbar.

2 Drag the right border of the field selector for the Bonbon Cost field to widen the field.

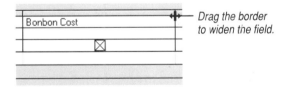

Drag the border
to widen the field.

Tip   Instead of widening the field, you can click the Criteria cell for Bonbon Cost and then press SHIFT+F2 to open the Zoom box.

---

3   In the Criteria cell below the Bonbon Cost field, type **Between [Enter low cost] And [Enter high cost]**

Bonbon Cost
⊠
Between [Enter low cost] And [Enter high cost]

You have added two prompts: one for the lowest cost and one for the highest cost.

Define the parameters' data types

1   From the Query menu, choose Parameters.

2   In the second Parameter cell, type the prompt **Enter low cost** and then press the TAB key to move to the Data Type cell.

Query Parameters	
Parameter	Data Type
Enter chocolate type	Text
Enter low cost	Text

Type the prompt here.

Microsoft Access displays the default data type, Text. Since the Box Cost field has a Currency data type, you need to change this data type.

3   Click the arrow in the Data Type cell. Then select Currency in the drop-down list. (You may need to scroll up to find Currency.)

Query Parameters	
Parameter	Data Type
Enter chocolate type	Text
Enter low cost	Text
	Long Integer
	Currency
	Single
	Double
	Date/Time
	Binary
	Text
	OLE Object

Select Currency as the data type.

4   In the third Parameter cell, type **Enter high cost** and press the TAB key. Change the data type to Currency.

Query Parameters		
Parameter	Data Type	
Enter chocolate type	Text	
Enter low cost	Currency	
Enter high cost	Currency	

5   Choose the OK button.

6   From the File menu, choose Save.

Tip   To delete a parameter from a query, first delete the parameter from the Criteria cell in the QBE grid. Then choose Parameters from the Query menu, and delete the parameter from the Query Parameters dialog box.

Try it out

Now when you run the query, you'll be prompted for all three parameters, with a different dialog box for each.

Datasheet View button

1   Click the Datasheet View button to run the query.

Microsoft Access displays the Enter Parameter Value dialog box.

2   Type **Dark**, and choose the OK button.

Enter Parameter Value
Enter chocolate type
Dark
OK   Cancel

Microsoft Access then displays the second dialog box prompting you for the low cost.

3   Type **.25** to find bonbons that cost a minimum of $0.25, and choose the OK button. Notice that you don't include a dollar sign ($).

Enter Parameter Value
Enter low cost
.25
OK   Cancel

Microsoft Access displays the third prompt.

4 Type **.35** to find bonbons with a maximum cost of $0.35, and choose the OK button.

Select Query: Bonbon Information			
Bonbon Name	**Chocolate Type**	**Bonbon Cost**	**Bonbon Description**
Almond Supreme	Dark	$0.30	Whole almond hand-dipµ
Cashew Supreme	Dark	$0.33	Giant whole cashew har
Chocolate Kiwi	Dark	$0.29	Brazil nut surrounded by
Classic Cherry	Dark	$0.28	Whole cherry in classic (

5 Save the query.

Basing a Report on a Parameter Query

Your research has shown that there's a huge market for moderately priced boxes that feature milk chocolate bonbons. So you're proposing a new line of boxes to Lillian Farber, the company president. As part of your presentation, you'll hand out an attractive report that lists milk chocolate bonbons that cost between $0.15 and $0.22.

For your report, you want the information about each bonbon displayed in a single-column list. To create this report, you use an AccessWizard. An AccessWizard asks questions about the report you want and then builds it for you according to your answers. You use FormWizards to build forms and ReportWizards to build reports.

You'll create this report based on the Bonbon Information query.

Create the report

Report button

1 Click the Report button in the Database window, and then choose the New button.

Microsoft Access displays the New Report dialog box. You use this dialog box to tell Microsoft Access which table or query in the database contains the data you want to print in your report and to choose whether to start with a blank report or have a ReportWizard build your report for you.

2 In the Select A Table/Query box, select the Bonbon Information query, and then click the ReportWizards button.

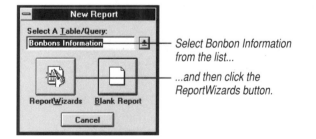

Microsoft Access asks which AccessWizard you want to use.

3 Double-click the Single-Column AccessWizard.

This AccessWizard will create the single-column list of data you want.

4 When Microsoft Access displays the next dialog box, choose the Fast Forward button. (The Fast Forward button lets you create a report very quickly by using default choices.)

5 Choose the Print Preview button.

Microsoft Access builds the report and then prompts you for the three parameters.

6 Enter the following parameters.

Chocolate type:	**Milk**
Low cost:	**.15**
High cost:	**.22**

Microsoft Access displays the report.

7 Save the changes, and name the report Bonbon Information.

One Step Further

Bob in the Shipping department has been using the Order Review query in the Sweet database so he can routinely check on orders for each customer. But the query always shows *all* the orders, and he would like to see orders only for a specific range of dates. Modify the Order Review query so Bob will be prompted for a beginning and ending date each time he runs the Order Review query.

Add parameters to the Order Review query

1   Open the Order Review query, and add the appropriate prompts to the Criteria cell below the Order Date field.

2   Open the Query Parameters dialog box, and type the prompts. Notice that the data type for the Order Date field is Date/Time.

3   Run the query. When you're prompted for dates, type each date using this format: 5-Nov-92. Remember that the orders in the Sweet database are for dates from 1-Oct-92 through 30-Dec-92.

The datasheet would look like this if you ran the query and asked to see orders with order dates between 1-Dec-92 and 15-Dec-92.

	Order ID	Last Name	First Name	Order Date
▶	205	Eddington	George	01-Dec-92
	206	Greenwald	Jasper	01-Dec-92
	207	Beauregard	Donna	01-Dec-92
	208	Abrams	Alice	01-Dec-92
	209	Fadiman	Ruth	01-Dec-92
	210	Ruter	George	01-Dec-92
	211	Snyder	Clara	01-Dec-92

Select Query: Order Review

Lesson Summary

To	Do this	Button
Set criteria with parameters	In the Criteria cell below the appropriate field, type the prompt that will appear when you run the query. Enclose the prompt in square brackets.	
Define the parameters	Choose Parameters from the Query menu. Type the same prompt that's in the Criteria cell but don't include the square brackets. Then select the data type.	
Run a parameter query	Click the Datasheet View button. Then type a value in the Enter Parameter Value dialog box.	

To	Do this	Button
Base a report on a parameter query	Create a parameter query and save it. With reports listed in the Database window, click the New button. In the Add Table dialog box, choose the parameter query you just created.	New

For more information on	See
Creating parameter queries	Chapter 7, "Designing Action Queries and Parameter Queries," in the *Microsoft Access User's Guide*. Or search Help for "parameter queries."

Preview of the Next Lesson

In the next lesson, you'll learn how to create queries that make changes to your data. You'll create a query that uses data in your tables to create a new table and makes changes to data in your existing tables.

Using Action Queries to Manipulate Data

Change is a fact of life for people and organizations, and you need to be able to easily integrate changes in your database. You change the prices of your products. You acquire a new company and inherit hundreds of customers. You get rid of products that aren't selling. You need to move selected data from one database to another.

In Microsoft Access, you use just one *action query* to make similar changes to large amounts of data. For example, suppose you want to lower the prices of all 12-ounce boxes of bonbons by 10 percent or raise the salaries of all employees in the Engineering department by 15 percent. You can have Microsoft Access do the calculations and make the updates for you—using only one query.

In this lesson, you'll learn how to create two types of action queries: make-table queries and update queries. You'll also learn some safeguards to make sure you change only the data that should be changed.

Quite simply, the best.

SWEET LIL'S
CHOCOLATES

Special 10% discount on all 12-oz. boxes

Call us at 1-800-555-1243

You will learn how to:

- Create a new table using a make-table query.
- Change prices with an update query.

Estimated lesson time: 35 minutes

What Are Action Queries?

All the queries you've created so far have selected data from your tables without making changes to this data. These queries are called *select queries*. With a select query, for example, you say, "Show me all the 12-ounce boxes." With *action queries*, you select data and make changes to it. With an action query, you say, "For all the 12-ounce boxes, lower the prices by 10 percent."

Table: Marketing Information		
Box Name	**Size**	**Box Price**
▶ All Seasons	8	$14.00
Alpine Collection	12	$20.75
Autumn Collection	16	$43.00
Bittersweets	16	$27.75
Cherry Classics	8	$16.25
Fudge Fondant Far	12	$18.00
Heavenly Hazelnut	8	$15.75
International	16	$34.00
Island Collection	16	$35.00
Lover's Hearts	8	$17.50
Marzipan Marvels	12	$32.25

Use one action query to select the 12-ounce boxes AND to lower their prices by 10 percent.

You can create four types of action queries:

- A *make-table query* creates a new table from selected data in your tables. For example, you could create a new table of Canadian customers selected from your Customers table.

- An *update query* changes data in your tables. For example, you could increase the cost of all milk chocolate bonbons by 5 percent.

- An *append query* adds records to your tables. For example, you could import a table that contains 100 new customers and add this data to your Customers table.

- A *delete query* removes records from your tables. For example, you could delete all orders placed last year.

For more information on action queries, see Chapter 7, "Designing Action Queries and Parameter Queries" in the *Microsoft Access User's Guide*.

In this lesson, you'll start by creating a make-table query. You'll then design an update query to change data in the table you just created.

Start the lesson

▶ Start Microsoft Access. If the Microsoft Access window doesn't fill your screen, maximize the window. Then open the Sweet database.

Creating a New Table from a Query

The Marketing manager asks you to create a table that she can then import to a sales database. She wants certain key information on Sweet Lil's boxes to help her decide whether to go ahead with a sales campaign.

You'll use a make-table query to create a table that contains the data she wants to import. This query will create a new table that extracts the information requested by Marketing: the name of each box, its size and price, and the total quantity that have sold.

Because these fields come from several tables, you may want to take a look at the Sweet database diagram to figure out which tables you'll need. As you can see, you'll use the Boxes and Box Details tables.

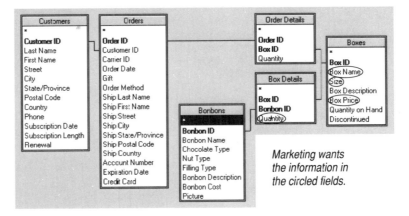

Marketing wants the information in the circled fields.

Create a select query

Now you're ready to create the query. Every time you create a new query, it is automatically a select query. So you'll first create a select query and then change it to a make-table query.

Query button

1   Create a new query. (Click the Query button in the Database window, and then choose the New button.)

2   Add the Boxes and Box Details tables to the query.

3   Choose the Close button to close the Add Table dialog box.

Notice that the title bar of the Query window says "Select Query: Query1."

Convert the select query to a make-table query

1   From the Query menu, choose Make Table.

Microsoft Access displays the Query Properties dialog box.

2   In the Table Name box, type **Marketing Information**, which is the name of the new table you'll create. Since you are adding this table to your current database, leave Current Database selected.

```
┌─────────────────────────────────────────────────────────────┐
│  ─                    Query Properties                       │
├─────────────────────────────────────────────────────────────┤
│ ┌─Make New Table──────────────────────────┐   ┌──────────┐   │
│ │ Table Name:  │ Marketing Information  │▼│ │   │    OK    │   │
│ │                                          │   ├──────────┤   │
│ │ ● Current Database                       │   │  Cancel  │   │
│ │ ○ Another Database:                      │   └──────────┘   │
│ │    File Name: │                        │ │                 │
│ └──────────────────────────────────────────┘                 │
│  ☐ Unique Values Only      ☒ Run with Owner's Permissions    │
└─────────────────────────────────────────────────────────────┘
```

3   Choose the OK button.

Microsoft Access changes the title bar of the Query window to Make Table Query: Query1.

4   From the Boxes table, drag the Box Name, Size, and Box Price fields to the QBE grid. From the Box Details table, drag the Quantity field to the QBE grid.

5   Click the Sort cell for Box Name, and then select Ascending.

Totals button

6   Click the Totals button on the toolbar.

7   Notice that the Total row appears in the QBE grid. Click in the Total cell below the Quantity field, and select Sum from the list. This will show the total number of each box that has been sold.

Field:	Box Name	Size	Box Price	Quantity	
Total:	Group By	Group By	Group By	Sum	
Sort:	Ascending				
Show:	☒	☒	☒	☒	
Criteria:					
or:					

For each box, find the quantity that have been sold.

8   Save the query, and name it Box Data.

> **Note**   You may have thought of giving this query the same name as the table, "Marketing Information." But in Microsoft Access, you can't use the same name for a query and a table.

9   Look at the query name in the Database window. (Press F11 to bring the Database window to the top of your screen.) Notice that the icon for your new query includes an exclamation mark (!). This is the icon for action queries.

Icon for action query

Run the make-table query

For select queries, you've been using the Datasheet View button to run the query. For action queries, you use the Run button. (Actually, you can also use the Run button for select queries, but you can't use the Datasheet View button for action queries.)

1   Click the Query window to bring it to the top again. Then click the Run button on the toolbar.

Run button

Microsoft Access displays a message telling you that 18 rows will be copied into the new table.

2   Choose the OK button to continue the make-table query. (Although you're choosing the OK button in this example, note that you can choose the Cancel button if you want to back out of the action query.)

Microsoft Access creates the table.

3   Close the query.

Whenever you run this query, it will create a new table.

Check the new table

Unlike a select query, you don't view a datasheet for a make-table query. To make sure your action query worked correctly, you'll look at the data in the new table.

1   In the Database window, click the Table button.

2   Double-click the Marketing Information table.

Table button

Table: Marketing Information			
Box Name	**Size**	**Box Price**	**SumOfQuantity**
▶ All Seasons	8	$14.00	12
Alpine Collection	12	$20.75	18
Autumn Collection	16	$43.00	24
Bittersweets	16	$27.75	24

Microsoft Access displays the new table. This table contains the data you asked for in your query. Marketing can import this table to their sales database.

3 Close the table.

Note   After you create a table with a make-table query, you can set the primary key of the new table and customize the table's design. For more information, see Lesson 6, "Adding a Table."

Changing Prices with an Update Query

As part of the new sales campaign, the Marketing manager decides to promote the 12-ounce boxes by temporarily reducing the price by 10 percent. Before she imports the Marketing Information table you just created, she'd like you to reduce the prices of 12-ounce boxes in the table.

You'll create an update query to make this change to the Marketing Information table.

Note   You'll practice an update query by changing data in the Marketing Information table rather than changing the data in the basic Sweet tables, such as Boxes and Bonbons, since these tables are used throughout the lessons.

The last thing you want to do is make the wrong changes to your data. To protect yourself from making unwanted changes, it's a good idea to use a three-step process in creating an update query. Although not required, this process is recommended.

Use a select query to make sure you're changing the records you want.

Convert the select query to an update query and run it to make the changes.

Convert the update query back to a select query and run it to make sure you've made the correct changes.

Create the select query

First you'll create a select query containing a calculated field that computes the new price. This calculated field does not change any data in your tables, but it does let you check to make sure you're using the right expression to lower the prices of the 12-ounce boxes.

1 Create a new query.

2 Add the Marketing Information table to your query.

3 Add all the fields to the QBE grid.

> **Tip** Double-click the title of the field list (Marketing Information) to select all the fields. Then drag the highlighted area in the field list to the QBE grid. This adds all the fields.

4 Select just the 12-ounce boxes (in the Criteria cell below the Size field, type **12**).

Add a calculated field

Now you'll add a new field that calculates a 10 percent price reduction.

1   Add a blank column between the Box Price field and the SumOfQuantity field. To do this, select the SumOfQuantity field. Then, from the Edit menu, choose Insert Column.

2   In this new field, type this expression to calculate the reduced box price: **[Box Price]*.9** This expression calculates 90 percent of the box price (which is the same as reducing the price by 10 percent).

3   Press the ENTER key.

Field:	Box Name	Size	Box Price	Expr1: [Box Price]*0.9
Sort:				
Show:	☒	☒	☒	☒
Criteria:				
or:				

Microsoft Access adds the name Expr1 for the calculated field.

4   Replace Expr1 with **New Price** (make sure that New Price is still followed by a colon).

Field:	Box Name	Size	Box Price	New Price: [Box Price]*0.9
Sort:				
Show:	☒	☒	☒	☒
Criteria:				
or:				

Check the results

1   Take a look at the datasheet.

Select Query: Query1				
Box Name	**Size**	**Box Price**	**New Price**	**SumOfQuantity**
Alpine Collection	12	$20.75	18.675	18
Fudge Café Fantasy	12	$18.00	16.2	30
Marzipan Marvels	12	$32.25	29.025	18
Peanut Butter Delights	12	$19.00	17.1	18
Sweet Creams	12	$23.00	20.7	18

New prices are 10 percent lower.

As you can see, the datasheet lists only 12-ounce boxes, and the calculation of the new price is correct. Check it out if you want: for example, 90 percent of $19.00 is $17.10. Although the values are correct, you'd like the new prices to appear in the same format as the prices in the Box Price field. To solve this problem, you'll use the **CCur** function to convert the New Price value to the Currency format.

2 Switch to Design view, click the New Price field in the QBE grid, and press SHIFT+F2 to open the Zoom box.

3 In the Zoom box, change the expression to **New Price:CCur([Box Price]*.9)** (be sure to include the parentheses). Then choose the OK button.

4 Look at the datasheet again to see the prices displayed as currency.

5 Save the query, and name it Promotional Prices.

Convert the select query to an update query

Now that you've made sure that your expression makes the correct change in prices, you can convert the select query to an update query. Then you can run the update query and change the values in the Marketing Information table.

1 In Design view, choose Update from the Query menu.

Microsoft Access changes the title of the Query window to Update Query: Promotional Prices and adds the Update To row to the QBE grid. You use this row to tell Microsoft Access how to change the prices of boxes. Since you have the correct expression already figured out, you'll just copy the expression to the Update To row.

You'll copy the expression from the New Price field...

...to the Update To cell below the Box Price field.

2 Click the New Price field, and press SHIFT+F2 to open the Zoom box.

3 In the Zoom box, select only the expression that calculates the new price, and press CTRL+C to copy the expression. Then choose the OK button in the Zoom box.

New Price: CCur([Box Price]*.9

Select the expression, but not the colon or the text before the colon.

3 Select the Update To cell below Box Price.

4 Press CTRL+V to paste the expression into the Update To cell.

This expression tells Microsoft Access how to change the Box Price value.

5 The New Price field was just a temporary field that allowed you to check the expression. Since you no longer need this field, delete it.

The New Price field has been deleted.

Field:	Box Name	Size	Box Price	SumOfQuantity
Update To:			CCur([Box Price]*0.9)	
Criteria:		12		
or:				

This expression updates the Box Price field.

6 Save the query.

Run the update query

Run button

1 Click the Run button on the toolbar.

Microsoft Access displays a message telling you that five rows will be updated.

2 Choose the OK button to continue the update query.

Microsoft Access updates the rows.

Check the changed records

As with other action queries, you do not see a datasheet after you run the query. There's a convenient way to check the results of an update query, though. If you want to make sure you made the changes you wanted, you can convert the update query back to a select query and then view the datasheet.

1 From the Query menu, choose Select.

Notice that the Update To row disappears.

2 Switch to Datasheet view.

As you can see in the datasheet, the prices for all the 12-ounce boxes have been changed correctly.

Box Name	Size	Box Price	SumOfQuantity
Alpine Collection	12	$18.68	18
Fudge Mocha Fantasy	12	$16.20	30
Marzipan Marvels	12	$29.03	18
Peanut Butter Delights	12	$17.10	18
Sweet Creams	12	$20.70	18

Select Query: Promotional Prices

3 Close the query without saving the changes.

You've already saved this query as an update query, so you don't need to save it also as a select query.

One Step Further

At the end of every month, you create a table that contains all the orders for that month. Later on, you export this table to another database that you use simply to store all these orders.

Make a table that contains November orders

1 Create a new query, and add the Orders table.

2 From the Query menu, choose Make Table. In the Query Properties dialog box, name the new table November Orders. (You don't need to fill in any other information in the dialog box.)

3 Add all the fields from the Orders table to your query.

4 Add criteria for the Order Date field that selects only orders between 1-Nov-92 and 30-Nov-92.

Hint   Use this expression: **Between 1-Nov-92 And 30-Nov-92**

---

5 Run the query.

6 Save the query, and name it Orders for November (remember that the query can't have exactly the same name as the table).

7 Open the November Orders table to check the data. (In the Database window, list tables, and choose the Open button.) The table should look something like the following illustration.

	Table: November Orders							
Order ID	Customer II	Carrier ID	Order Dat	Gift	Order Metho	Ship Last Name	Ship First Name	
1	237		11/2/92	-1	1	Burchard	Kristi	
2	386		11/2/92	-1	1	Carter	Bill	
3	158		11/2/92	-1	1	Dawousson	Helen	
4	332		11/2/92	-1	2	Gobi	Alice	
5	373		11/2/92	-1	1	Hertnagel	Rita	
6	1		11/2/92	-1	1	Kahn	Juliet	
7	275		11/2/92	0	1	Rivera	Juanita	

Change prices based on criteria

Use the Marketing Information table you created earlier in this lesson to raise the prices of all boxes by 10 percent.

1 Create a new query, and add the Marketing Information table.

2 Add the Box Name and Box Price fields from the Marketing Information table.

3 Add a calculated field that increases the price of these boxes by 10 percent. Name the field Higher Price.

Hint Type this expression into a blank field in the QBE grid: **CCur([Box Price]*1.1)**

---

4 Run the select query. The datasheet should look something like this.

	Select Query: Query1		
	Box Name	**Box Price**	**Higher Price**
▶	All Seasons	$14.00	$15.40
	Alpine Collection	$18.68	$20.54
	Autumn Collection	$43.00	$47.30
	Bittersweets	$27.75	$30.53
	Cherry Classics	$16.25	$17.88
	Fudge Mocha Fantasy	$16.20	$17.82
	Heavenly Hazelnuts	$15.75	$17.33

5 Go back to Design view and convert the query to an update query (from the Query menu, choose Update).

6 Copy the expression from the Higher Price field to the Update To cell below the Box Price field.

Hint Remember to copy only the expression, not the name of the field. That is, you'll copy this expression: **CCur([Box Price]*1.1)**

---

7 Delete the Higher Price field.

This field was just a temporary field you added to the original select query to test out your expression.

8 Run the update query. Then save the query, and name it New Prices.

9 To check the changes, convert the query back to a select query (from the Query menu, choose Select). Then run the select query, and view the datasheet, which should look something like this.

Select Query: New Prices	
Box Name	**Box Price**
All Seasons	$15.40
Alpine Collection	$20.54
Autumn Collection	$47.30
Bittersweets	$30.53
Cherry Classics	$17.88
Fudge Mocha Fantasy	$17.82
Heavenly Hazelnuts	$17.33

Lesson Summary

To	Do this	Button
Create a make-table query	Create a select query, and then choose Make Table from the Query menu.	
Create an update query	Create a select query, and then choose Update from the Query menu.	
Run a make-table or an update query	Choose the Run button on the toolbar.	!
Check the results of a make-table query	Open the new table.	
Check the results of an update query	From the Query menu, choose Select. Then choose the Datasheet View button.	▦

For more information on	See
Make-table queries, update queries, and other action queries	Chapter 7, "Designing Action Queries and Parameter Queries," in the Microsoft Access User's Guide. Or search Help for "action query."

Preview of the Next Lesson

In the next lesson, you'll learn how to customize your forms by adding graphical controls that make data entry quick and convenient. You'll also find out how to manipulate these controls and how to further customize them by setting properties.

4 Customizing Your Forms

Using Controls to Show Text and Data

When you want a quick form with standard features, an "off-the-rack" form that you create using FormWizards is perfect. It will look good and probably meet all your requirements. But what if you're looking for a form that provides a more custom fit? For example, you might want to add your own text, use colors to match your corporate look, or replace a standard field with a check box to make the form easier to use. All the tools you need are available in the form's Design view.

In this lesson, you'll learn how to add text and fields to a form, and you'll learn how to use the graphical tools available in Design view to make your form look great.

Half Year Inventory

Box ID: _____

Quantity on Hand: _____

☐ Check if Discontinued

*Fill —
We're taking inventory online this round. Can we get a custom online form to use instead of this?
— Herb*

You will learn how to:

- Add a text label to a form.
- Change the size of text and the colors on a form.
- Add a field (bound control) to a form.
- Create a check box.
- Set properties of a control.
- Align controls.

Estimated lesson time: 50 minutes

What Is a Control?

A *control* is an object on a form or report that displays data, performs an action, or decorates the form or report. The most common type of control used to display data from a field is called a *text box*. A text box can display text or numbers, and you can use it to type in new data or change existing data. Another type of control, called a *check box,* provides a graphical way to display Yes/No data. A third type of control, called a *label,* can display text that you use as a title for a form or to identify fields.

Labels

Text boxes

Check box

Microsoft Access provides many types of controls you can use to customize your forms, including lines, rectangles, and command buttons. It also provides controls that display lists of values and controls that display pictures, graphs, or other objects.

Each control on a form is a separate object. That means that when you're working on the design of a form, you can select any control, drag it to another location on the form, resize it — even copy it onto the Clipboard and paste it onto a different form.

In addition, each control has a set of *properties,* such as its color and position on the form, that you can set to determine how the control looks and operates. In the previous illustration, for example, the Box Name text box has a gray background that matches the background of the form. In contrast, the Quantity on Hand text box has a white background. The background color of a text box is a property that you can set.

Start the lesson

▶ Start Microsoft Access. If the Microsoft Access window doesn't fill your screen, maximize the window. Then open the Sweet database.

Changing the Design of a Form

Before you create a form, it's a good idea to figure out the form's purpose and plan how the form should look and function. If other people will use the form, talk to them and find out how they'll use it. Will they change data on the form or only view data? Do they intend to print the form? What fields should the form include? How will you arrange the fields so the data is displayed most effectively? By planning your form carefully, you'll save time creating it.

Sweet Lil's is about to conduct its semiannual inventory count. Herb, from the warehouse, stops by your office and asks you to design an online inventory form for him. He explains that his workers will use the form to update the quantity on hand of each box in inventory. "All we need on the form is the box ID code and the quantity on hand, so we can find the right box and update its quantity," says Herb. "Real simple. But can you make it look like all the other online forms? You know, with the blue and gray colors and everything?" You assure him that his inventory form will look just great.

Create a form

You'll use a FormWizard to create the basic form and then switch to the form's Design view to customize its appearance.

Form button

1   In the Database window, click the Form button, and then click the New button.

Microsoft Access displays the New Form dialog box. You use this dialog box to select the form's underlying table or query (the table or query that contains the fields you want to display on the form) and to choose whether or not you will use a FormWizard. Herb's workers will use the form you're creating to change the data in the Quantity on Hand field in the Boxes table, so you'll make Boxes the form's underlying table.

2   In the Select A Table/Query box, select the Boxes table, and then choose the FormWizards button.

Microsoft Access displays the first FormWizard dialog box, which asks which AccessWizard you want to use.

3 Double-click the Single-Column FormWizard.

The FormWizard displays a dialog box that asks which fields from the Boxes table you want to include on the form.

4 Double-click the Box ID field, and then double-click the Quantity on Hand field to add them to the form. Then choose the Next button.

5 Choose the Standard look for the form, and then choose the Next button.

6 For the title of the form, type **Inventory**, and then choose the Open button.

The box ID code and the quantity on hand for the first record in the Boxes table

The FormWizard creates the form and opens it in Form view.

7 From the File menu, choose Save Form. Type **Inventory** in the Form Name box, and then choose the OK button.

Microsoft Access saves your form.

Switch to Design view

You use Form view and Datasheet view to look at and change data. A form has one more view — Design view — that you use to look at and change the design of the form.

▶ Click the Design View button on the toolbar.

*Design View
button*

In Design view, you see the field name instead of data in the field. In Form view, this text box displays data from the Box ID field.

You use the toolbox to add more controls to your form. (You can drag the toolbox out of the way if it's blocking your work area.)

Notice that in Design view, the form is divided into three sections. When you're viewing data, the *form header* appears at the top of the window. In this form, the form header contains a label that shows the title of the form. The *detail* section makes up the main body of the form and contains the fields from the Boxes table. The *form footer* is empty, but you could add information to it that you wanted to appear at the bottom of the form when you're viewing data on screen and at the end of the form when you see it in print.

Adding a Label

A label is a control that contains text you want to display on the form. The text in the label doesn't come from a field; instead, you just type it right in the label control.

To add a label to a form, you use the label tool in the toolbox. The toolbox contains a tool for every type of control you can use on a Microsoft Access form.

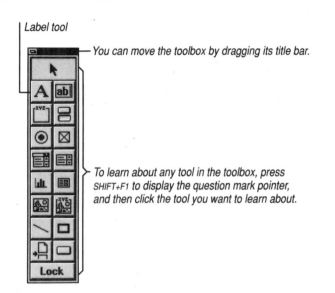

Label tool

— You can move the toolbox by dragging its title bar.

> *To learn about any tool in the toolbox, press*
> *SHIFT+F1 to display the question mark pointer,*
> *and then click the tool you want to learn about.*

When you switch to Design view for the first time, Microsoft Access displays the toolbox in the lower-left corner of the window. You can move the toolbox by dragging its title bar.

Note   If the toolbox isn't visible, choose the Toolbox command from the View menu to display it.

Add a label

Herb wants a label in the form header of the Inventory form that tells what period of time the inventory covers.

1   Click the label tool in the toolbox.

2   Click in the form header to the right of the Inventory label.

Label tool

Click inside this line — it marks the right edge of the form.

| Form: Inventory |

Form Header

Inventory   + A

Detail

The pointer changes to show which tool you're using.

3   Type (**Jan-Jun**) in the label, and then press the ENTER key.

| As you type, Microsoft Access expands the label to fit your text.

After you press ENTER, Microsoft Access selects the control. You can tell the control is selected, because it has *sizing handles* around it. (You resize a control by dragging one of its sizing handles.)

[Jan-Jun] ── Sizing handles

You don't need to resize this control, but you might want to move it to a different position in the form header.

Move a control

If your new label covers part of the Inventory label, you can move the new label. You move a control by dragging it with the mouse.

1   Move the pointer over the edge of the selected label control.

[Jan-Ju] ── When the pointer changes to a hand icon, you can move the control.

2   While the pointer is a hand icon, drag the control to the right, away from the Inventory label but still inside the right edge of the form. (To drag, click and hold down the mouse button while you move the mouse. When the control is where you want it, release the mouse button.)

| Right edge of the form

Form Header
0 ┤ **Inventory**   [Jan-Ju]
Detail

Don't worry about aligning the labels exactly at this point — you'll learn about aligning controls later in this lesson.

Changing Text Size and Setting Colors

The toolbar that appears in Design view contains options you can use to set the size of text in a control and the colors used in a control.

These options appear when you select a control that contains text. Use them to set the font, size, and alignment of text.

Click here to open the Pallette and set colors.

For quick help on options on the toolbar, press SHIFT+F1, and then click the toolbar.

Note   If the toolbar isn't visible, the Show Tool Bar option has been turned off. From the View menu, choose Options. Set the Show Tool Bar option in the General Category to Yes.

Change the text size and resize the label

You'd like the text in your new label to be bigger than it is. To change its point size, you use the Font-size box on the toolbar.

1   With your new label selected, set the Font-size box to 12 points.

Font-size box

Be sure the label is selected...

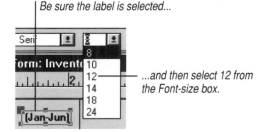

...and then select 12 from the Font-size box.

Tip   If you click the label after it's already selected, Microsoft Access puts an insertion point inside the label so that you can edit its text. As long as the insertion point is inside the label, you can't change the point size. If that happens, click outside the label, and then click the label once to select it again.

After you change the text's font size, the label is no longer big enough to display all the text. There's a fast way that you can resize the control to make it fit the text perfectly.

2 From the Layout menu, choose Size To Fit.

Microsoft Access resizes the control so that it fits the new text size.

3 If necessary, move the label to create some space between it and the Inventory label.

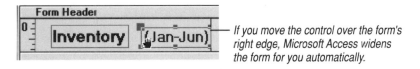

If you move the control over the form's right edge, Microsoft Access widens the form for you automatically.

Change a section's background color

Sweet Lil's corporate style calls for form headers to have a dark blue background with light gray text in the labels. Labels for fields are dark blue. You'll change your Inventory form so that it matches the corporate style. (To see an example of the corporate style, open the Bonbons form. You can leave the Bonbons form open while you work on the Inventory form, or you can close it.)

1 Select the form header section of the Inventory form.

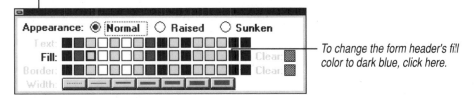

To select the form header section, click here...

...or here.

The title bar of the selected section is dark and sunken.

Palette button

2 Click the Palette button on the toolbar, and then select dark blue as the fill color.

You can use the Palette to change the appearance of a control.

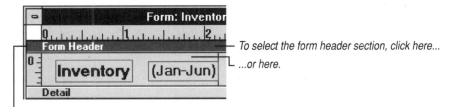

To change the form header's fill color to dark blue, click here.

Microsoft Access changes the background of the form header to dark blue.

Change the color of text

You want to change the text in the labels in the form header to light gray. You can do both labels at once by selecting both controls.

1 Click the Inventory label to select it, and then hold down the SHIFT key and click the (Jan-Jun) label. (If the Palette covers either label, drag the Palette out of the way first.)

| Click here... | ...then hold down the SHIFT key and click here.

Microsoft Access selects both labels.

2 In the Palette, set the text color to light gray.

Microsoft Access changes the text color of the labels.

3 Change the text of the two labels for the Box ID and Quantity on Hand fields to dark blue.

| Select the labels, and then change their text color to dark blue.

Close the Palette and save your changes

You're finished changing colors for the time being, so you can close the Palette.

1 Close the Palette.

2 From the File menu, choose Save to save your changes.

Adding a Field (Bound Control)

When you want to display information from a field or add new data to a field, you use a *bound control*. A bound control is tied to a specific field in the underlying table or query. For example, the Box ID text box on the Inventory form is bound to the Box ID field in the Boxes table — it displays the box ID codes that are stored in the Box ID field.

After looking over the form you designed, Herb comes back with a request for modifications. His workers think the form would be easier to use if it displayed the box name and size as well as the box ID. Also, Herb says he needs a discontinued field on the form so the workers can mark which boxes were discontinued during the past six months. You'll add three bound controls to the Inventory form, one for each of the three fields.

Make room for a new field

The detail section of the Inventory form that the FormWizard created is just big enough for its two text boxes. You need to make room for the new fields.

1 Drag the lower border of the detail section down to make the section taller. (Don't worry about its exact size for now; you can always adjust it again later if you need to.)

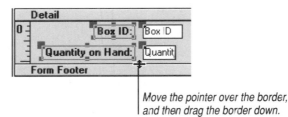

Move the pointer over the border,
and then drag the border down.

You'll put a text box bound to the Box Name field right under the Box ID text box. You need to move the Quantity on Hand text box down to make room.

2 Move the Quantity on Hand field to the lower portion of the detail section. (If the Box ID and Quantity on Hand labels are both still selected, click on the form outside the labels to cancel the selection. Then move the Quantity on Hand control.)

Now your detail section
looks something like this.

Notice that the Quantity on Hand label is *attached* to the text box — if you move
one, the other comes along for the ride.

Tip   To move a text box without moving its label, position the pointer over the
upper-left corner of the text box. The pointer changes to a pointing finger. Now
drag the text box. It moves separately from its attached label. The special, larger
handle on the upper-left corner of a control is called a *move handle*. You can use it
to move either a control or its attached label independently of the other.

Add a field

First, you'll add a text box that's bound to the Box Name field in the Boxes table. The
easiest way to add a bound control to your form is to drag the field from the *field list*
to the form. The field list lists the name of every field in the form's underlying table
or query.

1   Click the Field List button on the toolbar.

Field List button

Microsoft Access displays the field list. It includes every field in the Boxes table,
which you chose as the Inventory form's underlying table.

2   Drag the Box Name field from the field list to the spot on the form where you
want the field (not its label) to be.

Drag from the field list...

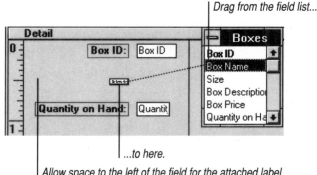

...to here.

Allow space to the left of the field for the attached label.

*Form View
button*

Microsoft Access creates a new text box where you drop the field, and it creates a label to the left of the field. Your new text box is bound to the Box Name field in the Boxes table.

3   Click the Form View button on the toolbar.

In Form view, the text box displays the name of the current box of chocolates. If you want, scroll through a few records to see the data in the text box change.

4   Click the Design View button on the toolbar to return to Design view.

*Design View
button*

Change the default appearance of a control

You probably noticed that the text in the label for the Box Name control is black. You can change it to blue to match the other controls; but what you'd really like is for Microsoft Access to automatically give every new label on this form blue text. You can do that by changing the default properties of labels.

Palette button

1   Change the text color of the Box Name label to dark blue. (Click the label, and then click the Palette button on the toolbar. Set the text color on the Palette.)

Now you can use this label to tell Microsoft Access how you want all new labels on this form to look.

2   With the Box Name label selected, choose Change Default from the Layout menu.

Any new label on the form will now have dark blue text. You'll see how that works when you add the Box Size and Discontinued fields.

3   Close the Palette.

Add more fields

1   In the field list, click the Size field, and then hold down the CTRL key and click the Discontinued field.

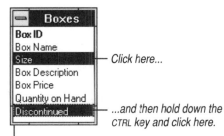

2   Drag the two fields to the detail section of the form and drop them below the Quantity on Hand field, but above the bar for the form footer section. (When you drop the fields on the form, Microsoft Access automatically makes the detail section taller if necessary to fit the two controls in the section.)

Drop the fields here.

Notice that the labels for the new controls are dark blue.

3 Switch to Form view to see how your form looks, and then switch back to Design view.

4 Rearrange the fields on the form so that Box ID, Box Name, and Size are on top and Quantity on Hand and Discontinued are on the bottom, with a space between the two sets of fields.

Now the detail section looks something like this.

Creating a Check Box

The Discontinued field in the Boxes table has a Yes/No data type. In a text box, it displays the value Yes or No. You realize you can make your form more graphical and easier to use by replacing the Discontinued text box with a check box. That way, the person using the form can just click the check box to indicate that a box has been discontinued.

Create a check box

First, you'll delete the Discontinued text box and its attached label. Then you'll replace it with a check box that's bound to the Discontinued field in the Boxes table.

1 Click the Discontinued text box to select it, and then press the DEL key.

Click here and then press DEL.

Microsoft Access deletes both the text box and its attached label. (If you select the attached label and press DEL, Microsoft Access deletes only the label. You can still delete the text box by selecting it and pressing DEL.)

Check box tool

2   Click the check box tool in the toolbox.

3   In the field list, select the Discontinued field. (If both the Size and Discontinued fields are still selected in the field list, click the Discontinued field to cancel the selection of the Size field.)

4   Drag the Discontinued field from the field list to the lower portion of the detail section.

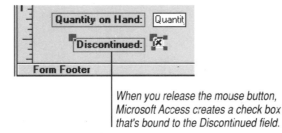

When you release the mouse button,
Microsoft Access creates a check box
that's bound to the Discontinued field.

Tip   If your check box's label says something like "Field19" instead of Discontinued, that means it's not bound to the Discontinued field. Delete the check box and try again. Be sure to select the check box tool first, and then drag the Discontinued field from the field list.

---

5   Switch to Form view and click the new check box to see how it works. Click it again to clear it, and then switch back to Design view.

Setting Properties

When you move a control or change its color, you're setting and changing properties of the control. You can set some properties, such as color and text size, by using tools on the toolbar. But to see and set all the properties of a control, you use the *property sheet*.

Box ID:	Box ID		Text Box	
		Control Name	Box ID	
Box Name:	Box Name	Control Source ...	Box ID	
		Format		
Size:	Size	Decimal Places ..	Auto	
		Status Bar Text ..	Unique 4-letter at	
		Validation Rule ..		
Quantity on Hand:	Quantit	Validation Text ...		
		Before Update ...		
Discontinued:	☒	After Update		
		On Enter		

Property sheet showing
the properties of the
Box ID text box

Each control on a form has its own set of properties that determine how the control looks and operates. For example, the ControlSource property of a bound control is the name of the field the control is bound to. You can bind the control to a different field simply by changing its ControlSource property.

Each form section also has its own set of properties. When you changed the background color of the form header section, for example, you were changing one of that section's properties.

And finally, the form as a whole has a set of properties that relate to how the entire form looks and operates. For example, if you plan to print a form, you can set its LayoutForPrint property to Yes. Then Microsoft Access uses printer fonts instead of screen fonts for all text and data on the form.

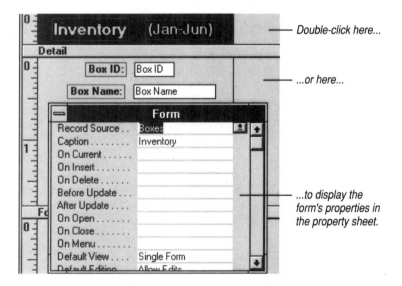

Properties button

To display the property sheet, you click the Properties button on the toolbar. A quick alternative method is to double-click the object whose properties you want to display. (This works if the object isn't already selected and if it's not an OLE object, such as a picture or graph.)

You're ready to adjust the position of the controls on the Inventory form so that they line up with each other. First, you'll set two form properties that will make it easier to align the controls: the GridX and GridY properties. These two properties determine the horizontal and vertical units of the alignment grid; you'll use the grid to position the controls precisely.

Display form properties

1 Double-click the form background, outside the right edge of the form.

— *Double-click here...*

— *...or here...*

...*to display the form's properties in the property sheet.*

Record Source ..	Boxes
Caption	Inventory
On Current	
On Insert	
On Delete	
Before Update . . .	
After Update	
On Open	
On Close	
On Menu	
Default View	Single Form
Default Editing	Allow Edits

The property sheet displays the properties of the form when the form is selected. To display the properties of a control or form section, you just select it.

2   Display the properties for different controls and form sections to see how the property sheet works. For example, click the Box ID text box to display its properties, and then click the label attached to this text box to display its properties. Click in the detail section (but not on a control) to display the section's properties.

For quick help on any property, click the property in the property sheet, and then press F1.

3   After looking at a few different sets of properties, click the form background again (outside the right edge) to display the form's properties.

Tip   In a large form, you might find that the sections take up all the space on your screen, and you don't have any form background to click to select the form. In those cases, you can select the form by choosing Select Form from the Edit menu.

Change the grid settings

1   In the property sheet for the form, scroll down until you see the GridX and GridY properties.

The FormWizard that created this form set each of these properties to 64. These grid settings make it easy for you to move controls by very small amounts using the mouse, but harder to align controls using the mouse. You'll change the fineness of the grid settings. Higher numbers indicate greater fineness.

2   If your default unit of measurement is inches, change the GridX property to 10. If it's centimeters, change the property to 4.

3   Change the GridY property to 12 (or 4.5 for centimeters).

4   Click outside the GridY box.

The grid helps you align controls.

Microsoft Access displays the new grid settings on the form. (If you don't see the grid marks on your form, choose the Grid command from the View menu.)

Aligning Controls

Microsoft Access provides a variety of tools that help you align controls. To align controls as you add and adjust them, you can use the rulers on the top and right side of the form's Design view, the grid itself, and the Snap To Grid command. (When the Snap To Grid command is on, it automatically aligns a new control to the grid.) To adjust controls after you've added them, you can use the Align command on the Layout menu.

For details about aligning controls and using the grid, search Help for "alignment: controls" or for "grid."

Turn on Snap To Grid

It's easier to align controls to the grid when Snap To Grid is on. To see whether this command is on, you'll look at it on the Layout menu.

1   Select the Layout menu.

```
Layout
  Apply Default
  Change Default

  Bring to Front
  Send to Back

√ Snap to Grid———— If Snap To Grid is on, then
  Size to Grid        the command is checked.
  Size to Fit
```

2   If Snap To Grid is off, choose it to turn it on. If it's already on, don't turn it off.

Align controls vertically to the grid

You'll align the controls vertically so that there's one vertical *grid subdivision* between controls. (There should be space between the controls, but no visible grid line.)

1   Move the Box ID text box slightly in any direction.

Because the Snap To Grid command is on, when you release the mouse button the control snaps to the nearest grid line.

2   Move the Box Name text box so that there's one vertical subdivision between it and the Box ID text box. Then move the Size control so that there's one vertical subdivision between it and the Box Name text box.

3   Align the Quantity on Hand and Discontinued controls at the bottom of the detail section so that there's one subdivision of vertical space between them.

Align controls horizontally

Next, you'll align the controls so that their left edges line up.

1   Select the attached labels for all five controls on the form.

Click the first label, then press the SHIFT key, and click the remaining labels.

2   From the Layout menu, choose Align, and then choose Left from the submenu.

Microsoft Access aligns the left edges of the labels. (If you accidentally give the labels the wrong alignment, just choose Undo Align from the Edit command, and Microsoft Access undoes the alignment. Then you can try it again.)

3   Select the Box ID, Box Name, and Size text boxes (the top three text boxes).

4   From the Layout menu, select Align, and then choose Left from the submenu.

Microsoft Access aligns the left edge of the text boxes.

5   Align the left edges of the Quantity on Hand text box and the Discontinued check box.

> *Now your detail section looks something like this.*

6   Switch to Form view to see how your changes look, then switch back to Design view, and save the form.

One Step Further

Your Inventory form is coming together — just a few more adjustments and it will be perfect.

You'll change the background of the first three text boxes so it matches the form's background...

...left-align the number displayed in the Size text box...

...and add a line to provide visual separation on the form.

Make a text box's background invisible

You want the data in the Box ID, Box Name, and Size text boxes to appear in Form view as though they're directly on the form background, not in a box. This is a visual cue to the people using the form that they don't change the data in these fields. The Palette has all the tools you need.

▶ Set the fill color of the three text boxes to the same color as the detail section (light gray). Then give them a clear border by selecting the Clear check box next to the border colors. (The border will still be visible in Design view. Switch to Form view to see how it looks with data on the form.)

Note   You can also *lock* a control, which prevents anyone from changing its data. You'll learn how to do that in Lesson 17, "Protecting Your Data."

Left-align number data in a text box

Sweet Lil's boxes come in three sizes: 8-ounce, 12-ounce, and 16-ounce. By default, Microsoft Access right-aligns the numbers in the text box. You'd rather have the number in the box displayed left-aligned, so it lines up with the text in the Box ID and Box Name text boxes.

Align-Left button

▶ Select the Size text box, and then click the Align-Left button on the toolbar. To see how a number in the box looks, switch to Form view, and then switch back to Design view.

Tip   The alignment buttons are displayed on the toolbar only when an object containing text is selected on the form. If you don't see the buttons, make sure the Size text box is selected.

Draw a line on a form

Sweet Lil's corporate style uses a heavy gray line to separate groups of fields. (To see an example, open the Bonbons form. The gray line on the form helps group related fields visually.) You'll draw a line between the first three fields on the Inventory form and the last two fields.

Line tool

▶ Use the line tool in the toolbox to draw the line. After selecting the tool, drag across the form to create a line the size you want. Then use the Palette to set the line's width and border color. (Select the third thickness for the width and dark gray for the border color.)

Size the window in Form view so it fits your form

Now your form has just the look you want, except that the window in Form view is bigger than necessary.

▶ To make the window fit the form exactly, switch to Form view, and then choose Size To Fit Form from the Window menu. When you're finished with the Inventory form, save it and close it.

Tip   If the Size To Fit Form command isn't available, check to see if your form is maximized. If it is, click the Restore button in the upper-right corner of the title bar so that your form is no longer maximized, and then choose the Size To Fit Form command.

Lesson Summary

To	Do this	Button
Switch to a form's Design view	Click the Design View button on the toolbar.	
Add a label to a form	Click the label tool in the toolbox, and then click on the form. Type the text you want to appear in the label.	
Move a control	Drag the control where you want it.	
Change the size of text displayed in a control	Select the control, and then change the size in the Font-size box on the toolbar.	
Resize a label so it exactly fits its text	Select the label, and then choose Size To Fit from the Layout menu.	
Change an object's color or a line's width	Select the object, and then click the Palette button to open the Palette.	
Add a field (bound control) to a form	Click the Field List button on the toolbar to display the field list, and then drag the field from the field list to the form.	

To	Do this	Button
Change the default properties of a type of control	Select a control that has the properties you want for the new default properties, and then choose Change Default from the Layout menu.	
Create a check box bound to a Yes/No field	Select the check box tool in the toolbox, and then drag the Yes/No field from the field list to the form.	
Display the property sheet	Select the object whose properties you want to display, and then click the Properties button on the toolbar.	
Align controls	Use the grid, or use the Align command on the Layout menu.	

For more information on	See
Designing forms	Chapter 8, "Form Basics," and Chapter 9, "Designing Forms," in the *Microsoft Access User's Guide*.

Preview of the Next Lesson

In the next lesson, you'll learn how to add pictures to your form's design and how to add a control bound to a field that contains pictures or other OLE objects.

Using Pictures and Other Objects

A picture may be worth a thousand words — but only if it's where people can see it. You can put pictures, graphs, and other objects created in other applications right on your Microsoft Access forms and reports. For example, you can put your company's logo on a report alongside a graph showing company sales. In addition, you can store objects in tables in your database and display the objects on a form just like the other data in the table.

In this lesson, you'll learn how to put a picture on a form, and you'll learn how to create a control that displays objects stored in a table.

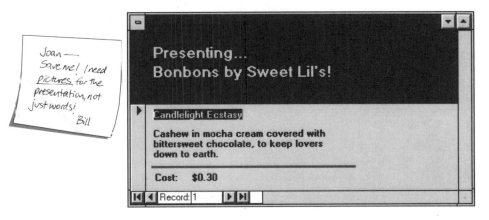

You will learn how to:

- Add a picture to a form.
- Add a control (object frame) that displays an object from a record.
- Make an object that's stored in a table fit in its frame.

Estimated lesson time: 20 minutes

Understanding OLE

An *OLE object* is any piece of information created with an application for Windows that supports *object linking and embedding* (OLE). With the OLE features in Microsoft Access, you can put OLE objects — such as pictures, sounds, and graphs — on your forms and reports, and you can store objects as data in your tables. In addition, OLE makes it easy to edit these objects directly from the form or report.

When you put an object on a form or report, it's displayed in a control called an *object frame*. Microsoft Access provides two kinds of object frames — unbound and bound.

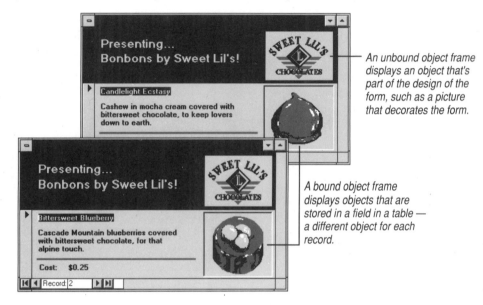

An unbound object frame displays an object that's part of the design of the form, such as a picture that decorates the form.

A bound object frame displays objects that are stored in a field in a table — a different object for each record.

You can either embed or link an object in an object frame. When you *embed* an object, Microsoft Access stores the object in your database file. You can easily modify the object from within Microsoft Access. If the object came from another file, only the embedded object in your database is changed, not the object in the original file.

On the other hand, when you *link* an object, Microsoft Access doesn't put the object in the object frame; instead, it puts a link to the object's source file in the frame. You can still look at the object and make changes to it on the form or report, but your changes are saved in the object's source file, not in your database file.

In this lesson, you'll create an unbound object frame and embed a picture in it. You'll also create a bound object frame that displays pictures stored in the Bonbons table. You won't be linking any objects in this lesson: For more information about linking, see Chapter 13, "Using Pictures, Graphs, and Other Objects," in the *Microsoft Access User's Guide*.

Start the lesson

▶ Start Microsoft Access. If the Microsoft Access window doesn't fill your screen, maximize the window. Then open the Sweet database.

Adding a Picture to a Form

An outside vendor wants to package Sweet Lil's bonbons in his own products, and it's your job to present the bonbons to him in their best light. In your presentation to the vendor, you'll use an online form that displays information about each of Sweet Lil's bonbons. The Sweet database already has a form called Presenting Bonbons with some of the right data on it, but the form could use a little more visual appeal.

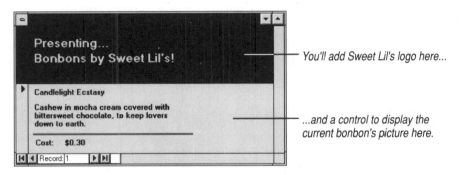

You'll add Sweet Lil's logo here...

...and a control to display the current bonbon's picture here.

Note To do the steps in this lesson, you must be using Windows version 3.1 or later. That's because Windows 3.1 comes with a version of Paintbrush that supports OLE. The version of Paintbrush that comes with Windows version 3.0 does not support OLE. If you're using Windows 3.0, you can still display pictures you've created with Paintbrush on your form by copying and pasting the pictures between Paintbrush and your form. For details, search Help for "copying OLE objects."

Open a form in Design view

You'll start by adding Sweet Lil's logo to the form header of the Presenting Bonbons form. To add a picture to the design of the form, you must be working in Design view.

Form button

1 Click the Form button in the Database window.

Microsoft Access displays the list of forms in the Sweet database. The Presenting Bonbons form is near the bottom of the list.

2 Select the Presenting Bonbons form, and then choose the Design button.

Microsoft Access opens the form in Design view.

3 If the form window isn't large enough to display all of the detail section, resize it to make it bigger.

Add a picture

The Sweet Lil's logo is in a Paintbrush file named LOGO.BMP. You'll add an unbound object frame to the form header of the Presenting Bonbons form and then embed the logo in the frame.

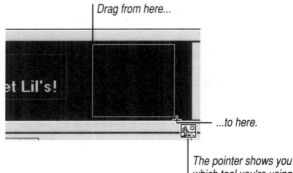

*Unbound object
frame tool*

1   Click the unbound object frame tool in the toolbox. (If the toolbox isn't displayed, choose Toolbox from the View menu to display it. If you don't see the Toolbox command on the View menu, check to make sure you're in Design view, not Form view.)

If you simply clicked in the form header, Microsoft Access would create an unbound object frame in the default size. But the default size is a lot bigger than Sweet Lil's logo, so instead you'll draw a control that's closer to the size of the picture it will contain.

2   Drag the pointer to create a square-shaped control that fits in the form header beside the title. (Don't worry about the exact size of the square; you can adjust it slightly to fit the picture after the picture is embedded.)

Drag from here...

et Lil's!

...to here.

*The pointer shows you
which tool you're using.*

When you release the mouse button, Microsoft Access displays the Insert Object dialog box.

3   Scroll down the Object Type list and select Paintbrush Picture.

If you were going to draw the logo now, you'd choose the OK button or double-click Paintbrush Picture, and Paintbrush would start with an empty drawing area for you to draw your picture. But since the logo already exists in a file, you'll tell Microsoft Access where to find it instead.

*If you don't have a
PRACTICE directory,
see "Getting Ready"
at the beginning of
this book.*

4   Choose the File button.

Microsoft Access displays the Insert Object From File dialog box. The LOGO.BMP file was copied to your PRACTICE directory when you copied the practice files to your hard disk.

5   If necessary, use the Directories list to switch to the PRACTICE directory, and then double-click LOGO.BMP.

Microsoft Access embeds the picture from the file into the object frame on your form.

6   From the Layout menu, choose Size To Fit.

Microsoft Access sizes the object frame so that it fits the logo perfectly.

— *Now the logo is embedded in the design of the form.*

Look at the picture in Form view

Form View button

1   Click the Form View button to see how the logo looks with a record of data.

2   Move from record to record on the form.

Because the logo is embedded in the design of the form, it appears on the form background for every record.

3   Switch back to Design view.

Start Paintbrush to edit the picture

1   Double-click the logo.

— *To edit a picture that's not bound to a field, double-click it in Design view.*

Paintbrush starts and displays the logo in its window. If you want, use Paintbrush to change the logo. (You don't have to make changes to continue with this lesson, but you can if you want.)

2   When you're finished editing the picture, choose Exit & Return To Microsoft Access from the Paintbrush File menu.

If you changed the picture, Paintbrush asks if you want to update it in Microsoft Access. You can update the picture with your changes (choose Yes) or discard your changes (choose No). Because the picture is embedded rather than linked, changes you make are saved only in the picture on the form, not in the LOGO.BMP file.

> **Tip**   A handy way to display the properties of most controls is to double-click the control; but as you saw in the preceding steps, that won't work for a Paintbrush picture. Instead of displaying the property sheet, Microsoft Access starts Paintbrush. To display the properties of an unbound object frame, first select the frame, and then click the Properties button on the toolbar.

Adding a Control That Displays a Picture from a Record

The Bonbons table includes a field named Picture that contains pictures of Sweet Lil's bonbons. You'll add a control to the detail section of the Presenting Bonbons form that displays the pictures in Form view. Your control will be bound to the Picture field, so you'll use the bound object frame tool.

Add a bound object frame to a form

Bound object frame tool

1   Select the bound object frame tool in the toolbox.

> **Tip**   Here's a tip to help you remember which tool is for the bound object frame and which is for the unbound object frame. Notice that the picture on the tool for the bound object frame includes some letters at the top, similar to an attached label. You can think of those letters as the name of the field that the control is bound to. When you create a bound object frame, Microsoft Access adds an attached label to the frame, just as it does when you create a text box.

2   Drag the pointer to create a square-shaped control that fits in the detail section.

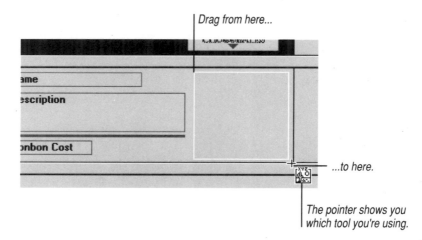

Drag from here...

...to here.

The pointer shows you which tool you're using.

When you release the mouse button, Microsoft Access creates a bound object frame with an attached label. You don't need the label, so you'll delete it.

3 Delete the label that's attached to your new control.

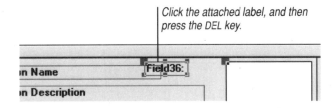

Click the attached label, and then press the DEL key.

Bind the object frame to the Picture field

In Lesson 13, you learned how to create a control that's bound to a field by dragging the field from the field list to the form. Now you'll learn another way to bind a control to a field — by setting the control's ControlSource property.

1 If the property sheet isn't displayed, double-click the new bound object frame to display its properties. (If the property sheet is displayed but shows the properties for another control, just click the bound object frame to display its properties.)

2 Set the ControlSource property to Picture (that's the name of the field that contains the pictures of bonbons). You can either click in the box and select Picture from the list of fields, or you can type **Picture** in the ControlSource property box and then press the ENTER key.

Properties of the bound object frame

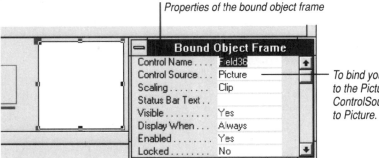

To bind your new control to the Picture field, set its ControlSource property to Picture.

Look at the data

Do you know why a picture of a bonbon didn't appear in the bound object frame after you bound it to the Picture field? The answer is clear when you think about which view of the form shows the data from the table. You're looking at the form in Design view, but the pictures of bonbons aren't part of the form's design. They're part of the data in the Bonbons table.

1   Switch to Form view.

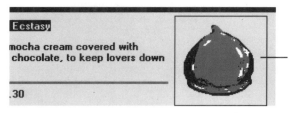

The picture is stored in a field in the Candlelight Ecstasy record in the Bonbons table, the same as the bonbon's name, description, and cost.

You see the picture for Candlelight Ecstasy, the first bonbon in the table.

2   Move to the next record in the table.

Now the control displays the picture for Bittersweet Blueberry.

Edit the picture

You use the same method to modify a picture in a bound control as in an unbound control — except that you do it in Form view, where the data is displayed, rather than in Design view.

For steps on adding a new bonbon to the Bonbons table, including its picture, see Lesson 2, "Getting the Best View of Your Data."

1   In Form view, double-click the picture of the Bittersweet Blueberry bonbon.

Paintbrush starts and displays the picture in its window. If you want, use Paintbrush to change the picture. (You don't have to make changes to continue with this lesson, but you can if you want.)

2   When you're finished editing the picture, choose Exit & Return To Microsoft Access from the Paintbrush File menu.

If you changed the picture, Paintbrush asks if you want to update it in Microsoft Access. You can update the picture with your changes (choose Yes) or discard your changes (choose No). If you update the picture, your changes are saved in the Bonbons table.

3   Look at a few more records, and then switch back to Design view.

Only the first five bonbons and a few bonbons that appear later in the table have pictures. In the other records, the Picture field is empty.

Making an Object from a Table Fit in a Frame

If the pictures of bonbons don't fit in your bound object frame exactly, you might see an empty white area on the edge of the frame (showing that the frame is too big), or the frame might cut off a portion of the picture (showing that it's too small).

With an *unbound* object frame, such as the logo in the form header, you can use the Size To Fit command on the Layout menu to size the frame so it fits the picture exactly. But that doesn't work for a *bound* object frame, because the objects displayed in the frame could be different sizes. In the Bonbons table for example, each picture is the same size, but they don't have to be. You could have a tiny picture in one record and a giant one in the next.

To choose the best way to display an object in its bound object frame, you set the frame's Scaling property. The Scaling property has three possible settings:

- *Clip* displays as much of the object as will fit in the frame with no changes to the size of the object and no distortions. This is the default setting.

- *Scale* enlarges or shrinks the object to fit the size of the frame. This may distort the proportions of the object, especially if its size is quite different from the frame's size.

- *Zoom* enlarges or shrinks the object to fit the frame as well as it can without changing the proportions of the object.

Because your frame is close to the same size as the pictures in the Bonbons table, you can set the Scaling property to Scale, and each picture will fit the frame with a minimum of distortion.

Scale the picture to fit the control

1   In Design view, set the Scaling property of the bound object frame to Scale.

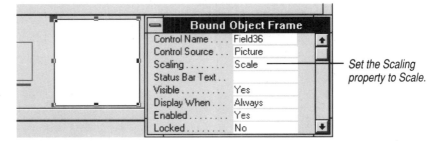

Set the Scaling property to Scale.

2   Switch to Form view.

Microsoft Access scales the picture so that it fits in the frame perfectly.

3   Switch back to Design view.

Give the object frame a sunken appearance

You'll give the object frame for the Picture field one more visual touch.

Palette button

1   With the object frame selected, click the Palette button on the toolbar to open the Palette.

2   Click the Sunken option.

Click here to give the frame a sunken look.

3 Switch to Form view to see how the form looks now.

4 To size the form's window so it fits the form, choose Size To Fit Form from the Window menu.

The form looks great — you're ready for your presentation.

5 Save the Presenting Bonbons form, and then close it.

One Step Further

So far, all the examples in this lesson use pictures that had already been created and saved in a file before you put them on your form. But you can also create an object at the same time you embed it. You'll embed your own drawing of a bonbon in the Picture field in the Bonbons table.

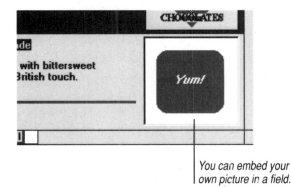

You can embed your
own picture in a field.

Add your own bonbon picture

Pictures of bonbons are stored in the Bonbons table. You can use the Presenting
Bonbons form to add your own picture of a bonbon to the table.

1   Open the Presenting Bonbons form in Form view. Go to a record that doesn't have
a picture (such as the sixth record).

2   Click the empty Picture field, and then choose Insert Object from the Edit menu.
When the Insert Object dialog box appears, double-click Paintbrush Picture. Paint
your picture of a bonbon, and then return to Microsoft Access.

Microsoft Access displays your picture in the object frame. Because the control's
Scaling property is set to Scale, the entire Paintbrush work area is scaled to fit in
the control. For that reason, your picture might appear very small. Either change
the Scaling property to Clip, or paint a larger picture.

3   When you're finished, save the changes, and close the form.

Microsoft Access saves the picture you drew in the Bonbons table.

Lesson Summary

To	Do this	Button
Add a picture to the design of a form or report	In Design view, use the unbound object frame tool in the toolbox to draw an object frame on the form. Choose the type of object you want from the Insert Object dialog box. If the object already exists in a file, chose the File button. Otherwise, choose the OK button and create the object.	![button]
Size an unbound object frame to fit the object it contains	In Design view, select the object frame, and then choose Size To Fit from the Layout menu.	

To	Do this	Button
Display objects on a form or report that are stored in a table	In Design view, use the bound object frame tool to draw an object frame on the form. Set the ControlSource property of the object frame to the name of the field that contains the objects. To view, edit, or add objects, switch to Form view.	
Scale an object so it fits in a bound object frame	Set the Scaling property of the bound object frame to Scale.	
Modify a Paintbrush picture on a form or report	For an unbound object, double-click the object in Design view. For a bound object (stored in a table), double-click the object in Form view.	

For more information on	See
Using OLE objects on forms and reports	Chapter 13, "Using Pictures, Graphs, and Other Objects" in the *Microsoft Access User's Guide*.

Preview of the Next Lesson

In the next lesson, you'll learn how to create a form that shows customer information at the top and then lists each order the customer has placed in the lower portion of the form. In addition, you'll learn how to use a calculated control to display the result of a calculation on a form.

Showing Related Records and Calculations on Forms

How data is arranged and presented can make all the difference. A customer's phone number is in one table; the orders that the customer placed are in another. But when you call the customer, you want to see a list of the customer's orders along with the customer's name and number. Likewise, a customer's first and last names are stored in separate fields, but you want to see or print them together, as a whole name.

You can design your forms to display the data the way you want to see it. In this lesson, you'll learn how to create a form that shows one record at the top (such as a customer's record) and related records in a subform at the bottom (such as a record for each order the customer placed). You'll also learn how to create a control that combines text values from other fields and a control that displays the result of a calculation.

You will learn how to:

- Use a FormWizard to create a form with a subform.

- Combine text values in a control.

- Show the result of a calculation in a control.

Estimated lesson time: 20 minutes

Two Forms That Work Together

When you work with data on a form, it's often convenient to see related records grouped together under one main record. To do that, you use a form with a *subform*. A subform is a form within a form. In most cases, the subform is linked to the main form, so that it shows records that are related to the record on the main form. For example, the Boxes form in the Sweet database shows information about a box of bonbons. The subform is linked to the main form — it lists the bonbons in the box.

The main form shows the record for a single box.

The subform shows the records for all the bonbons in the box.

If you open the Boxes Subform by itself, it shows the records for all the bonbons in the Bonbons table.

A subform is saved as a separate form in the database. The form that appears as the subform on the Boxes form is named Boxes Subform. If you open this form separately, apart from the Boxes form, it shows all the bonbons in the database.

In this lesson, you'll create a form that shows customer information on the main form — the customer's name and phone number — and displays a list of the customer's orders on a subform. If one customer placed ten orders, then you'll see all ten orders listed under the customer's name. You'll also learn how to create a control that combines text values from other fields and one that displays a calculation.

Start the lesson

▶ Start Microsoft Access. If the Microsoft Access window doesn't fill your screen, maximize the window. Then open the Sweet database.

Using a FormWizard to Create a Form with a Subform

The easiest way to create a form with a subform is to use the Main/Subform FormWizard. This FormWizard creates both forms and makes them work together for you. It can even link the two forms automatically, as long as both of these conditions are met:

■ The main form is based on a table.

For details about creating relationships between tables, see Lesson 9, "Relating Tables."

■ The subform is based on a table that's related to the main form's table; or the subform is based on a table or query that contains a field with the same name and data type as the primary key of the main form's table.

For example, the main form that you create in this lesson will be based on the Customers table. The primary key of that table is the Customer ID field. The subform will be based on a query named Orders with Subtotals. That query includes a Customer ID field that contains the customer ID numbers. The query also includes other information about an order that you want to display on the subform.

Microsoft Access uses the Customer ID fields in the underlying table and query to link the main form and the subform automatically.

Table: Customers			
Customer ID	**Last Name**	**First Name**	**Street**
1	Hanson	Rita	304 King Edward Pl.
2	Pence	Stephen	312 6th Ave.
3	Carter	Dale	14 S. Elm Dr.
4	Jefferson	Wal	23 Tsawwassen Blvd.
5	Morales	M.	1001 West Pender
7	Wojack		
8	Grant		
10	Murray		
11	Smith		
12	Herron		
13	Hernandez		
14	Peterson		
15	MacIntyre		
16	Silverman		
18	Hollings-Aldric		
19	Foster		

Record: 15

Select Query: Orders with Subtotals			
Customer ID	**Order ID**	**Order Date**	**Total**
1	6	02-Nov-92	$218.25
1	300	14-Dec-92	$200.00
2	214	02-Dec-92	$149.75
2	363	23-Dec-92	$106.25
3	345	20-Dec-92	$128.75
4	141	21-Nov-92	$98.50
5	26	05-Nov-92	$27.75
7	10	03-Nov-92	$76.50
8	308	15-Dec-92	$47.75
10	196	29-Nov-92	$135.75
11	76	12-Nov-92	$125.50
12	288	12-Dec-92	$196.25
13	299	14-Dec-92	$62.75

The query for the subform also has fields for the order ID and order date, as well as a calculated field showing the total value of each order.

Note If the two conditions for automatically linking a main form and a subform are not met, you can still link the two forms yourself. Both the underlying table or query for the main form and the underlying table or query for the subform must still contain *linking fields* — fields that have the same value for linking records. For details on linking the forms yourself, see Chapter 10, "Creating Forms Based on More Than One Table" in the *Microsoft Access User's Guide*.

Begin a form with a subform

When you use a FormWizard to create a form with a subform, you need to select the underlying table or query for both the main form and the subform. You select the underlying table or query for the main form in the New Form dialog box. Later, as you work with the Main/Subform FormWizard, you'll select the underlying table or query for the subform.

Form button

1 In the Database window, click the Form button to display the list of forms, and then click the New button.

Microsoft Access displays the New Form dialog box.

2 In the Select A Table/Query box, select the Customers table, and then choose the FormWizards button.

3 Select the Main/Subform FormWizard, and then choose the OK button.

Enter information in the FormWizard dialog boxes

When you use a FormWizard, you work with a series of dialog boxes. Each of the following steps tells you what to enter in each dialog box. After completing a step, choose the Next button to go to the next dialog box.

1 Select the Orders with Subtotals query as the underlying query for the subform.

2 Add these fields to the main form in this order: First Name, Last Name, State/Province, and Phone.

3 Add these fields to the subform: Order ID, Order Date, and Subtotal.

4 Choose the Standard look for the form.

5 Change the title of the form to Customers and Orders, and then choose the Open button.

You will see a message about the subform. Microsoft Access creates two forms: the main form and its subform. The subform must be named and saved before Microsoft Access can put it on the main form.

6 Choose the OK button in response to the message, and then name the subform Customers and Orders Subform.

Microsoft Access creates the Customers and Orders form and opens it for you.

```
┌─────────────────────────────────────────┐
│ ▬            Customers and Orders         │
│                                           │
│    Customers and Orders                   │
│ ▶                                         │
│       First Name:  │Rita│                 │
│                                           │
│        Last Name:  │Hanson        │       │
│                                           │
│    State/Province: │British Columbia│     │
│                                           │
│           Phone:   │(604) 555-2933  │     │
│                                           │
│       ┌──────────┬───────────┬──────────┐ │
│       │Order ID│Order Date:│ Subtotal:  │ │
│     ▶ │       6│  02-Nov-92│   $218.25  │ │
│       │     300│  14-Dec-92│   $200.00  │ │
│       │        │           │            │ │
│       └──────────┴───────────┴──────────┘ │
│                                           │
│   │◀│◀│Record:│1   │▶│▶│                  │
│                                           │
│ │◀│◀│Record:│1   │▶│▶│                    │
└─────────────────────────────────────────┘
```

Rita Hanson is the first customer in the Customers table.

The subform shows you Rita's orders.

See how the form works

Microsoft Access automatically linked the subform to the main form. To see how that works, look at other customers' records.

1   Go to the next customer record, using the navigation buttons at the bottom of the Form window.

You can see that the records in the subform change to display that customer's orders.

Design View button

2   Click the Design View button on the toolbar to switch to Design view.

In Design view, you can see the controls on the main form and one large control for the subform. The subform control has properties that link the records on the subform to the appropriate record on the main form.

3   If the property sheet isn't displayed, click the Properties button on the toolbar to display it.

Properties button

4   Select the control for the subform to display its properties.

Click once on the subform control to select it.

```
1 ┌─────────────────────────────────────────────┐
  │ Customers and Orders Subform                 │
  │                       ┌──────────────────────┤
  │                       │▬   Subform/Subreport  │
  │                       │                       │
  │ ◀│                    │Control Name . . . . Customers and │ ▲
  │                       │Source Object . . . Customers and  │
  │                       │Link Child Fields . . Customer ID ─┐│
  │                       │Link Master Fields  Customer ID ──┘│
  │                       │Status Bar Text . .                │
```

The FormWizard set these properties to link the record on the main form with matching records on the subform.

5   Click outside the subform control to cancel the selection.

To see and modify the subform itself, you'll need to open it in Design view.

6   Double-click the subform control to open the subform form in Design view.

Design view of the subform

Form: Customers and Orders Subform		
Form Header		
Detail		

Order ID: [Order ID]

Order Date: [Order Date]

Subtotal: [Subtotal]

Form	
Record Source . .	Orders with Subtotals
Caption	
On Current	
On Insert	
On Delete	
Before Update . . .	
After Update	
On Open	
On Close	
On Menu	
Default View	Datasheet
Default Editing . . .	Allow Edits

Form Footer

Notice that the FormWizard put a text box on the form for each field you selected from the subform's underlying query. The FormWizard also set the form's DefaultView property to Datasheet. When you open the main form, the subform automatically opens in Datasheet view rather than Form view. Datasheet view is appropriate for a subform, because it displays all the related records in a list.

7   Close the subform.

8   Save the main form, naming it Customers and Orders.

Note   A subform doesn't have to be displayed in Datasheet view. For example, the subform in the Boxes form (Boxes Subform) is designed to be displayed in Form view. The DefaultView property of the form is set to Continuous Forms, which means Microsoft Access displays the form in Form view and shows as many records as fit in the subform's control.

Combining Text Values in a Text Box

The First Name and Last Name text boxes on the Customers and Orders form are bound to the First Name and Last Name fields in the Customers table. But suppose you want to show a customer's first name and last name together in one text box.

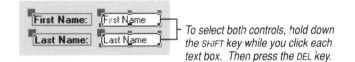

Instead of this...   *...you want this.*

To do that, you use a *calculated* control. A calculated control is tied to an expression instead of a field. The expression can combine text values from more than one field in the underlying table or query, or it can perform calculations on values from the fields.

For more about expressions, see Appendix C, "Using Expressions."

To tie a text box to an expression, you type the expression in the text box in Design view. Always start the expression with an equal sign (=). You can see how it works now.

Delete two controls

You'll replace the First Name and Last Name text boxes on the Customers and Orders form with one text box that shows both names. Start by deleting the two bound text boxes.

▶   Delete both the First Name and Last Name text boxes.

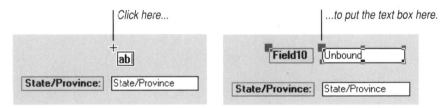

To select both controls, hold down the SHIFT key while you click each text box. Then press the DEL key.

Add a text box

Next, add an unbound text box to the form.

1   Click the text box tool in the toolbox.

2   Click in the detail section where you want the upper-left corner of the text box (not its attached label) to be.

Text box tool

Click here...   *...to put the text box here.*

Microsoft Access adds a text box that's not bound to any field in the Customers table.

Tie a text box to an expression

A text box that's bound to a field displays the field name in Design view. To bind a text box to an expression instead, you just type the expression in the box. You'll use the **&** operator in the expression to display one text value followed by another.

1   Move the pointer over the text box. When the pointer turns into a vertical line, click in the text box.

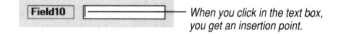

Field10   When you click in the text box,
                         you get an insertion point.

2   Type =**[First Name] & " " & [Last Name]** in the text box, and then press the ENTER key. Be sure to start the expression with an equal sign and to put a space between the two quotation marks in the expression.

This expression tells Microsoft Access to...

=[First Name] & " " & [Last Name]

...display the value in | ...followed by | ...followed by the value
the First Name field... | a space... | in the Last Name field.

You use brackets around field names in an expression and double quotation marks around a space or other text characters.

3   Click the Form View button on the toolbar to switch to Form view and see the results.

Form View button

Field10:   Rita Hanson   *Microsoft Access displays the*
                                  full name in the text box.

4   Switch back to Design view.

Fix up the form's appearance

When you added the text box to the form, Microsoft Access gave it a default label, such as Field10. You'll replace the text in the label with something more descriptive.

1   Click the text box's attached label to select it, and then click it again to make an insertion point appear in the label.

2   Replace the text in the label with **Name:**

3   Press ENTER.

Microsoft Access selects the label.

4   From the Layout menu, choose Size To Fit.

Microsoft Access sizes the label to fit its new text.

5 Move the controls on the form closer together to fill in the extra space between the text boxes.

Note To move a control, select it, position the pointer over the edge of the control so that the pointer turns into a hand icon, and then drag the control.

---

6 Switch to Form view, and then choose Size To Fit Form from the Window menu so that the window fits the form.

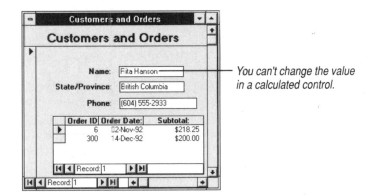

You can't change the value in a calculated control.

7 Try to change Rita Hanson's name. Because the control is bound to an expression, Microsoft Access won't let you change its value.

8 When you're finished looking at the Customers and Orders form, save it and close it.

Showing the Result of a Calculation in a Control

Often, the most important piece of data you want to see is the result of a calculation. For example, suppose you want to find out the value of the inventory of each box of bonbons that Sweet Lil's sells. The Boxes table includes a Box Price field that contains the selling price of each box, and it also includes a Quantity on Hand field that contains the total number of units in inventory. The value you want to see is the box price multiplied by the quantity on hand.

This text box shows the box price multiplied by the quantity on hand.

Microsoft Access provides two approaches for displaying this calculation on a form:

For details on creating a calculated field in a query, see Lesson 10, "Selecting the Records You Want."

- You can create a query that includes a calculated field that performs the calculation, and then base your form on that query. That way, you can put the calculated field from the query on the form.

- As long as the form's underlying table or query includes both the Box Price and Quantity on Hand fields, you can create a calculated control on the form. Remember, a calculated control isn't tied to a field in the underlying table or query; instead, it's tied to an expression that performs a calculation.

You'll take the second approach in this lesson.

Note   In most cases, you won't store the result of a calculation in a field in a table. It's not necessary, because you can always see the result in a calculated control on a form or in a calculated field in a query.

Create the Value of Inventory form

1 Begin a new form. In the Select a Table/Query box, select the Boxes table, and then choose the FormWizards button.

2 Choose the Single-Column FormWizard.

3 Add the Box Name, Box Price, and Quantity on Hand fields to the form.

4 Choose the Standard look.

5 Change the title of the form to Value of Inventory, and then choose the Design button to open the form in Design view.

The FormWizard creates the form and displays it in Design view.

6   Save the form, naming it Value of Inventory.

Display the result of a calculation in a text box

Next, you'll add a calculated control that displays the value of the box's inventory: the box price multiplied by the quantity on hand.

1   Drag the lower border of the detail section down to make room for a new control.

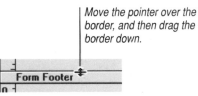

Move the pointer over the border, and then drag the border down.

Text box tool

2   Use the text box tool in the toolbox to add an unbound text box to your form below the Quantity on Hand field.

3   Click in the text box, and then type **=[Box Price] * [Quantity on Hand]** in the box.

This expression tells Microsoft Access to multiply the value in the Box Price field by the value in the Quantity on Hand field and then display the result in the text box.

4   Change the text box's label to **Value of Box's Inventory:**

5   Switch to Form view.

Microsoft Access displays the result of the calculation in the text box, but it's not formatted as currency. You can fix that by setting the control's Format property.

Display your result as currency

1   Switch to Design view.

Properties button

2   Display the properties of the calculated control. (Select the calculated control. If the property sheet isn't displayed, click the Properties button on the toolbar.)

3   Set the control's Format property to Currency.

Click the Format property box, and then click the
arrow to open the list. Select the Currency setting.

4   Switch to Form view to see the results.

Now the text box displays
the result as currency.

5   Save and close the Value of Inventory form.

One Step Further

The calculated control you added to the Value of Inventory form shows the value
of *one* box's inventory. But what if you want to see the total value of your
inventory — the sum of all the boxes' values? To do that, you use the **Sum** function in
a calculated control. The **Sum** function calculates the total for a group of records.

Here's the syntax for the **Sum** function:

Sum(*expression*)

The *expression* argument (the information in parentheses after the word Sum) can be
the name of a field in the form's underlying table or query, or it can be an expression.
So to show the total of all the boxes' values, you can use the same expression with the
Sum function that you used to calculate the value of one box.

Show the sum of all the records in the form footer

1 Add an unbound text box to the form footer of the Value of Inventory form. Display the sum of all the boxes's values, formatted as currency. Change the text in the attached label to **Total Value of Inventory**:

Hint The text box should be bound to this expression:

=Sum([Box Price] * [Quantity on Hand])

Be sure you include the equal sign and all the required parentheses and brackets in your expression.

---

2 Set the form's DefaultView property to Continuous Forms, and then resize the form's window in Form view so that you can see two records at the same time. Use the scroll bars to scroll through the records.

Properties button

Hint To display the form's properties, choose Select Form from the Edit menu. If the property sheet isn't displayed, click the Properties button on the toolbar.

When you're finished, here's what your form should look like in Form view.

Value of Inventory	
Value of Inventory	
Box Name:	All Seasons
Box Price:	$14.00
Quantity on Hand:	700
Value of Box's Inventory:	$9,800.00
Box Name:	Alpine Collection
Box Price:	$20.75
Quantity on Hand:	400
Value of Box's Inventory:	$8,300.00
Total Value of Inventory	$199,750.00

To see more than one record at a time in the detail section, set the form's DefaultView property to Continuous Forms.

This text box shows the sum of all the boxes' values.

Note The Total Value of Inventory control shows the total value of the inventory for the current set of records in the Value of Inventory form. If you create a filter that limits the set of records displayed on the form, then the value in the control changes. For example, you could filter the set to show only 12-ounce boxes. When you do, the control shows just the total value of those boxes, not the value of all the boxes in the Boxes table.

Lesson Summary

To	Do this	Button
Create a form with a subform	Create a new form based on the table or query that contains the data you want on the main form. Choose the Main/Subform FormWizard.	
Combine text values in a text box	Use the text box tool in the toolbox to create a new text box, and then type an expression (starting with an equal sign) in the text box that combines the values. Example: **=[First Name] & " " & [Last Name]**	abl
Display the result of a calculation in a text box	Use the text box tool in the toolbox to create a new text box, and then type an expression (starting with an equal sign) in the text box that performs the calculation. Example: **=[Box Price] * [Quantity on Hand]**	
Calculate a total for a group of records	Use the **Sum** function in a calculated control. Example: **=Sum([Box Price])**	

For more information on	See
Creating a form with a subform	Chapter 10, "Creating Forms Based on More Than One Table," in the *Microsoft Access User's Guide*.
Creating calculated controls	Chapter 9, "Designing Forms," and Chapter 11, "Using Expressions in Forms," in the *Microsoft Access User's Guide*.
Using expressions in calculated controls	Appendix C, "Using Expressions," in this book.

Preview of the Next Lesson

In the next lesson, you'll learn how to make your forms easier to use by providing choices in lists and option groups.

Part 5

Making Your Forms Easy to Use

Providing Choices in Combo Boxes

When looking up customer information on a form, you'd probably find it easier and friendlier to identify the customer by name, rather than by a number. If you can pick the name from a list instead of typing it, that's even better. But computers and databases are different — Microsoft Access can find the customer information faster if you give it the customer's ID number, not the name. How do you make your form friendly to both you and Microsoft Access?

The answer is to design a list box or combo box on your form that lets you pick a name but that tells Microsoft Access the ID number associated with the name. In this lesson, you'll learn how to create a combo box that displays customer names in a list and then stores the selected customer's ID number in the field.

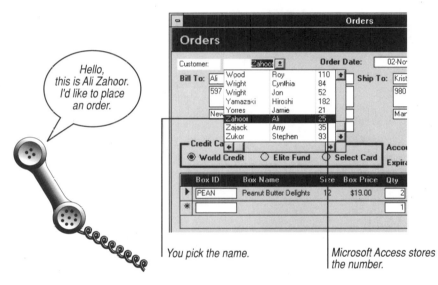

You pick the name.

Microsoft Access stores the number.

You will learn how to:

- Create a combo box.
- Define the rows in the combo box's list.
- Define the columns in the combo box's list.
- Limit entries in the combo box to values already in the list.

Estimated lesson time: 30 minutes

How Combo Boxes and List Boxes Work

Microsoft Access has two types of controls that provide a scrollable list of choices: list boxes and combo boxes. Because looking up a value in a list is often easier and quicker than remembering the value you want, these controls can make your forms easier to use. In addition, picking from a list of choices rather than typing helps ensure that the value entered in the table is correct.

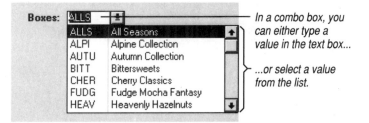

*A list box is a simple list of values
you can select from.*

*A combo box is like a text box and list box combined
in one control.*

The list in a list box or combo box consists of a number of rows of data. Each row can have one or more columns. You can specify which column contains the data you want stored in the field, and you can use other columns to display informational data, such as full names, that help you pick the right row.

In many cases, you'll want to display names in the list but store ID numbers in the field that the control is bound to. You can display the column with the ID numbers, or if you prefer, you can hide it and display only the names.

Start the lesson

▶ Start Microsoft Access. If the Microsoft Access window doesn't fill your screen, maximize the window. Then open the Sweet database.

Creating a Combo Box

When operators take new telephone orders for Sweet Lil's chocolates, speed and accuracy are their top priorities. To make their job easier, you plan to make several enhancements to the online form they use.

Currently, operators enter the ID number of the customer placing the order in a text box on the form. You'll start by replacing the text box with a combo box that shows customer names as well as ID numbers.

You'll replace this text box...

...with this combo box.

You make these changes in the form's Design view.

Delete a text box

Before adding the combo box, make room for it by deleting the Customer ID text box and its label.

1   Open the Orders form in Design view.

The Orders form in Design view

```
┌──────────────────────────────────────────────────────────┐
│ ▭                            Form: Orders                  │
│   0⌊⌊⌊⌊⌊⌊⌊⌊⌊1⌊⌊⌊⌊⌊⌊⌊⌊⌊2⌊⌊⌊⌊⌊⌊⌊⌊⌊3⌊⌊⌊⌊⌊              │
│  Form Header                                               │
│ 0                                                          │
│ ┌─ Orders                                              ─┐  │
│  Detail                                                    │
│ 0                                                          │
│   ┌Customer ID:┐  ┌Customer┐        ┌Order Date:┐ ┌Orc    │
│   ┌Bill To:┐ ┌First Name────┐ ┌Last Name──────┐ ┌Ship To │
│              ┌Street──────────────────────────┐           │
│ 1            ┌City─────────┐ ┌State/Province┐ ┌Postal Co│ │
│                                              ┌Country┐    │
│            ┌Credit Card────────────────────────────┐      │
│            │ ◉ World Credit   ◉ Elite Fund  ◉ Select Card││
│            └───────────────────────────────────────┘      │
│ 2  Orders Subform                                          │
│ ▭                                                          │
│   ┌────┐                                                   │
│   │  ▶ │                                                   │
│   ├─┬──┤                                                   │
│   │A│ab│                                                   │
│   └─┴──┘                                                   │
└──────────────────────────────────────────────────────────┘
```

2 If the form's window is too small for you to see all its controls, resize the window to make it larger.

3 Click the Customer ID text box, and then press the DEL key.

Create a bound combo box

Your combo box on the Orders form will be bound to the Customer ID field in the Orders table. When the operator selects a customer from the combo box list on the form, Microsoft Access will store the customer's ID number in the bound field in the table. To create a bound combo box, you first select the combo box tool in the toolbox, and then drag the field you want from the field list to the form.

Combo box tool

1 Click the combo box tool in the toolbox. (If the toolbox isn't visible, choose the Toolbox command from the View menu.)

Now when you drag the Customer ID field from the field list, Microsoft Access will create a combo box that's bound to the field.

· Field List button

2 If the field list isn't visible, click the Field List button on the toolbar to display it.

3 Drag the Customer ID field from the field list to the upper-left corner of the form.

Drag from here...

...to here.

Orders

Detail

Bill To: First Name   La

Street

Orders Form

Order ID

Customer ID

First Name

Last Name

Street

City

When you release the mouse button, Microsoft Access puts a combo box bound to the Customer ID field on the form.

Combo box bound to the Customer ID field

Detail

Customer ID: Customer ID   ±   Order D

Bill To: First Name   Last Name

4 Check to make sure your combo box looks like the previous illustration. If its label says something other than Customer ID (such as Field139), then your combo box isn't bound to the Customer ID field. If there's no down arrow on the right of the control, you've created a text box instead of a combo box. In either case, delete it and go through the steps to create it again. When your combo box looks like the previous illustration, go on to the next steps.

Put a control in the right tab order

The *tab order* of a form is the order in which the insertion point moves through fields when you tab from field to field in Form view. When you create a new control, Microsoft Access puts the new control last in the tab order of the form, regardless of where you place the control on the form. You'll edit the tab order of the form so that the new Customer ID combo box you just created is first in the tab order, not last.

1 From the Edit menu, choose Tab Order.

Microsoft Access displays the Tab Order dialog box.

2 Scroll down the list of controls until you see the Customer ID control, which is last in the list.

3   Select the Customer ID control and drag it to the top of the list.

| Orders Subform |
| Subtotal |
| Customer ID |

Click here to select Customer ID...

Custom Order:

| Customer ID |
| Order Date |
| Order ID |

...then click again and drag it to the top of the list.

4   Choose the OK button.

Now your new control is first in the tab order, where it belongs.

Defining the Rows in the List

Your new combo box is bound to the Customer ID field, a field with a Number data type, in the Orders table. If you use the form to look at an order, the value of the control will be the ID number of the customer who placed the order.

But the combo box's list can display other values — values that aren't in the form's underlying table or query. In many cases, the best way to define the list is to create a separate query that selects and arranges the data just the way you want it to appear in the list. Then you can tell Microsoft Access to use the fields in the query as columns in the list.

In this case, you want the list to show the last name, first name, and ID number of each of Sweet Lil's customers. The database already contains a query named Customer List that has exactly the data you want.

Look at the Customer List query

Before refining your combo box any further, take a look at the query you'll use to define the rows that will be displayed in the combo box's list.

1   Press the F11 key to switch to the Database window.

2   Click the Query button, and then double-click the Customer List query to open it.

Query button

Select Query: Customer List		
Last Name	**First Name**	**Customer ID**
▶ Abrams	Alice	205
Adams	Cathy	48
Adams	Melissa	232
Addison	Sarah	88
Ahern	Rolf	122
Albert	Joseph	66
Anchor	Paula	295
Ardley	Felicia	70
Babbitt	Edwina	152

This query displays three fields from the Customers table, sorted by the Last Name field.

Customer ID: Abrams

Abrams	Alice	205
Adams	Cathy	48
Adams	Melissa	232
Addison	Sarah	88
Ahern	Rolf	122
Albert	Joseph	66
Anchor	Paula	295
Ardley	Felicia	70

You'll use the three fields as the three columns in your list.

The records in the query's dynaset will be the rows in your list.

Design View button

3   Click the Design View button on the toolbar to switch to Design view.

As you can see, this query includes fields from only one table — the Customers table.

4   Close the Customer List query.

5   Click the Orders form to switch to it.

Tell Microsoft Access where to get the rows for the list

Just like other controls, a combo box has a set of properties. You use two of these properties to tell Microsoft Access where to get the rows for the combo box's list: the RowSourceType property and the RowSource property. The RowSourceType property tells Microsoft Access whether the source is a table or query, a list of values you provide, or some other source. The RowSource property identifies the actual source of the list. For example, to get the rows from a query, you set the RowSourceType property to Table/Query, and then you set the RowSource property to the name of the query that contains the values you want in the list.

Properties button

1   If the property sheet isn't displayed, click the Properties button on the toolbar to display it.

2   Select the Customer ID combo box to display its properties.

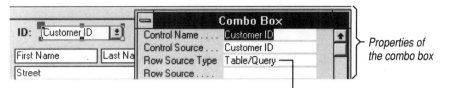

Because the rows in lists commonly come from a table or query,
the RowSourceType property is already set to Table/Query.

Notice that the RowSourceType property is already set to Table/Query. Now you'll tell Microsoft Access which table or query to use.

3   Click the box for the RowSource property.

Microsoft Access displays an arrow in the box, signaling that you can set the property by selecting a value from a list.

4   Click the arrow to open the list, and then select Customer List.

Combo Box	
Control Name	Customer ID
Control Source . . .	Customer ID
Row Source Type	Table/Query
Row Source	Customer List

Set the RowSource property
to Customer List.

Now Microsoft Access will use the values in the Customer List query to fill the rows in the combo box's list.

Defining the Columns in the List

Next, you'll answer three key questions that define the columns in your combo box's list.

Column Count . . .	3
Column Heads . . .	No
Column Widths . .	0.75 in;0.85 in;0.25 in
Bound Column . . .	1
List Rows	8
List Width	2.1 in

—— How many columns are in the list?

—— How wide is each column?

—— How wide is the whole list?

After answering these questions, you'll tell Microsoft Access which of the combo box's three columns contains the values that should be stored in the Customer ID field in the Orders table.

Define the number of columns in the list

The Customer List query has three fields: Last Name, First Name, and Customer ID. You want to display the customer's last name and first name in the list, so that you can select the customer by name. In case there are two customers with the same name, you also want to display the Customer ID field. That way, you can use the ID number to confirm which customer to pick. So you'll use all three fields in your list, and you need three columns to display them.

▶ Set the combo box's ColumnCount property to 3.

Define the width of the columns

Now you'll tell Microsoft Access how wide to make each of the three columns. You enter a measurement in the ColumnWidths property for each column in the list, starting with the first column. Separate the three measurements with semicolons.

▶ If your default unit of measurement is inches, type **0.75; 0.85; 0.25** in the ColumnWidths property box. If your default unit of measurement is centimeters, type **2; 2.12; 0.51** in the box. (The ruler at the top of your form displays in your default unit of measurement.)

Define the width of the list

Next, you'll use the ListWidth property to tell Microsoft Access how wide to make the entire list. You set the width of the list to a little more than the width of all three columns combined. That way, there's room for a scroll bar, too.

▶ If your default unit of measurement is inches, type **2.1** in the ListWidth property box. If it's centimeters, type **5.3** in the box.

There's one more question to answer for your combo box to work correctly: Which column in the list contains the customer ID numbers?

Define the bound column

Your combo box is bound to the Customer ID field in the Orders table. Microsoft Access needs to know which one of the three values in a selected row should be stored in this field. Customer ID is the third field in the Customer List query, which means that the ID numbers appear in the third column in the list.

1   Set the BoundColumn property to 3.

Take a look at your new combo box.

2   Click the Form View button on the toolbar to switch to Form view, and then click the combo box's arrow to open the list.

Form View button

The text box portion of the combo box shows
the value from the first column in the list.

The list shows all three columns.

When you take a new order, you can use this combo box to pick the customer by
name. When you save the order, Microsoft Access stores the customer's ID
number in the Orders table.

Tip   Suppose you decide that you want to display only names in your list, without
displaying ID numbers, but that you still want to bind the combo box to the Customer
ID field. It's simple. Define the combo box exactly as you've done here, but set the
ColumnWidths property so that the width of the third column is zero (0).

Limiting Entries to Values Already in the List

What if you're using the Orders form to take an order, but the customer's name
doesn't appear in the combo box's list? Maybe it's a new customer who doesn't have
a record in the Customer's table yet. Should you be able to simply type the customer's
name in the combo box and take the order anyway?

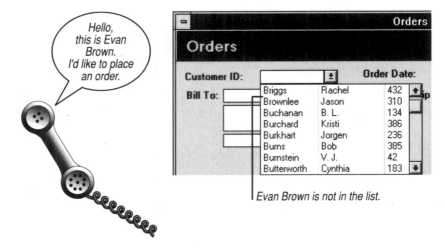

Evan Brown is not in the list.

At first glance, that might seem like the easiest way to get the task done, but in fact, it could cause you problems later. If you go ahead and take an order with the intention of adding the customer to the Customers table at another time, you could end up with an "orphan" order that has no corresponding customer record. Then your reports that include both customer and order information would be inaccurate.

You might think that you could use the Orders form both to add an order to the Orders table and to add a customer to the Customers table in one operation. But the Orders form isn't set up to add customers — it doesn't include all the fields in the Customers table, for example. If you use it to add a new customer, you'll end up with incomplete information in the Customers table.

In situations like this, it's usually better to add the customer information to the Customers table *first*, in a separate operation, and then take the order. To ensure that you already have the customer in the Customers table before adding the order, you can limit the values accepted in the combo box to those that are already in the list. That way, you know the customer is in the Customers table before you take the customer's order.

Note   One way to expedite adding a new customer would be to put a command button on the Orders form that opens a New Customer form. If the customer doesn't appear in the list on the Orders form, you can press the command button, add the customer to the Customers table, and then return to the Orders form to take the order. For more about creating command buttons that open other forms, see Lesson 21, "Customizing Your Work Environment."

Set the LimitToList property

Now you'll limit the values accepted in your Customer ID combo box to the values that are already in the list.

1   Switch to Design view of the Orders form.

2   Set the combo box's LimitToList property to Yes.

Limit To List	Yes		— Select Yes from
Validation Rule . .	Yes		the property's list.
Validation Text . . .	No		

Setting the LimitToList property to Yes actually makes it easier for you to select a value from the list. You can see how it works now.

Use incremental typing to select a value in the list

1   Switch back to Form view.

2   From the Records menu, choose Go To, and then choose New from the submenu.

Microsoft Access displays a new, blank record so you can add a new order.

3 Open the list for the Customer ID combo box, and then type **bro** in the text box portion of the combo box.

Microsoft Access scrolls the list to the first row that matches the letters you type. It selects the row for Jason Brownlee because that's the only last name in the list that matches "bro." (You must have the list open for this to work.)

4 Press the TAB key to move to the next field on the form.

Customer:	Brownlee ±	Order Date
Bill To:	Jason	Brownlee
	888 Hudson St.	
	Locust Valley	NY	11560
		USA

Microsoft Access fills in these fields automatically after you pick the customer from the list in the combo box.

The Orders form is based on a query that includes fields from both the Orders table and the Customers table. Once Microsoft Access knows which customer is placing the order, it fills in the fields from the Customers table automatically.

Tip If you get a blank record after pressing TAB in the combo box, it could be that the combo box isn't in the right tab order for the form. See "Put a control in the right tab order" earlier in this lesson for details on how to correct the problem.

One Step Further

The Orders Subform contains a text box in which operators type the ID code of the box the customer wants. The control is bound to the Box ID field in the Order Details table. It would be easier for operators if they could select the code from the list and if the list also displayed the full name of the box.

You'll replace this text box...

...with this combo box.

Create the query for the list

To learn how to create queries, see Lesson 10, "Selecting the Records You Want."

You'll probably use queries to define most lists in list boxes or combo boxes, so it would be a good idea to create the query for the Box ID combo box's list yourself, if you can. Or you can use the Box List query that's already in the Sweet database. (To use the Box List query, just skip this exercise and go on to "Create the combo box.")

▶ Create a new query that lists all the boxes in the Boxes table. Include both the box ID code and the box name in the query's dynaset. Sort the records by Box ID. Name your query My Box List.

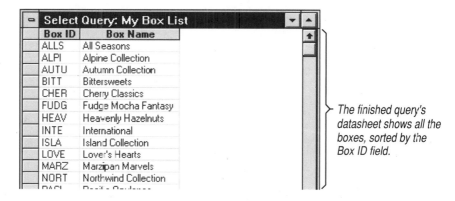

The finished query's datasheet shows all the boxes, sorted by the Box ID field.

Create the combo box

1 Open the Orders Subform form in Design view.

Tip   You can open the form from the Database window, or you can open it from the Design view of the Orders form by double-clicking the subform control. However, to see the changes that you make to the subform reflected on the Orders form, you must first save and close both forms, and then open the orders form in Form view.

---

2   Delete the Box ID text box in the detail section, and then replace it with a combo box bound to the Box ID field.

3   Delete your new combo box's attached label. (The combo box is probably covering part of the label. Click the label to select it, and then press DEL.) Resize the combo box so that it fits in the space.

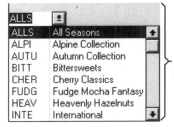

Here's how your combo box should look in Design view.

4   Define the list so that it displays the values from the Box List query. (Use the My Box List query instead if you created it in the previous exercise.)

ALLS		
ALLS	All Seasons	
ALPI	Alpine Collection	
AUTU	Autumn Collection	
BITT	Bittersweets	
CHER	Cherry Classics	
FUDG	Fudge Mocha Fantasy	
HEAV	Heavenly Hazelnuts	
INTE	International	

Here's how the finished combo box looks in Form view.

Hint   You'll probably have to experiment with the settings of the ColumnWidths and ListWidth properties to display your columns and list just the way you want. Also, notice that you don't have to change the BoundColumn property. By default, it's set to the first column, Box ID.

---

5   Set the tab order of the subform so that the Box ID combo box is first. (Be sure that the subform is open in Design view; otherwise you'll be working with the tab order for the main form.)

6   When you're finished with the Orders form and the Orders Subform, save them and close them.

Lesson Summary

To	Do this	Button
Create a combo box bound to a field	Click the combo box tool in the tool box, and then drag the field from the field list to the form.	
Tell Microsoft Access where to get the rows for the combo box list using a query	First create a query that contains the same records you want to use as rows in your list. Then set the control's RowSourceType property to Table/Query, and set the RowSource property to the name of the query.	
Define the number of columns in the list	Set the ColumnCount property to the number of columns you want.	
Define the width of the columns	Type the width of each column in the ColumnWidths property box, separated by semicolons.	
Define the width of the entire list	Type the width in the ListWidth property box.	
Determine which column contains the same values as the field that the control is bound to	Type the number of the column in the BoundColumn property box.	
Limit entries in a combo box to values already in the list	Set the LimitToList property to Yes.	

For more information on	See
Creating list boxes and combo boxes	Chapter 9, "Designing Forms," in the *Microsoft Access User's Guide*.

Preview of the Next Lesson

In the next lesson, you'll learn how to protect your data by having Microsoft Access enter default values in controls automatically. You'll also learn how to prevent people using your form from changing the data in some controls, and how to write validation rules that check the data entered in controls to make sure it meets your specifications.

Protecting Your Data

Anyone can make a mistake. When writing today's date, you might accidentally put down the previous year instead of this year. When viewing data on a form, you could inadvertently change a value in a field. It's no big deal — unless you don't notice the mistake and correct it.

Microsoft Access provides a variety of ways you can protect your data from everyday mistakes like these. In this lesson, you'll learn how to display a value such as today's date automatically, so you don't have to type it yourself. You'll find out how to design controls and forms so that you can't change the data on them. And you'll design a control so that it automatically displays a message if you enter invalid data in it.

You will learn how to:

- Set an initial (default) value for a control.
- Lock or disable a control.
- Validate data entered in a control.

Estimated lesson time: 20 minutes

How You Can Protect Your Data and Ensure Accuracy

The information you get out of your database is only as good as the data you put into it. For example, suppose you want to look at all the orders placed on 7-Mar-93. You can create a filter or query that asks for records with that order date. But if some of the order dates were entered incorrectly in the first place, you can't be sure you're seeing the records you really want.

By having Microsoft Access enter the order date automatically, you can make your order form easier to use and ensure the accuracy of the data at the same time. To do this, you set the DefaultValue property of the Order Date control.

Instead of typing the date yourself...

...you can have Microsoft Access fill it in for you.

Giving a control a default value is only one way you can protect your data. In addition, you can:

- Prevent others from selecting and copying data in a control by setting its Enabled property.

- Prevent others from changing data in a control by setting its Locked property.

- Describe what data is correct for a control by setting its ValidationRule property. And by setting the control's ValidationText property, you can also have Microsoft Access display a message that tells you how to fix an incorrect entry.

- Prevent changes from being made to data on a form by setting the form's DefaultEditing and AllowEditing properties.

In this lesson, you'll modify the Orders form so that it helps employees enter the right data for a new order. In addition, you'll modify another form that's used only to view (not change) data so that the person using the form can't change its data.

Start the lesson

▶ Start Microsoft Access. If the Microsoft Access window doesn't fill your screen, maximize the window. Then open the Sweet database.

Setting an Initial (Default) Value for a Control

Customer orders are the heart of Sweet Lil's business — a mistake on an order can mean lost revenue and lost customers. You plan to make a number of enhancements to the Orders form that will help ensure that the data on the form is correct. You'll start by giving the form's Order Date text box a default value, so the operators don't have to type the date themselves.

<table>
<tr><td colspan="3">Orders</td></tr>
<tr><td colspan="3">Orders</td></tr>
<tr><td>Customer ID: 1</td><td>Order Date: 07-Mar-93</td><td>Order ID:</td></tr>
</table>

You'll have Microsoft Access automatically enter today's date in each new record...

...by setting the DefaultValue property of the control.

Text Box	
After Update	
On Enter	
On Exit	
On Dbl Click	
Default Value	=Date()
Visible	Yes
Display When . . .	Always
Enabled	Yes
Locked	No
Scroll Bars	None
Can Grow	No
Can Shrink	No
Left	3.31 in

You can set the DefaultValue property either to an expression or to a constant value, such as text or a number. In this case, you'll set it equal to an expression that includes the **Date** function. The **Date** function is a small program that retrieves the current date from your computer's system clock.

Display today's date in a text box

1   Open the Orders form in Design view. (Remember to click the Form button in the Database window first; otherwise, you could open the Orders table instead of the Orders form.)

2   If the property sheet isn't displayed, click the Properties button on the toolbar. Then display the properties of the Order Date text box.

Properties button

Select the text box to display it's properties.

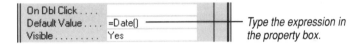

3 Set the DefaultValue property to the expression **=Date( )**

On Dbl Click	
Default Value	=Date()
Visible	Yes

Type the expression in the property box.

4 Switch to Form view.

Since Microsoft Access enters the default value when you start a new record, you'll go to a new record to see your property setting work.

5 From the Records menu, choose Go To, and then choose New from the submenu.

Microsoft Access displays a new record with today's date in the Order Date text box.

Locking and Disabling a Control

Not all controls on a form work the same way. Some controls provide a way for you to add and change data; others simply display data that you don't change.

Box ID	Box Name	Size	Box Price	Qty	Ext Price
BITT	Bittersweets	16	$27.75	2	$55.50
ALPI	Alpine Collection	12	$20.75	1	$20.75
SWEE	Sweet and Bitter	16	$27.75	3	$83.25

Total: $159.50

The operator can change the quantity ordered...

...but not the total charge, which is calculated automatically.

Microsoft Access provides two properties — the Locked and Enabled properties — that you can use to protect the data in a control.

The *Locked* property determines whether you can change data in the control in Form view. If you set this property to Yes, you can't change the data, but you can still select it and copy it onto the Clipboard.

The *Enabled* property determines whether you can select the control in Form view. If you set this property to No, you can't select, change, or copy the data in the control.

These two properties provide flexibility in how you make your controls work. As you'll see in this lesson, in some cases you may want to lock a control without disabling it; in others, you may not want the person using the control to even be able to select its value.

Locking a Control

The Total text box on the Orders form is a calculated control that displays the total charge for the order. You don't want operators to change its value, but you do want to be able to select the value and copy it onto the Clipboard. That way, you can paste it into a Word for Windows document or a Microsoft Excel spreadsheet. To get the functionality you want, you'll lock the Total text box but leave it enabled.

Lock a control

Design View button

1   Click the Design View button on the toolbar to switch to Design view.

2   Display the properties of the Total text box. (The Total text box is near the bottom of the Form's detail section.)

Select the text box to display its properties.

Total: =[Orders Su	**Text Box**	
	Control Name . . . . Subtotal	↑
	Control Source . . . =[Orders Subform].Foi	
	Format . . . . Currency	
	Decimal Places . . Auto	
	Status Bar Text . .	
	Validation Rule . .	
	Validation Text . . .	

3   Set the Locked property to Yes.

4   Switch to Form view, and then click the First Record button in the lower-left corner of the window.

◄◄ ◄	Record: 407	► ►►

Click here to go to the first record.

5 Try to change the value in the Total field.

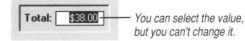

Total: [$38.00] —— *You can select the value,*
but you can't change it.

6 Select the value in the Total field, and then choose Copy from the Edit menu.

Microsoft Access lets you copy the value onto the Clipboard. Now you could paste the value from the Clipboard into a Microsoft Excel spreadsheet cell, for example.

Note The Total text box is a calculated control that displays the sum of the Extended Price field for all the records on the subform. For more information about creating calculated controls, see Lesson 15, "Showing Related Records and Calculations on Forms." For an example of an expression that totals values on a subform, see Appendix C, "Using Expressions," in this book. Also, see the example "Displaying the Order Subtotal on the Main Form" in Chapter 11 of the *Microsoft Access User's Guide*.

Disabling a Control

The Order ID text box on the Orders form is a control whose value can't be changed regardless of whether it's locked or disabled. That's because the Order ID field in the Orders table has a Counter data type — Microsoft Access automatically assigns an order ID number to an order when it's saved. The operators don't type the number themselves; in fact, because the field has a Counter data type, the operators *can't* type or change an order ID.

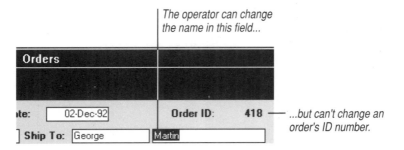

The operator can change
the name in this field...

Orders

te: [02-Dec-92]   **Order ID**:   418 —— *...but can't change an*
order's ID number.

] **Ship To**: [George]   [Martin]

You've noticed that when new operators start taking orders, they sometimes try to enter an Order ID in the text box themselves by selecting the contents of the text box and trying to type in it. Microsoft Access doesn't accept what they type, but some operators still find it confusing. You think that the form would be less confusing if operators couldn't even click in the text box or select its value, so you'll disable the control.

Disable a control

1   Switch to the Orders form's Design view.

2   Display the properties of the Order ID text box.

Select the text box to display it's properties.

Order ID Order ID	Text Box
Ship Last Name	Control Name . . . . Order ID
	Control Source . . . Order ID
	Format . . . . General Number
	Decimal Places . . Auto
	Status Bar Text

3   Set the Enabled property to No.

The text in the control and its label fades. That's because Microsoft Access changes the text color on disabled controls. You can restore the text to its original color by locking the control as well as disabling it.

4   Set the Locked property to Yes.

The text appears in its normal color.

5   Switch to Form view.

6   Try to select the contents of the Order ID text box.

Nothing happens. Now if new operators try to enter an order ID, they'll see right away that this field doesn't accept data entry.

Validating Data Entered in a Control

You've seen how to make data entry easier and more accurate by setting default values, and how to prevent changes to data by locking and disabling controls. Microsoft Access provides a third way you can protect your data — by adding validation rules to controls. A validation rule checks the data that you enter in the control against a rule that you define. If the data doesn't meet the rule's requirements, Microsoft Access displays an error message that you create yourself. Microsoft Access won't save the incorrect data in your table.

For example, operators enter the expiration date of the customer's credit card in the Expiration Date text box on the Orders form. If the date entered has already passed, you want to display a message alerting the operator that the card has expired. You can do that by setting a validation rule that requires the date entered to be greater than or equal to today's date. You'll also write an error message that tells the operator what to do if the card has expired.

Set the ValidationRule and ValidationText properties

1   Switch to the Orders form's Design view.

2   Display the properties of the Expiration Date text box.

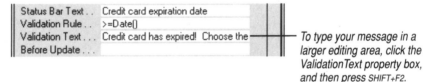

3   Set the ValidationRule property to this expression:

>=Date( )

4   Set the ValidationText property to the following message:

Credit card has expired! Choose the OK button, and then press Esc. Pick a different card or cancel the order.

To type your message in a larger editing area, click the ValidationText property box, and then press SHIFT+F2.

Your validation text message can be up to 255 characters long.

Test your validation

1   Switch to Form view.

2   Change the value in the Expiration Date text box to 11/92.

3   Press TAB.

Microsoft Access displays your error message.

4   Choose the OK button.

5   Press the ESC key.

Microsoft Access replaces 11/92 with the original value in the text box. Now you can enter a different credit card, or cancel the order.

6   Save and close the Orders form.

One Step Further

Suppose you want to create a number of different order forms, all feeding data to the Orders table. You'd probably want the same default value for the Order Date control on all the forms and the same validation rule for the Expiration Date control. Do you have to set the properties again and again on every form?

Microsoft Access provides an easier way. You can set a default value for the Order Date field in the Orders table rather than on the forms. And you can give the Expiration Date field in the Orders table a validation rule. Then Microsoft Access will set the DefaultValue and ValidationRule properties automatically for new controls that are bound to those fields. You can still change or delete the validation rule on a form if you want.

Give fields a default value and validation rule

1   Open the Orders table in Design view. (Be sure to click the Table button in the Database window first, so that you open the table and not the form.)

If you left the property sheet open in the Orders form's Design view, then you'll see a property sheet for the table as well. You won't be changing the table's properties, so you can close the property sheet.

2   Set the DefaultValue property of the Order Date field so that the field's default value is today's date.

3   Switch to the Expiration Date field, and then set its ValidationRule and ValidationText properties to the same settings these properties have for the Expiration Date text box on the Orders form.

While you're changing the design of the Orders table, you can't open the Orders form in Form view. However, you can open it in Design view.

Tip   If you're using Windows version 3.1 or later, here's a quick tip for copying a control's property setting from one place to another. Select the property setting you want to copy, and then press CTRL+C. To paste the setting in a new location, click in the new location, and then press CTRL+V. (You can't use the Copy command on the Edit menu to copy a control's property setting to the Clipboard. The Copy command copies the whole control instead.)

Make a form read-only

The Presenting Bonbons form in the Sweet database is used in presentations of Sweet Lil's product line to outside vendors. To prevent inadvertent changes to the data, you'll make the form read-only, so that Microsoft Access doesn't accept any changes to data on the form.

1   Open the Presenting Bonbons form in Design view.

2   Set the form's DefaultEditing property to Read Only.

Tip   To display the form's properties, click inside the Form window, but outside the border of the form. Or choose Select Form from the Edit menu.

---

3   Switch to Form view and try to change data on the form.

Microsoft Access won't let you change the data. However, you can still turn editing on by choosing the Editing Allowed command from the Records menu. To make it really impossible to use this form to edit data, you can make that command unavailable.

4   Switch back to Design view, and then set the AllowEditing property of the form to Unavailable.

Now you can't use this form to change data in the Bonbons table.

5   When you're finished working with the Presenting Bonbons form, save and close it.

Lesson Summary

To	Do this
Set an initial (default) value for a control	Set the control's DefaultValue property. You can set the property to text, a number, or an expression.
Display today's date in a text box	Set the text box's DefaultValue property to this expression: **=Date( )**
Modify a control so you can't change its data but can select and copy its data	Set the control's Locked property to Yes.
Modify a control so you can't change or select its data	Set the control's Enabled property to No.
Check the value entered in a control and display a message if it's incorrect	Set the control's ValidationRule and ValidationText properties.

To	Do this
Make a form read-only	Set the form's DefaultEditing property to Read Only. To prevent the person using the form from turning on editing, also set the AllowEditing property to Unavailable.
Give a field in a table a default value	Set the field's DefaultValue property in the table's Design view.
Give a field in a table a validation rule	Set the field's ValidationRule property in the table's Design view.

For more information on	See
Setting default values and validation rules for controls on a form, and setting the default editing mode of a form	Chapter 9, "Designing Forms," in the *Microsoft Access User's Guide*.
Setting field properties in a table	Chapter 3, "Changing and Customizing Tables," in the *Microsoft Access User's Guide*.

Preview of the Next Lesson

In the next lesson, you'll learn how to use a ReportWizard to create a quick report. You'll also learn how to modify the report in Design view to show groups of records.

Customizing
Your Reports

Creating a Quick Detail Report

How do you get a quick report that shows off your data in print? You may want a sales report to take to a meeting right away or an attractive list of products for a prospective customer. Ideally, you'd like to create a great-looking report in a few minutes—a report that looks like it was designed by a professional.

What you need are ReportWizards, the report design experts in Microsoft Access that do most of the work for you. They ask you a series of questions and then build a professional-looking report. You can use the report as is, or you may want to touch it up and add a few custom details.

In this lesson, you'll learn how to create a simple report with a ReportWizard. You'll preview the report and then switch to Design view to make a few changes.

You will learn how to:

- Use a ReportWizard to create a report.
- Preview and print a report.
- Understand the design of a report.
- Change the design of a report.
- Show groups of records by hiding duplicates.

Estimated lesson time: 30 minutes

What Is a Detail Report?

Although you can print a table or query directly, you can take a little more time and create a report that presents your information in an easier-to-read, more professional-looking format. A *detail report* displays basically the same information you see when you print a table or query, but it contains additional elements, such as *report headers*, *page headers*, and *page footers*.

The query displays the raw data...

...but the report presents the data attractively in print.

In this lesson, you'll create a detail report. In the following lesson, you'll learn how to create a *grouped report*, which combines your data into groups and calculates totals or other information for each group.

Usually, the fastest way to create a report is with a ReportWizard. The ReportWizard places fields on the report and presents the data in one of several presentation styles. If you want, after you've created the report, you can customize it, making small- or large-scale changes.

Important If you haven't read Lesson 13, "Using Controls to Show Text and Data," it would be a good idea to work through that lesson before continuing with this one.

Start the lesson

▶ Start Microsoft Access. If the Microsoft Access window doesn't fill your screen, maximize the window. Then open the Sweet database.

Using a ReportWizard to Create a Report

You're planning new advertisements that promote your most popular boxes of bonbons. At a meeting with other people from the Marketing department, you plan to hand out a report that shows sales by state or province. You don't need anything elaborate — just an easy-to-create, easy-to-read report.

The Sales by State/Province query in the Sweet database contains the records you need for this report.

Decide which ReportWizard to use

Since you want to create a report quickly and easily, you'll use a ReportWizard. Microsoft Access gives you three ReportWizards to choose from: the Single-Column ReportWizard, the Groups/Totals ReportWizard, and the Mailing Label ReportWizard. Since you're not interested in mailing labels, it's a choice between the Single-Column and Groups/Totals ReportWizards.

The two reports in the following illustration show the differences between these two ReportWizards. The Single-Column report displays the data in one long column, while the Groups/Totals report uses a more compact format and presents the data in a table.

Single-Column report

Sales by State/Province
18-Oct-92

State/Province:	AK
Box Name:	Bittersweets
Amount:	$27.75
State/Province:	AK
Box Name:	Cherry Classics
Amount:	$16.25

Groups/Totals report

Sales by State/Province
18-Oct-92

State/Province	Box Name	Amount
AK	Bittersweets	$27.75
AK	Cherry Classics	$16.25
AK	Lover's Hearts	$17.50
AK	Marzipan Marvels	$64.50
AK	Sweet and Bitter	$55.50

▶   You want a shorter, more compact report. So you'll choose the Groups/Totals ReportWizard.

Note   You can also use the Groups/Totals ReportWizard to create more complex reports that divide your data into groups and calculate group totals. In this lesson, you'll use the Groups/Totals ReportWizard because it provides the tabular format you want, but you won't use all the grouping features. In Lesson 19, you'll create a report that takes greater advantage of the power of the Groups/Totals ReportWizard.

Begin a new report

Report button

1 In the Database window, click the Report button, and then choose the New button.

Microsoft Access displays the New Report dialog box.

2 In the Select A Table/Query box, select the Sales by State/Province query.

3 Choose the ReportWizards button.

Microsoft Access asks which AccessWizard you want to use.

4 Select Groups/Totals, and then choose the OK button.

Microsoft Access displays the first ReportWizard dialog box.

Enter information in the ReportWizard dialog boxes

When you use a ReportWizard, you go through a series of dialog boxes. Each of the steps below shows you how to enter information in one dialog box. The first dialog box lists the available fields (the fields from the Sales by State/Province query) and asks which fields you want to include on the report.

1 Add all three available fields to the report, and then choose the Next button.

Click here to add all fields.

2 When you're asked which fields to group by, choose the Next button. (Because you don't need the grouping feature for this report, you don't need to make any selections in this dialog box.)

3 When you're asked which fields you want to sort by, choose State/Province first and then Box Name. Then choose the Next button.

To choose a field, first select it...

Available fields:

> State/Province
> Box Name
> Amount

`>`
`>>`
`<`
`<<`

Field order on report:

...and then click here.

This means that Microsoft Access will first sort state and province names alphabetically, and then it will sort the box names within each state or province.

4   When you're asked what kind of look you want, choose Executive, and then choose the Next button.

5   Leave the title unchanged, and click the Print Preview button to see how your report will look when you print it.

Sales by State/Province

18-Oct-92 ——————————————————————————————

The ReportWizard automatically adds the date the report was printed.

State/Province	Box Name	Amount
AK	Bittersweets	$27.75
AK	Cherry Classics	$16.25
AK	Lover's Hearts	$17.50
AK	Marzipan Marvels	$64.50
AK	Sweet and Bitter	$55.50
AL	Bittersweets	$27.75
AL	Fudge Mocha Fantasy	$18.00

All three available fields are included in the report.

First the state and province names are alphabetized...

...and then the box names within each state or province are alphabetized.

Note   The text in your report may differ from that in the illustration, depending on the printer that is selected.

6   Save the report, and name it Sales by State/Province.

Previewing and Printing a Report

By previewing your report, you can make sure you've designed it the way you want before you print it. The Sales by State/Province report is magnified in Print Preview. The magnifying glass pointer means you can switch between viewing data in magnified view and seeing the layout of the entire page.

Switch views in Print Preview

1 To see the whole page, click anywhere on the report.

Microsoft Access displays a view of the whole page.

2 To return to viewing data, click the report again.

Move from page to page

▶ Use the navigation buttons at the bottom of the window to page through your report.

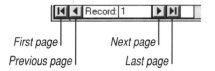

First page   Next page
Previous page   Last page

Print the report

For more information on printing, see Appendix A, "Installing and Setting Up Your Printer."

If your system is set up for printing, try printing the report now.

▶ Click the Print button on the toolbar (or from the File menu, choose Print).

Note When you have the report open in Design view, you can print by choosing Print from the File menu. You can also print a report from the Database window. First select the report, and then choose Print from the File menu.

Exploring the Design of the Report

As you preview the report, you can see how Microsoft Access displays the records from your query along with added information that makes the report easier to read. If you page through this report, you'll see:

■ A *report header* at the top of the first page of the report. In your report, the report header includes the title of the report and today's date.

■ A *page header* at the top of every page of the report. The page header displays the heading for each column of data.

- Between the page header and the page footer is the *detail*—the records from the Sales by State/Province query, which you selected as the report's underlying query when you created the report.

- A *page footer* at the bottom of every page of the report. In this case, the page footer shows the page number.

- A *report footer* at the very end of the report. For this report, the report footer shows the total sales amount.

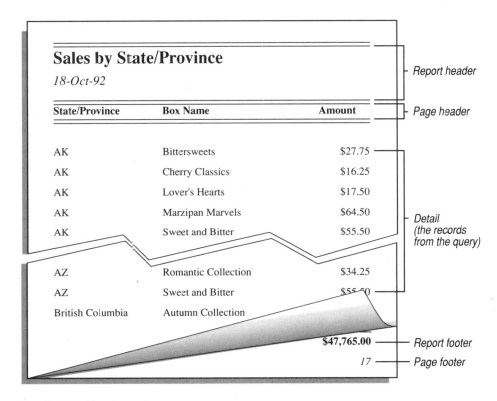

Switch to Design view

Cancel button

1 Choose the Cancel button on the toolbar to switch to Design view.

Microsoft Access displays the design of the report.

Note   If you open the report in Print Preview directly from the Database window and then choose the Cancel button, you will close the report. Choosing the Cancel button to switch to Design view works only if you originally opened the report in Design view.

---

2   If the Report window is too small for you to see all the controls, resize the window to make it larger.

In Design view, the different sections represent the elements you saw in Print Preview. Design view is a blueprint for the report: It shows Microsoft Access how to display each element when you preview or print the report. For example, the detail section in Design view shows how the records from the underlying table or query should look. When you look at the report in Print Preview, you'll see many records, each formatted as shown in Design view.

Move the design tools out of the way

When you switch to Design view, Microsoft Access may display the toolbox and the property sheet. You'll use these tools to customize your report. For now, though, you may want to move these tools so you can see the report better.

```
Report Header
0
  Sales by State/Province
  =Now()
Page Header
0
  State/Province        Box Name                    Amount
Detail
0  State/Province       Box Name                    Amount
Page Footer
0
                                                    =Page
Report Footer
0
                                           =Sum([Amount])
```

To move the design
tools, drag their title
bars.

```
Report
Record Source . .  Sales by State/Province
On Open . . . . . . .
On Close . . . . . . .
```

Toolbox   Property sheet

What ReportWizards do for you

When you created this report, the ReportWizard did a lot of work for you behind the scenes. These are just some of the things the ReportWizard did:

- Created the sections on your report
- Placed the data and other information in the appropriate sections
- Aligned the columns and added some decorative lines to create an attractive report
- Selected fonts and font sizes for all text on the report
- Added today's date to the report header
- Added an expression to calculate the total in the report footer

When you become more proficient with Microsoft Access, you'll be able to create your own reports from scratch if you want. But you can often save hours of time if you start with a ReportWizard and then customize the report after the ReportWizard creates it.

Changing the Design of a Report

It took only a short time to create this report, and it attractively presents the data you need for your meeting. There are a few minor things you'd like to change, though. Working in Design view, you'll:

- Change the text in the Amount label so it's more descriptive, and move the label so it lines up better with the sales values below it.

- Add some information to the page footer.

Change the label in the page header

1 Select the Amount label.

2 Move the pointer inside the label, place it to the left of the word Amount, and then click the mouse button.

3 Type **Sales** followed by a space, and then press the ENTER key.

Page Header		
State/Province	Box Name	Sales Amount

Detail

Move the label

1 Move the Sales Amount label to the right edge of the report.

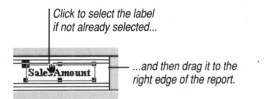

Click to select the label if not already selected...

...and then drag it to the right edge of the report.

Print Preview button

2 Click the Print Preview button on the toolbar to see how your changes will look on the printed report.

Sales by State/Province

18-Oct-92

State/Province	Box Name	Sales Amount
AK	Bittersweets	$27.75
AK	Cherry Classics	$16.25

The Sales Amount label now appears directly above the sales values.

Add more information to the page footer

To help other Marketing people understand the purpose of the report, you'll add a footer to each page of the report.

1 Switch to Design view.

Label tool

2 In the toolbox, click the label tool. (If the toolbox isn't displayed, choose Toolbox from the View menu to display it.)

3 Click in the lower-left corner of the page footer section to add the label. (If necessary, move the toolbox out of the way.)

```
┌─────────────────────────────────────────────────────────┐
│ │ Page Footer                                            │
│ 0 ┤ +                                                     │
│   ┤   A                                      =Page       │
│   ┤ Report Footer                                        │
└─────────────────────────────────────────────────────────┘
```

| Click here.

4 In the new label, type **Data for Marketing Meeting on 15-Dec-92**, and then press ENTER.

```
┌─────────────────────────────────────────────────────────┐
│ │ Page Footer                                            │
│ 0 ┤                                                       │
│   ┤  Data for Marketing Meeting on 15-Dec-92    =Page    │
│   ┤ Report Footer                                        │
└─────────────────────────────────────────────────────────┘
```

Bold button

Microsoft Access displays the label in bold type, which is the default font style for labels in this report. But you want it to be italic and not bold, just like the page number in the page footer.

5 While the label is still selected, click the Bold button on the toolbar to cancel bold for the text.

6 Click the Italic button on the toolbar to make the text italic.

7 Look at the report in Print Preview.

Italic button

You'll see the page footer at the bottom of every page.

Hiding Duplicates to Show Groups of Records

What's wrong with the report? When you look down the left side, you see the name of the state or province repeated over and over. But you need to see each name only once for each group. In Lesson 19, you'll learn how to create a grouped report, which will solve this problem. But for the report you're working on now, there's another quick way to fix this.

As the report is now, Microsoft Access displays data for the State/Province field even if this field contains duplicate values. You can change the HideDuplicates property for the Sales/Province text box so that duplicate values are shown only once.

Hide the duplicate values

1   Switch to Design view.

2   In the detail section, select the State/Province text box.

3   In the property sheet, change the setting of the HideDuplicates property to Yes. (If the property sheet isn't displayed, choose Properties from the View menu.)

Select the State/Province text box in the detail section...

Detail		Text Box
0 State/Province	Control Name	State/Province
Page Footer	Control Source . . .	State/Province
	Format	
0	Decimal Places . .	Auto
Data for Marketing Me	Visible	Yes
Report Footer	Hide Duplicates . .	Yes
0	Can Grow	No
	Can Shrink	No
	Running Sum	No

...and then change its HideDuplicates property to Yes.

4   Switch to Print Preview.

Sales by State/Province

18-Oct-92

State/Province	Box Name	Sales Amount
AK	Bittersweets	$27.75
	Cherry Classics	$16.25
	Lover's Hearts	$17.50
	Marzipan Marvels	$64.50
	Sweet and Bitter	$55.50
AL	Bittersweets	$27.75
	Fudge Café Fantasy	$18.00

Each state or province appears only once.

5   Save the report and close it.

One Step Further

An international gourmet food company is interested in ordering large quantities of individual bonbons from Sweet Lil's. The international company's representative wants a report that shows all of Sweet Lil's bonbons categorized by chocolate type. Since he wants it immediately, you decide to make a quick report similar to the one you've already made in this lesson.

Create the report

Create a report similar to the one below. As the underlying query for this report, use the Chocolate Types query. Save the report, and name it Chocolate Types.

Hint   Use the Groups/Totals ReportWizard, but don't select any fields to group by.

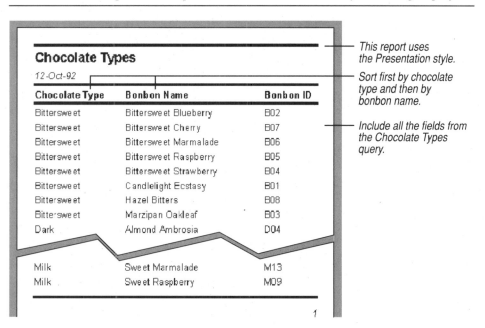

This report uses the Presentation style.

Sort first by chocolate type and then by bonbon name.

Include all the fields from the Chocolate Types query.

Customize your report

You're hoping this report will help you make a big sale, so you want it to look as good as possible. To improve the appearance of the report, customize it so that each type of chocolate appears only once. For example, Bittersweet should appear only once.

Hint   Set the HideDuplicates property for the Chocolate Type text box.

To emphasize the chocolate type in the detail section, make it bold. When you're done, your report will look something like the following illustration.

Chocolate Types
19-Oct-92

Chocolate Type	Bonbon Name	Bonbon ID
Bittersweet	Bittersweet Blueberry	B02
	Bittersweet Cherry	B07
	Bittersweet Marmalade	B06
	Bittersweet Raspberry	B05
	Bittersweet Strawberry	B04
	Candlelight Ecstasy	B01

Change the report so that each chocolate type
appears only once and is displayed in bold type.

Lesson Summary

To	Do this	Button
Create a tabular detail report using a ReportWizard	Click the Report button, and then choose the New button. Select the underlying table or query, and then click the ReportWizards button. Select the Groups/Totals ReportWizard and answer the questions in the dialog boxes. Don't select any grouping for the report.	Report
Preview a report	In the Database window, select the report, and then click the Print Preview button on the toolbar. In Design view, click the Print Preview button on the toolbar.	
View the design of a report	In the Database window, click the report, and then choose the Design button. In Print Preview, choose the Cancel button if the report was originally opened in Design view.	Design
Print a report	In the Database window, select the report, and then choose Print from the File menu. In Print Preview, click the Print button. In Design view, choose Print from the File menu.	

To	Do this	Button
Hide duplicates in the detail section	Select the control for which you want to hide duplicates. In the property sheet for this control, set the HideDuplicates property to Yes.	

For more information on	See
Creating reports	Chapter 9, "Creating Reports, Graphs, and Mailing Labels" in *Microsoft Access Getting Started.*
	Chapter 17, "Report Basics," and Chapter 18, "Designing Reports" in the *Microsoft Access User's Guide.*

Preview of the Next Lesson

In the next lesson, you'll learn how to create a report that includes groups and subtotals for each group. Then you'll customize the report by adding descriptive text for each group, calculating a percentage for each group, and changing the sort order.

Creating a Grouped Report

Your data becomes more meaningful when it's grouped, or divided into categories. When you're looking at regional sales patterns, for example, you don't want to see just a long list of sales data—what you'd rather see is a list of sales for each region. What would be even better is a list of sales with a subtotal for each region so that you can see at a glance where your sales are strongest.

Using Microsoft Access ReportWizards, you can design grouped reports that make your data easier to understand. In this lesson, you'll find out how to create a report that groups your data and automatically calculates subtotals for each group. Then you'll create another grouped report that calculates a percentage, and you'll change the sort order of that report.

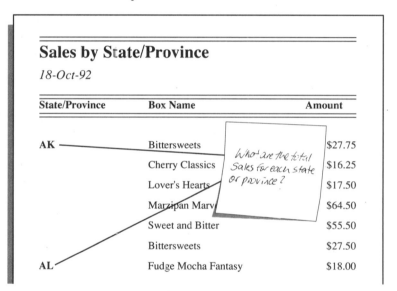

You will learn how to:

- Create a grouped report.
- Customize the group footer.
- Calculate a percentage.
- Change the sort order.

Estimated lesson time: 30 minutes

What Are Groups and Totals?

A *group* is a collection of similar records. By creating a grouped report, you can often improve your reader's understanding of the data in the report. That's because a grouped report not only displays similar records together; it also shows introductory and summary information for each group.

In the following report, the records are grouped by state or province. The state of Alaska (AK), for example, makes up the first group.

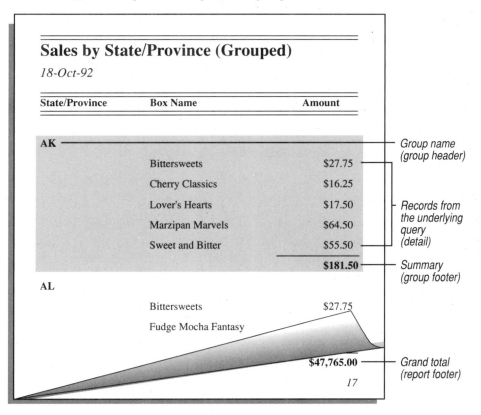

The *group header* (AK, in this case) identifies or introduces the group. The body of the group, or the *detail* section, displays the appropriate records from the underlying query. The *group footer* summarizes the data for the group, showing the total sales for Alaska. The report footer at the very end of the report includes the grand total for the sales from all states and provinces.

In this lesson, you'll use the Groups/Totals ReportWizard to create grouped reports. This ReportWizard is a real time-saver: It asks how you want to group records in your report, and then it adds the group header and group footer sections for you. It even adds the expressions that perform the subtotal and total calculations.

Start the lesson

▶   Start Microsoft Access. If the Microsoft Access window doesn't fill your screen, maximize the window. Then open the Sweet database.

Creating a Grouped Report

As Sweet Lil's new Marketing manager, you plan to expand sales through a mail order campaign. You'll start by sending the mail order advertisement only to people in the states and provinces where your products have been most successful.

What you'd like to see is a report that shows the total sales for each state and province. The quick report you created in Lesson 18 shows a list of sales, but it doesn't show you the totals for each state and province.

To get the report you want, you'll create a new report using the Groups/Totals ReportWizard. In this report, you want to see sales totals for each state and province, so you'll choose State/Province as the field to group by. The Sales by State/Province query in the Sweet database provides the records you need.

Begin a new report

Report button

1   In the Database window, create a new report (remember to click the Report button and then choose the New button).

2   In the Select A Table/Query box, select the Sales by State/Province query, and then click the ReportWizards button.

3   When you're asked which AccessWizard you want, select Groups/Totals and choose the OK button.

Enter information in the ReportWizard dialog boxes

Now that you've selected a ReportWizard, you'll go through a series of dialog boxes. Each of the steps below shows how to enter information into one dialog box.

1   Add all three available fields to the report, and then choose the Next button.

Available fields:		Field order on report:
State/Province	>	
Box Name	>>	——— *Click here to add all fields.*
Amount	<	
	<<	

2   When you're asked which fields to group by, select the State/Province field, and then choose the Next button.

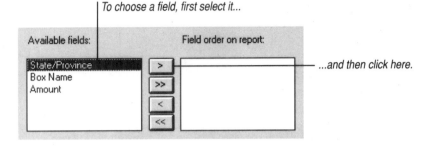

To choose a field, first select it...

...and then click here.

> **Note**   Because you're selecting State/Province as the field to group by, your report will show totals for each state and province. Grouping by State/Province also means that your report will display the states and provinces in alphabetical order.

3   When you're asked how you want to group data, choose the Next button to accept the default, Normal grouping.

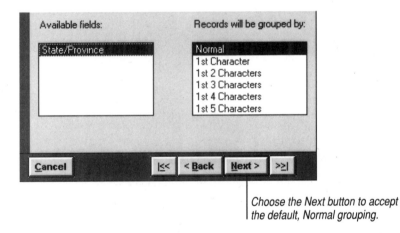

Choose the Next button to accept the default, Normal grouping.

> **Note**   Normal means that each group will consist of one state or province. If you selected 1st Character rather than Normal, the first group would consist of all the states and provinces beginning with A, the second group would be all the states and provinces beginning with B, and so on.

4   When you're asked what fields to sort by, select Box Name field, and then choose the Next button.

This means that Microsoft Access will list the box names for each state and province in alphabetic order.

5 When you're asked what type of look you want, choose Executive, and then choose the Next button.

6 Change the title of the report to Sales by State/Province (Grouped), and then click the Print Preview button.

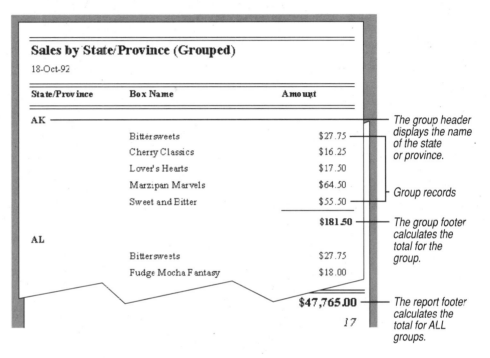

Sales by State/Province (Grouped)

18-Oct-92

State/Province	Box Name	Amount
AK		
	Bittersweets	$27.75
	Cherry Classics	$16.25
	Lover's Hearts	$17.50
	Marzipan Marvels	$64.50
	Sweet and Bitter	$55.50
		$181.50
AL		
	Bittersweets	$27.75
	Fudge Mocha Fantasy	$18.00
		$47,765.00

17

The group header displays the name of the state or province.

Group records

The group footer calculates the total for the group.

The report footer calculates the total for ALL groups.

7 Save the report, and name it Sales by State/Province (Grouped).

Check the report in Design view

1 Click the Cancel button to switch to Design view so you can compare the two views.

[**Cancel**]

Cancel button

2 If the Report window is too small, resize it so you can see more of the controls on the report.

Tip You may want to move the toolbox and the property sheet or other design tools out of the way for a better view of the report.

When you look at the report in Design view, notice that the ReportWizard has added these elements:

A group header and group footer The ReportWizard has added a group header and a group footer for the State/Province group. In Design view, they're identified as the State/Province Header and the State/Province Footer. In more complex reports, you might have several group headers with different names.

Expressions that calculate totals Notice that the expression in the State/Province footer is exactly the same as the expression in the report footer: **=Sum([Amount])**. When you place an expression in the State/Province footer or the State/Province header, it performs calculations for the records in each State/Province *group*. When you place an expression in the report footer or header, it calculates a value for *all records* in the report. Later on, when you're customizing the report, remember that while it's important to create the right expression, it's just as important to place the expression in the right section.

Customizing the Group Footer

You'd like to make it really easy to skim the report and find the total sales figure for each state or province. So you'll add some text to identify each sales total. For example, to the left of the Alaska total, you'd like to see "Sales for AK."

To add this text, you'll use a text box with an expression. Microsoft Access will use the expression to fill in the appropriate name for each state or province.

Note The toolbox includes both a label tool and a text box tool. Since you're adding descriptive text, you might think you'd use a label. But you can't use expressions in labels, so you'll use a text box instead.

Add a text box in the State/Province footer

Text box tool

1 In the toolbox, click the text box tool. (If the toolbox isn't open, choose Toolbox from the View menu.)

2 Click near the middle of the State/Province footer to add the text box.

State/Province Footer
0 ⫶ ⫿ ....⏉ ⫿ab⫿.................................⫿=Sum([Amount])⫿
Page Footer

Click here.

3 Click in the text box you've just added. Type this expression:

="Sales for " & [State/Province]

Then press the ENTER key.

Be sure to start the expression with the equal sign (=), and leave a space before the second quotation mark. If you don't leave a space, your label will contain text like this: Sales forAK.

Here's what the expression means.

For more information on expressions, see Appendix C, "Using Expressions."

Display this text... | | ...followed by...

$$=\text{"Sales for"} \& [\text{State/Province}]$$

...the name of the state/province for this group.

4   Make the text box wider, and move it so it's roughly in the position shown below.

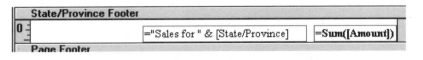

Note   You need to make the text box wider to allow enough room for the text to
fit. Otherwise, the text box will not be wide enough to display longer state or
province names, such as "Sales for Yukon Territories."

Change the format of the text box

Now you'll emphasize the text box with bold text.

Bold button

1   Click the Bold button on the toolbar. (Be sure the text box is still selected.)

2   Switch to Print Preview to see the report.

Sales by State/Province (Grouped)

18-Oct-92

State/Province	Box Name	Amount
AK		
	Bittersweets	$27.75
	Cherry Classics	$16.25
	Lover's Hearts	$17.50
	Marzipan Marvels	$64.50
	Sweet and Bitter	$55.50
	Sales for AK	**$181.50**

3   Save the report.

Showing a Percentage on Your Report

Now you can skim through your report easily and find the totals you're interested in.
For your mail order campaign, you want to target those states and provinces with the
most sales.

You'd like to see at a glance what percentage of total sales is brought in by each state
and province, and you'd like to display this information next to the name of the state
or province. The report you create will look like this.

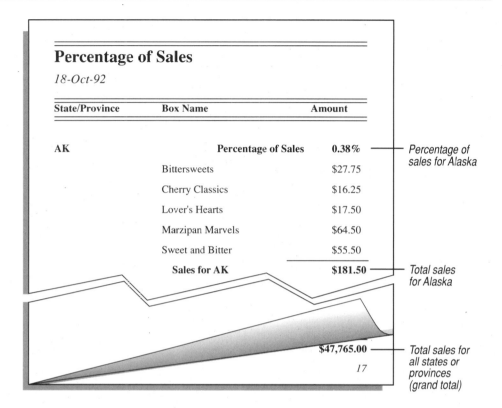

Percentage of Sales

18-Oct-92

State/Province	Box Name	Amount
AK	**Percentage of Sales**	**0.38%**
	Bittersweets	$27.75
	Cherry Classics	$16.25
	Lover's Hearts	$17.50
	Marzipan Marvels	$64.50
	Sweet and Bitter	$55.50
	Sales for AK	**$181.50**

Percentage of sales for Alaska

Total sales for Alaska

$47,765.00

17

Total sales for all states or provinces (grand total)

Name the report

You'll start with the Sales by State/Province (Grouped) report you've already created and add the percentage information.

1 Switch to Design view of the Sales by State/Province (Grouped) report.

2 From the File menu, choose Save As, and name the report Percentage of Sales.

3 In the report header, select the label that contains the title of the report. Click in the label and replace the existing title with this new title: **Percentage of Sales**

Change the report's title.

Report Header

0

Percentage of Sales

=Now()

Page Header

Rename the totals text boxes

To calculate a percentage of sales, you'll add an expression to the State/Province header. Because the expression is in the State/Province header, it will automatically calculate a value based on all the records in each group.

You'll use an expression that divides the total for each state or province by the grand total. This expression will refer to the text box that calculates the State/Province total and the text box that calculates the grand total.

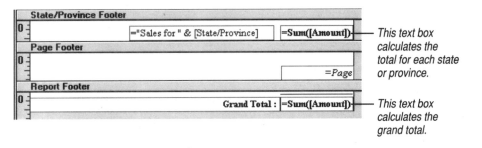

This text box calculates the total for each state or province.

This text box calculates the grand total.

When you created the report, the ReportWizard gave default names to the text boxes containing the State/Province total and the grand total. These text boxes have generic names like Field9. When you create your expression to calculate a percentage, you need to use these names. But an expression like **=[Field9]/[Field10]** wouldn't be very easy to understand when you looked at the report in the future. So before creating the expression, you'll give these two text boxes more meaningful names.

1 In the State/Province group footer, click the text box that displays the expression **=Sum([Amount])**.

2 In the property sheet for this text box, notice the ControlName property. It's set to a name such as Field9. (If the property sheet isn't displayed, choose Properties from the View menu.)

3 In the ControlName property box, replace the existing name with State/Province Total.

Now that you've changed this control name, you'll change the name of the text box that displays the grand total.

4 In the report footer, select the text box that displays **=Sum([Amount])**.

5 In the property sheet, change the ControlName property to Grand Total.

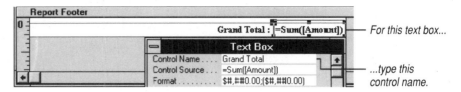

Add a text box to the State/Province header

Next, you'll add a text box in the State/Province header to display the percentage of sales. Then you'll add an expression to calculate the percentage. The expression you'll use is =[**State/Province Total**]/[**Grand Total**].

Note   This expression uses the new names you have given to the text boxes. It divides the value in the State/Province Total text box by the value in the Grand Total text box.

Text box tool

1 Use the text box tool in the toolbox to add a text box to the State/Province header.

2 Click in your new text box.

3 Type this expression:

=[**State/Province Total**]/[**Grand Total**]

Then press ENTER.

Bold button

4 To make the text bold, click the Bold button on the toolbar.

5 Move the text box until it's in this position.

Add a label and preview the report

Label tool

So far, you've added just a number. You also need a label that describes what this number is.

1 Use the label tool in the toolbox to add a label to the left of the text box you just created.

2   In the label, type **Percentage of Sales** and press ENTER.

3   Move the label so it's roughly in this position.

Move the label to this location.

4   Preview the report.

Fix the percentage format

The report looks great—except that you wanted to display a percentage such as
0.38%, not a number like 0.00379985345. To display this value as a percentage,
you'll need to set the Format property.

1   Switch to Design view.

2   In the State/Province header, click the text box with the expression that calculates
percentage.

3   In the property sheet for the text box, set the Format property to Percent.

For this text box...

*...set the
Format property
to Percent.*

4   Preview the report again. Now you should see the percentages formatted correctly.

5   Save the report.

Changing the Sort Order

The Percentage of Sales report is lacking just one more detail. In the advertisements you send to a particular state or province, you want to feature boxes of bonbons that are the best sellers in that region.

When you originally created your report, you grouped by the State/Province field and then sorted by the Box Name field. Now you'd like to change the sort order. Within each state or province, you'd like to see a list of boxes starting with the box that brought in the most money and ending with the one that brought in the least. In other words, you want to sort by the Amount field rather than the Box Name field, and you want to sort in descending order.

Percentage of Sales

18-Oct-92

State/Province	Box Name	Amount
AK	Percentage of Sales	0.38%
	Marzipan Marvels	$64.50
	Sweet and Bitter	$55.50
	Bittersweets	$27.75
	Lover's Hearts	$17.50
	Cherry Classics	$16.25
	Sales for AK	$181.50

The box that brought in the most revenue

The box that brought in the least revenue

When you create reports with a ReportWizard, you're asked about how you want to group and sort your data. If you decide to change sorting or grouping after you've created a report, you don't have to start from scratch and rerun the ReportWizard. Instead, you can use the Sorting and Grouping box to make the changes.

Open the Sorting and Grouping box

1 Switch to Design view.

2 Click the Sorting and Grouping button on the toolbar.

Sorting and Grouping button

Sort first by state or province...

...and then sort by box name.

Sorting and Grouping		
Field/Expression	Sort Order	
State/Province	Ascending	
Box Name	Ascending	

Group Properties

Group Header .	Yes	
Group Footer . .	Yes	Select a field or type an expression to sort or group on.
Group On	Each Value	
Group Interval .	1	

This icon indicates the field is used for grouping and sorting.

Microsoft Access displays the Sorting and Grouping box. You can see the settings that were established when you answered the ReportWizard's questions.

The Field/Expression column shows fields that are used either for grouping and sorting or for sorting only. To the left of the State/Province field is the Grouping icon, which tells you that this field is used for grouping and sorting. The Box Name field doesn't have this icon, so you can tell it is used solely for sorting.

Change the sort order

Using the Sorting and Grouping box, you'll change the second field to group by from Box Name to Amount.

1 In the Field/Expression column, click the Box Name cell, and then click the arrow to display a list of fields.

This list displays the fields on the report.

Sorting and Grouping		
Field/Expression	Sort Order	
State/Province	Ascending	
Box Name	Ascending	
State/Province		
Box Name		
Amount		

2 Select the Amount field from the list.

The Amount field replaces the Box Name field.

3 Click the Sort Order cell to the right of the Amount field, and then click the arrow.

4   Select Descending from the list.

Sorting and Grouping		
Field/Expression	Sort Order	↑
State/Province	Ascending	
Amount	Descending	±

By selecting Descending, you're asking Microsoft Access to display amounts starting with the largest and working down to the smallest.

5   Close the Sorting and Grouping box, and preview the report.

It should look like the report shown previously under "Changing the Sort Order."

6   Save the report, and close it.

One Step Further

Lillian Farber, the company president, is trying to reduce box costs again. She wants a report that lists the bonbons in each box along with the cost of each bonbon. She also wants to know the total cost of bonbons in each box.

Display the total cost of bonbons in each box

Use a ReportWizard to make a report that shows the information Lillian wants.

Cost of Boxes
18-Dec-92

Box Name	Bonbon Name	Cost of Bonbons
All Seasons		
	Bittersweet Blueberry	$0.50
	Bittersweet Raspberry	$0.50
	Bittersweet Strawberry	$0.46
	Sweet Blueberry	$0.50
	Sweet Raspberry	$0.52
	Sweet Strawberry	$0.40
		$2.88
Alpine Collection		
	Bittersweet Blueberry	$1.00
	Bittersweet Strawberry	$1.15
	Sweet Blueberry	$1.00

1   Create a new report using all the fields in the Bonbons by Box query. Use the Groups/Totals ReportWizard.

2   Group by box name and use Normal grouping.

3 Sort by bonbon name.

4 Use any type of look for your report.

5 Give your report the title Cost of Boxes.

6 Save the report, and name it Cost of Boxes.

Add a text box that describes the group totals

Make it easier for Lillian to skim this report by making these changes to the Box Name footer.

Cost of Boxes 18-Dec-92		
Box Name	**Bonbon Name**	**Cost of Bonbons**
All Seasons		
	Bittersweet Blueberry	$0.50
	Bittersweet Raspberry	$0.50
	Bittersweet Strawberry	$0.46
	Sweet Blueberry	$0.50
	Sweet Raspberry	$0.52
	Sweet Strawberry	$0.40
	Total Cost for All Seasons	**$2.88**
	Add this text box and make the text bold.	*Add this line.*

Hint   In the text box, use this expression: **="Total Cost for " & [Box Name]**. Then widen the text box, and make the text bold.

Lesson Summary

To	Do this	Button
Create a grouped report	Click the Report button, and then choose the New button. Select a table or query, and then click the ReportWizards button. Select the Groups/Totals ReportWizard, and answer the questions in the dialog boxes.	Report

To	Do this	Button
Add a percentage of total to your report	Add a text box in the group header or footer. In the text box, add the expression that calculates the percentage of total (the group total divided by the grand total).	
Change the sort order in a report	Click the Sorting and Grouping button on the toolbar. In the Field/Expression column, select the field for which you want to change the sort order. Then select Ascending or Descending in the Sort Order cell for this field.	

For more information on	See
Creating reports	Chapter 17, "Report Basics," and Chapter 18, "Designing Reports," in the *Microsoft Access User's Guide*.
Creating grouped reports	Chapter 19, "Sorting and Grouping Data," in the *Microsoft Access User's Guide*.
Calculating percentages on a report	Chapter 20, "Using Expressions in Reports," in the *Microsoft Access User's Guide*

Preview of the Next Lesson

In the next lesson, you'll learn how to convert an existing grouped report into a summary report.

Summarizing Data

Sometimes all you care about is the big picture, and you'd like to sweep the distracting details out of the way. You may find some of your reports too detailed, and you'd like to simplify them to focus on summary data only. For example, you might want a report that shows only the sum of sales for each month, rather than all the details on each sale. Or you might want a report that shows the total cost for each of your products, but not the cost of each ingredient.

You can use Microsoft Access to change a report so that it shows summary data only. In this lesson, you'll learn how to convert a grouped report into a summary report, and you'll learn how to change the width of the report so it's narrower.

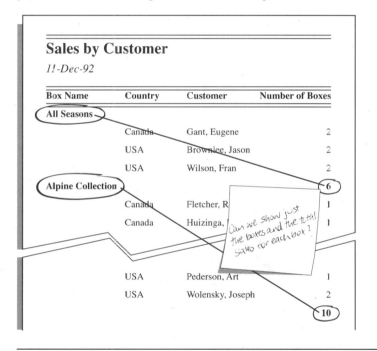

You will learn how to:

- Create a summary report.
- Change the width of a report.

Estimated lesson time: 20 minutes

What Is a Summary Report?

A *summary report* shows only summary values, such as the total number of boxes or the average value of orders.

Weekly Sales	
11-Dec-92	
Box Name	**Number of Boxes**
All Seasons	6
Alpine Collection	10
Autumn Collection	9
Bittersweets	23
Cherry Classics	11
Fudge Mocha Fantasy	17
Heavenly Hazelnuts	8
International	11
Island Collection	9
Lover's Hearts	30
Marzipan Marvels	4
Northwind Collection	30
Grand Total :	236

This report shows only total values for each box.

You can create a summary report in two ways: You can create a query that calculates the summary values you want and then create a report based on that query; or, if you have an existing report that contains the values you want along with excess detail, you can modify the report and change it to a summary report. Sometimes it's faster to make changes to an existing report — you don't have to create a new query, and you can maintain the same general look of the first report.

If you compare the report on this page with the report on the previous page, you'll see that the summary report is greatly simplified. In this lesson, you'll learn how to convert an existing report to a summary report.

Start the lesson

▶ Start Microsoft Access. If the Microsoft Access window doesn't fill your screen, maximize the window. Then open the Sweet database.

Creating a Summary Report

As manager of the bonbon factory, you need to keep in close touch with the demand for Sweet Lil's boxes of bonbons. This information helps you decide which boxes and how many boxes to manufacture throughout the year.

To examine this information, you want to print a report at the end of every week. The report will show the names and numbers of boxes sold during the past week. You'll use the Sales by Customer report and eliminate the extra detail that you don't need.

You could start over and create a new report. But since the Sales by Customer report is close to what you want, you'll simply modify the existing report so that it displays summary information only.

Rename the report

You'll start by changing the report title to Weekly Sales.

1   Open the Sales by Customer report in Design view.

2   In the report header, select the Sales by Customer label, click in the label, and replace the text with **Weekly Sales**

Report Header	
Weekly Sales ————	*Change the title of the report.*
=Now()	
Page Header	

Tip   To get a better view of the report, you may want to move the design tools, such as the toolbox, out of the way. Also, you may want to make the Report window larger so you can see more of the report on the screen.

---

3   From the File menu, choose Save As. Name the report Weekly Sales.

4   Preview the report (choose the Print Preview button on the toolbar).

Print Preview button

Delete the text boxes from the detail section

The detail section of the report contains the information you *don't* need — information on individual customers. All you want is the total information.

Weekly Sales

11-Dec-92

Box Name	Country	Customer	Number of Boxes
All Seasons			
	Canada	Gant, Eugene	2
	USA	Brownlee, Jason	2
	USA	Wilson, Fran	2
			6

You don't need any of this information.

So the next step is to delete the Country, Customer, and Number of Boxes text boxes in the detail section.

Tip   Before you make any changes to a report, always check first to make sure that you're making the change in the correct section.

Cancel

Cancel button

1   Switch to Design view (choose the Cancel button).

2   Select all three text boxes in the detail section. (Press and hold down the SHIFT key while you click each text box.)

Detail			
0	Country	Customer	Numbe

Box Name Footer

Press the SHIFT key, and then click these text boxes.

3   Press the DEL key.

4   Preview the report.

5   Save your changes (from the File menu, choose Save.)

Weekly Sales
11-Dec-92

Box Name	Country	Customer	Number of Boxes
All Seasons			

You don't need these labels anymore.   *You'll move this total value up.*

6

The report has the data you want, but it contains a couple of labels that you don't need anymore. And the spacing still needs some work—the Number of Boxes value should appear on the same line as the box name.

Note   The report you're working with is based on the Sales by Customer query. This query returns information for one week only (6-Dec-92 through 12-Dec-92). If you were to use this report in the future, you'd probably change the Sales by Customer query to a parameter query. Then, whenever you ran the report, you could specify which week's data you were interested in. For information on parameter queries, see Lesson 11, "Creating User-Friendly Queries."

Delete the extra labels

Now you'll delete the Country and Customer labels. After you've deleted them, the page header will contain only the labels for the information you're interested in: the box name and the number of boxes.

1 Switch to Design view.

2 In the page header section, select the Country and Customer labels, and press DEL.

Page Header				
Box Name	Country	Customer		Number of Boxes
Box Name Header				

Delete these fields from the page header section.

Move the total to the Box Name header

Now you'll move the text box containing the expression that calculates the total number of boxes sold from the Box Name footer to the Box Name header, so that the total number of boxes sold is displayed on the same line as the box name. As long as this text box is placed in the Box Name header or the Box Name footer, it will calculate the total number of boxes for the Box Name group. (If you placed the text box by mistake in the report footer, though, it would calculate the total number of boxes for the entire report.)

1 Select the text box in the Box Name footer, and drag it to the Box Name header.

Drag from here...   *...to here.*

Box Name Header	
Box Name	
Detail	
Box Name Footer	
	=Sum([Numbe]
Page Footer	

2 Preview the report.

Weekly Sales
11-Dec-92

Box Name	Number of Boxes
All Seasons	6
Alpine Collection	10

Hide the detail and group footer sections

The report contains exactly the information you want. But there's too much space between each row on the report. That's because the report is still displaying space for the detail section and the group footer section, even though you've removed all the text boxes from these two sections.

1 Switch to Design view.

2 Click the lower border of the Box Name footer, and then drag the border upward to close the section.

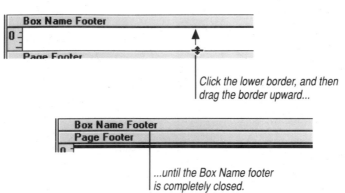

Click the lower border, and then drag the border upward...

...until the Box Name footer is completely closed.

3 Use the same method to close the detail section.

The detail section and Box Name footer section are both closed.

4 Preview the report, and then save your changes.

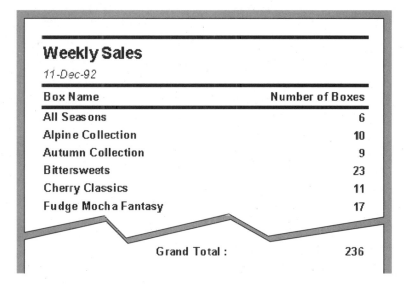

You're almost there — but you'd like to make the report still more compact. Now that you've deleted all the controls in the middle of the report, the Box Name column and the Number of Boxes column are too far apart.

Changing the Width of a Report

After you've created a report, you may find that there's too much (or too little) space between the columns of data, making the report difficult to read. Or you may want to make a report wider or narrower just to fit better on the paper you're using.

In this case, you want to close the big gap in the middle of your Weekly Sales report. You'll make this report much narrower so that it's about 4 in. (or 10 cm) wide.

Find the controls that you'll have to move

▶ Switch to Design view to see which controls are placed against the right edge of the report. You'll either move or shorten these controls, which include lines, labels, and text boxes.

Controls that you'll move or shorten

Shorten the lines

You'll shorten all four lines so that they're only 4 in. (or 10 cm) wide. The trick to shortening the lines is to keep them perfectly straight. You can shorten a line by dragging its right edge, but sometimes this results in a crooked line. The way to make sure a line stays straight is to select the line and then set its Width property.

1 Select the line in the report header.

2 In the property sheet, set the Width property to 4 in (or 10 cm). (If the property sheet isn't displayed, choose Properties from the View menu.)

Selected line

Set the Width property to 4 in (or 10 cm).

3 Select the next line, and set the Width property. Continue with the other lines on the report, making them all 4 in. (or 10 cm) long.

Modify the other controls

You'll shorten the long label in the report header and then move the other controls to the left. Use the ruler at the top of your screen to help you make the changes.

1 Shorten the Weekly Sales label in the report header until its right edge is also at 4 in. (or 10 cm). (Select the label, and then drag its corner to the left.)

2 Before you can move the text box in the report footer to the left, you'll have to shorten the Grand Total label. Select the Grand Total label, and then drag its corner to the left to shorten it.

> Report Footer
> 0 ┆ Grand Total : =Sum([Number of I

3 Click outside the Grand Total label so that it's no longer selected.

4 Select all four controls located at the right edge of the report, and drag them until their right edges are at 4 in. (or 10 cm). Use the ruler at the top of the report to position them.

Tip To select all four controls, hold down the SHIFT key and click each control. Move the pointer over the edge of one of the text boxes until it changes to the move handle icon. Then drag the controls as a group.

> Report Header
> Weekly Sales
> =Now()
> Page Header
> Box Name   Number of Boxes
> Box Name Header
> Box Name   =Sum([Numbe
> Detail
> Box Name Footer
> Page Footer
>   =Page
> Report Footer
> Grand Total :   =Sum([Number of I

Drag the controls to the left until their right edges are at 4 in. (or 10 cm).

5 Click the right edge of the report, and then drag the border to the left until the report is 4 in. (or 10 cm) wide.

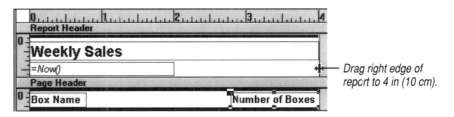

> Report Header
> Weekly Sales
> =Now()
> Page Header
> Box Name   Number of Boxes

Drag right edge of report to 4 in (10 cm).

6   Preview the report.

Weekly Sales
11-Dec-92

Box Name	Number of Boxes
All Seasons	6
Alpine Collection	10
Autumn Collection	9
Bittersweets	23
Cherry Classics	11
Fudge Mocha Fantasy	17
Heavenly Hazelnuts	8
International	11
Island Collection	9

---

7   Save your changes, and then close the report.

One Step Further

Convert the Bonbons by Box report in the Sweet database to a summary report.

Remember to:

To find out how to add a picture to a report, see Lesson 14, "Using Pictures and Other Objects."

1. Delete the text boxes from the detail section.

2. Delete the Bonbon Name label from the page header.

3. Move the total text box from the Box Name footer to the Box Name header.

4. Close the detail section and the Box Name footer section.

5. If you have time, make the report narrower like the one shown below.

Convert this report...

Bonbons by Box

15-Dec-92

Box Name	Bonbon Name	Cost of Bonbons
All Seasons		
	Bittersweet Blueberry	$0.50
	Bittersweet Raspberry	$0.50
	Bittersweet Strawberry	$0.46
	Sweet Blueberry	$0.50
	Sweet Raspberry	$0.52
	Sweet Strawberry	$0.40
		$2.88

...to this summary report.

Bonbons by Box

15-Dec-92

Box Name	Cost of Bonbons
All Seasons	**$2.88**
Alpine Collection	**$4.15**
Autumn Collection	**$8.58**
Bittersweets	**$5.54**

Lesson Summary

To	Do this
Convert an existing report to a summary report	Delete the text boxes and other controls in the detail section, and close the detail section. Move the total text box or boxes from the group footer to the group header, and close the group footer section.
Close a section	Click the lower border of the section, and drag it upward.
Change the length of a horizontal line on a report	Select the line, and then open the property sheet. Set the Width property to the new line length.

To	Do this
Change the width of a report	Click the right border of the report, and drag it to the left or right. If you are making the report narrower, you may have to first move some controls to the left.

For more information on	See
Creating summary reports	Chapter 19, "Sorting and Grouping Data," in the *Microsoft Access User's Guide*.

Preview of the Next Lesson

In the next lesson, you'll learn how to customize your work environment so you can open forms or print reports at the click of a button.

7 Automating with Macros

Customizing Your Work Environment

By using a database, you gain a great deal of control over your data. But even after you've designed a database that works well for you, you may find yourself spending a lot of time performing the same database tasks over and over. How can you adapt the database so that it can help simplify your work?

Using macros, you can automate those repetitive tasks so that they are completed efficiently and accurately. In this lesson, you'll learn how to create a form that opens several other forms in the Sweet database. And you'll make the form more attractive by adding a picture to a command button.

You will learn how to:

- Create a Control Center form.
- Create a macro to open a form.
- Create a macro to close a form.
- Attach a macro to a command button.
- Add a picture to a command button.

Estimated lesson time: 40 minutes

What Is a Macro?

If you perform certain tasks in Microsoft Access repeatedly, you can probably write a macro to do them for you. A *macro* is a set of actions that correspond to tasks you could do using Microsoft Access. Each *action* in a macro does a task such as opening a form or a report.

For example, say you have to print four reports at the end of every month. Instead of selecting the first report and printing it, selecting the next report and printing it, and so on, you could write a macro that would print all the reports at one click of a button. Or you could write a macro that would open or close a form at the click of a button.

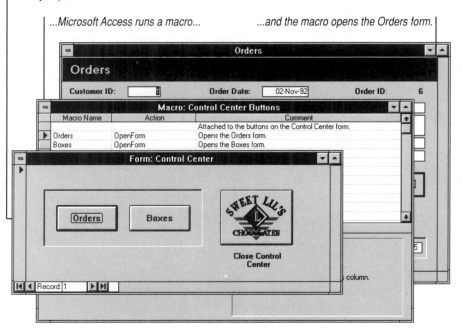

When you press the Orders button...

...Microsoft Access runs a macro...   ...and the macro opens the Orders form.

In this lesson, you'll learn how to create a macro that you run by pressing a button on a form. To create this macro and make it work, you'll complete three steps:

1 You'll create a form that contains several buttons.

2 You'll create the macros that will run when you press the buttons.

3 You'll attach the macros to the buttons on the form.

Start the lesson

▶ Start Microsoft Access. If the Microsoft Access window doesn't fill your screen, maximize the window. Then open the Sweet database.

Creating the Control Center Form

You take orders on the phone all day for Sweet Lil's products. You use only two forms, but you use them constantly — the Orders form for entering orders and the Boxes form for answering customers' questions about your products.

To streamline your job, you'll create a Control Center form. When you come to work in the morning, you'll open this form and then use it to open the forms you work with all day long. The Control Center form is your own custom workspace.

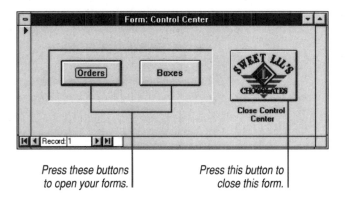

Press these buttons | Press this button to
to open your forms. | close this form.

The Control Center form doesn't display data from any tables; it just contains buttons to automate your work. So you won't base this form on a table or query when you create it. You'll build this form from the ground up rather than relying on a FormWizard. You'll start with a blank form and place all the controls on the form yourself.

Note You'll start off by designing your own custom form. If you haven't already done so, read Lesson 13, "Using Controls to Show Text and Data," before continuing with this lesson.

Create a blank form

Form button

1 In the Database window, click the Form button, and then choose the New button.

2   In the New Form dialog box, choose Blank Form.

Microsoft Access opens a form that doesn't include any controls or background colors.

Select a background color for the form

All of Sweet Lil's forms have a light gray background. You want your form to have the same look. Open the Boxes form if you want to see an example.

1   Select the detail section of the new form. (Notice that this form has only one section, the detail section.)

Form: Form1

To select the detail section, click here.

Tip   The grid may not be displayed on your form. If you want to display the grid, choose Grid from the View menu.

Palette button

2   Click the Palette button on the toolbar.

3   In the Palette, select light gray as the fill color. (In the Fill row of colors, light gray is the third color from the left.)

Click here.

Appearance: ○ **Normal**   ○ **Raised**   ◉ **Sunken**
Text:
Fill:
Border: Clear:⊠
Width:

Microsoft Access changes the form background to light gray.

Add a rectangle to group the command buttons

The form you design will have two buttons you'll use to open other forms. To group these two buttons together, you'll create a rectangle and give it a sunken appearance. After that, you'll add the buttons on top of the rectangle.

1 Drag the bottom edge of the form down to make more room for the rectangle. (If necessary, drag the design tools, such as the toolbox or the property sheet, out of the way.)

Move the pointer over the border, and then drag the border down.

Rectangle tool

2 In the toolbox, click the rectangle tool. (If the toolbox isn't visible, choose Toolbox from the View menu.)

3 On the form, click where you want the upper-left corner of the rectangle. Continue to hold the mouse button down, and drag the pointer until the rectangle is roughly the size shown in the following illustration. Then release the mouse button.

4 In the Palette, select the Clear check box for the fill color.

Select Clear.

Because you've chosen a clear fill color, the rectangle will be transparent, and the background color of the form will show through.

Tip   You could select light gray for the fill color rather than choosing clear. But if you choose a clear fill color, you'll be able to see through to the grid on the form's background. The grid will help you align the buttons more easily.

---

5   With the rectangle still selected, select Sunken at the top of the Palette.

The rectangle now looks sunken.

Add the Orders command button

Now you're ready to add command buttons that will open Orders and Boxes, your two most frequently used forms. *Command buttons* are controls on forms. Unlike most other controls, command buttons don't display data, and you don't enter data them. Instead, when you press a command button, it performs an action.

First, you'll add the Orders command button to your form.

Command button tool

1   Click the command button tool in the toolbox.

2   Click in the upper-left corner of the rectangle. Continue to hold the mouse button down, and drag the pointer until the button looks like the one in the following illustration. Then release the mouse button.

Microsoft Access adds a command button to your form. The default caption on the button is Button1.

3   With the command button selected, move the pointer inside the button so that the pointer turns into an I-beam. Then double-click to select the caption Button1.

Button1 ———— *Double-click to select the caption on the command button.*

4   Type **Orders** to give the button a new caption, and then press the ENTER key.

5   To match the other forms in the Sweet database, make the text in the button dark blue. (In the Palette, select a text color of dark blue.)

Add the Boxes command button

Now you'll add the command button that will open the Boxes form. Since the Orders command button is the size you want, you'll copy and paste this button.

1 With the Orders button selected, press CTRL+C to copy the command button.

2 Press CTRL+V to paste the copy of the command button.

Microsoft Access adds a second command button with the caption Orders. This command button overlaps the original command button.

3 Change the caption of the new command button to **Boxes** (with the new command button selected, double-click the button to select the caption, type **Boxes** and then press ENTER).

4 Move the buttons so that they're centered in the rectangle.

Center the command buttons in the rectangle.

Tip If you can't select a command button, it's probably because the rectangle itself is selected. To cancel the selection of the rectangle, click anywhere on the form outside the rectangle.

Add the Close command button

You're also going to add a button to close the form.

1 Add a third command button to the right of the rectangle, dragging until the button is the size shown below. (You may have to enlarge the detail section.)

Add the third button.

2 Change the caption on the command button to **Close** and then press ENTER.

3 Make the text on the button dark blue.

4   Save the form, and name it Control Center.

5   Close the form.

Creating Macros to Open Forms

The Control Center form looks great, but it's not ready to use yet. If you switch to Form view and press a button, nothing happens! That's because you haven't yet created the macros that tell Microsoft Access what action to perform when you click each button.

Now you'll create a macro for each button. Although you'll create several macros, you'll group them together into one *macro group* called Control Center Buttons. It's a good idea to group related macros together into one macro group. Later, when you want to make changes to these related macros, they'll all be in one place, and it will be easier to see how they work.

A macro consists of a list of *actions*. Microsoft Access provides a predefined set of actions for you to use in your macros. For example, the OpenForm action opens a form, and the Hourglass action displays the hourglass. Most actions let you provide *arguments* to specify exactly how you want the actions carried out.

Create a new macro

First you'll create a new macro containing one action that opens the Orders form.

1   In the Database window, click the Macro button, and then choose the New button.

Microsoft Access opens the Macro window.

Macro button

2   From the Window menu, choose Tile.

Macro: Macro1			Database: SWEET		
Action	Comment		**New** **Run** **Design**		
			Macros		
			Table Show Box Sales		
			Query		

Tip   If you have other windows open in addition to the Macro window and the Database window, close them. Then choose Tile from the Window menu.

3   In the Database window, click the Form button to display the list of forms.

4   Drag the Orders form from the Database window to the first Action cell in the Macro window.

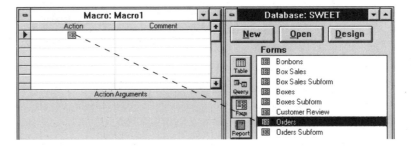

Drag the Orders icon to the first Action cell.

Microsoft Access adds
the OpenForm action...

...and sets the Form Name
argument to Orders.

Notice that Microsoft Access set the Form Name argument to Orders, the name of the form you dragged to the macro. When you run the macro, Microsoft Access will know which action to take and which object the action applies to.

Add a comment

You can include a comment that explains the purpose of an action. Maybe you'll want to modify this macro at a later date. Your job will be a lot easier if you add comments when you create the macro.

1 In the Comment column, type **Open the Orders form.**

Action	Comment
▶ OpenForm	Open the Orders form.

2 Save the macro, and name it Control Center Buttons.

Give the action a name

You've added an OpenForm action to your macro. Later on, you'll need a specific name for this action so you can attach it to the Orders button on the Control Center form. That way, Microsoft Access will know which action to take when you choose the Orders button.

Once you give an action a name, the action becomes a macro in itself. You'll name this macro Orders. Once it's named, Orders becomes the first macro in the Control Center Buttons macro group.

Macro Names button

1 Click the Macro Names button on the toolbar.

Microsoft Access displays a column where you can type a name.

2 In the Macro Name column, type **Orders**

3 Save your changes.

Macro: Control Center Buttons		
Macro Name	Action	Comment
Orders	OpenForm	Open the

Add a macro name.

Run the macro

When you run a macro, Microsoft Access performs the action in the macro. You'll add more actions later, but go ahead and run this one to make sure it opens the Orders form.

Run button

1 Click the Run button on the toolbar.

Microsoft Access runs the macro and opens the Orders form.

2 Close the Orders form.

Add an OpenForm action that opens the Boxes form

Now you'll add another action to the macro group you just created. This action will open the Boxes form, and you'll name the action Boxes.

1 Drag the Boxes form from the Database window to the second Action cell in the Macro window.

Microsoft Access adds the OpenForm action to your macro group and sets the action's Form Name argument to Boxes.

2 In the second row of the Macro Name column, type **Boxes**

Macro Name	Action	Comment
Orders	OpenForm	Open the
Boxes	OpenForm	

This OpenForm action...

Action Arguments	
Form Name	Boxes
View	Form
Filter Name	
Where Condition	
Data Mode	Edit
Window Mode	Normal

...opens the Boxes form.

3   In the Comment column, type **Open the Boxes form.**

4   Since you no longer need to use the Database window, choose Cascade from the Window menu.

5   Save your changes.

Creating a Macro to Close a Form

You still need a macro to close the Control Center form. To create this macro, you won't drag and drop a form. Instead, you'll select an action from a list.

Create another macro in the Control Center Buttons macro group

1   In the third row of the Macro Name column, type **Close**

This macro will close the Control Center form.

2   Click the Action cell for this new macro, and then click the arrow.

A list of available actions appears.

3   Select the Close action.

	Macro: Control Center Buttons	
Macro Name	Action	Comment
Orders	OpenForm	Open the Orders form.
Boxes	OpenForm	Open the Boxes form.
▶ Close		
	AddMenu	
	ApplyFilter	
	Beep	rguments
	CancelEvent	
	Close	
	CopyObject	
	DoMenuItem	
	Echo	Enter an action in this column.

Select the Close action.

4   In the Comment column, type **Close the Control Center form.**

Enter arguments for the Close action

In the lower portion of the Macro window, you'll specify arguments for the Close action. The arguments tell Microsoft Access the type of object you want to close and the name of the object.

1   In the lower portion of the Macro window, click the Object Type argument box. Select Form from the list.

2 Click the Object Name argument box. Select Control Center from the list.

	Action Arguments
Object Type	Form
Object Name	Control Center

Enter a comment that describes the macro group

Now you'll add a comment that describes the entire Control Center Buttons macro group. It may seem pretty obvious to you now what this macro group does. But months from now, if you decide to make a change, you'll be glad that you added a comment.

1 Click in the first row in the Macro window.

2 From the Edit menu, choose Insert Row.

Microsoft Access adds a new row at the top of the Macro window.

3 In the Comment column of the new row, type this comment: **Attached to the buttons on the Control Center form**.

Add a comment that describes the macro group.

Macro: Control Center Buttons		
Macro Name	Action	Comment
		Attached to the buttons on the Control Center form.
Orders	OpenForm	Opens the Orders form.
Boxes	OpenForm	Opens the Boxes form.
Close	Close	Closes the Control Center form.

4 Save and then close the macro.

Attaching Macros to Command Buttons

You've created your form. You've created the macros that will run when you press the buttons on the form. All that remains is to attach the macros to the command buttons on the form so that Microsoft Access knows what to do when you press a button.

To attach a macro to a button, you set the OnPush property of the button to the name of the macro. Remember that you've created a macro group called Control Center Buttons. It contains the three macros you'll attach to the buttons on your form. To refer to these macros, you use the name of the macro group followed by a period and the name of the macro. So, for example, the macro that opens the Orders form is named Control Center Buttons.Orders.

Attach the Orders macro to the Orders command button

1 Open the Control Center form in Design view.

2 Select the Orders command button.

*Properties
button*

3 If the property sheet isn't displayed, click the Properties button on the toolbar.

4 In the property sheet, click the OnPush property.

5 From the list, select Control Center Buttons.

Detail		
0		
		Command Button
	Control Name	Button1
	Caption	Orders
	Picture	(none)
Orders	Transparent	No
	Auto Repeat	No
1	Status Bar Text . .	
	On Push	
	On Enter	Control Center Buttons
	On Exit	Show Box Sales
	On Dbl Click	

Click Control Center Buttons.

6 Drag the right edge of the property sheet to widen it.

7 In the OnPush property box, place the insertion point directly after the word Buttons, and type **.Orders**

On Push	Control Center Buttons.Orders

Microsoft Access now knows which macro to run when you push this button — the Orders macro in the Control Center Buttons macro group.

Attach the Boxes macro to the Boxes command button

1 Select the Boxes command button. (You may need to move the property sheet so you can select the button.)

2 Set the OnPush property for the Boxes command button to **Control Center Buttons.Boxes**

Attach the Close macro to the Close command button

1 Select the Close command button.

2 Set the OnPush property for the Close command button to **Control Center Buttons.Close**

3 Save the form.

Try it out

Now you're ready to give the whole form a test run.

1   Switch to Form view.

Notice that the Orders button has a darker outline than the others. This is the default button when you first open the Control Center form. If you press ENTER while this button still has the focus, you'll open the Orders form.

2   From the Window menu, choose Size To Fit Form.

The extra space around the form disappears.

Note   When you open the Control Center form in Form view from the Database window, it will automatically be the right size. But when you open the form in Design view and then switch to Form view, it may be sized incorrectly. You can choose Size To Fit Form from the Window menu to size the form correctly.

---

3   Choose the Orders button.

Microsoft Access opens the Orders form.

4   Close the Orders form, and choose the Boxes button.

Microsoft Access opens the Boxes form.

5   Close the Boxes form, and choose the Close button.

Microsoft Access closes the Control Center form.

Adding a Picture to a Command Button

You'd like to make the Control Center form more attractive by adding Sweet Lil's logo to the Close button. This logo is in a file named LOGO.BMP in your \ACCESS\PRACTICE directory.

To add the logo, you set the Picture property for the Close button to the path and file name of the file containing the logo.

Add the logo

1   Open the Control Center form in Design view.

2   Select the Close command button.

3   Set the Picture property for the Close command button to
c:\access\practice\logo.bmp

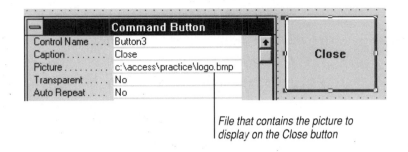

File that contains the picture to
display on the Close button

Note   If you have installed your files on another drive or directory, type the
appropriate path instead.

---

4   Press ENTER.

Logo displayed
on Close button

5   If the logo doesn't fit on your button, choose Size To Fit from the Layout menu.

Add a label

Now that the button contains a picture, you'd like to add a label that tells you what
this button does.

Label tool

1   In the toolbox, choose the label tool.

2   Click below the command button on the form to add a label.

3   Type **Close Control Center** and then press ENTER.

You'll adjust the label's appearance next.

Improve the appearance of the label

Bold button

Center button

1 Open the Palette if it's not already displayed.

2 Make the text dark blue, and select the Clear check box for the fill color.

This gives the label the same appearance as the other buttons on Sweet Lil's forms.

3 Click the Bold button on the toolbar to make the text bold.

4 Click the Center button on the toolbar to center the text in the label.

5 Change the size and shape of the label until it looks something like this.

> Close Control
> Center

6 Preview the form to see how it looks.

7 Save and close the form.

One Step Further

With the Control Center form, you've customized the Sweet database to help you take orders more efficiently. Now you'll make your job even easier by creating a macro that opens the Control Center form automatically whenever you open the Sweet database. To do this, you create a macro with an OpenForm action and name the macro AutoExec.

Create a new macro and add an OpenForm Action

1 Create a new macro.

2 Drag the Control Center form from the Database window to the first Action cell in the Macro window.

Hint Choose Tile from the Window menu if you want to display the Database window and the Macro window side by side.

Microsoft Access adds an OpenForm action and sets the Form Name argument to Control Center.

3 Add a comment that describes what the OpenForm action does. Then add a comment in the first line that describes the purpose of the macro. A good comment for the macro might be " Runs when you first open the database; opens the Control Center form."

4 Save the macro, and name it AutoExec.

Try it out

▶ Close and then reopen the Sweet database.

Microsoft Access opens the Control Center form, from which you can conveniently open the Orders and Boxes forms.

Tip   If you don't want to run the AutoExec macro when you open the database, hold down the SHIFT key when you open it.

Lesson Summary

To	Do this	Button
Create a new macro	In the Database window, click the Macro button, and then choose the New button.	
Create an OpenForm action that opens an existing form in your database	Click the Form button in the Database window. Then drag the form you want to open from the list to the first empty Action cell in the Macro window.	
Run a macro (from the Macro window)	Click the Run button on the toolbar.	
Create a macro group	In the Macro window, choose the Macro Names button. Then in the Macro Name column, type macro names for each macro in the group.	
Add an action to a macro without dragging an object from the Database window	Click the first empty Action cell. Select the action you want from the list.	
Enter arguments for an action	Select the action in the Macro window. Enter the arguments for that action in the lower part of the window by typing a value or selecting from a list.	
Attach a macro to a command button	Set the OnPush property of the command button to the name of the macro that performs the desired action.	
Create a macro that runs automatically when you open a database	Create the macro, and name it AutoExec.	
Add a picture to a command button	Set the Picture property of the command button to the path and file name of the file containing the picture.	

For more information on	See
Creating macros	Chapter 10, "Customizing and Automating," in *Microsoft Access Getting Started.*
	Chapter 21, "Macro Basics," Chapter 22, "Using Macros with Forms," and Chapter 24, "Using Macros for Application Design," in the *Microsoft Access User's Guide.*

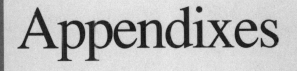

Appendixes

Installing and Setting Up Your Printer

This appendix provides information about installing and selecting a printer for use with Microsoft Access. For more information about printing in Windows, see your Windows documentation.

Installing a New Printer

There are two ways to install a new printer after you've installed Microsoft Access.

Control Panel   The easiest way is to use Control Panel, a utility application that comes with Windows.

Setup program   The Setup program you use to install Windows includes printer and plotter setup. You can rerun the Windows Setup program and specify new printers.

Using Control Panel is the most convenient way to install a new printer because you can make the changes without leaving Microsoft Access. This appendix explains how to use Control Panel to install a new printer and connect to a printer port.

Start Control Panel

1   Open Windows Program Manager.

2   In the Main group of Program Manager, double-click the Control Panel icon.

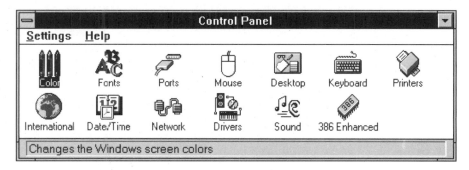

Windows displays the Control Panel window. The exact positions of the icons may vary.

Note   You can do more than install a printer with Control Panel. For example, you can choose the Mouse icon and change the double-click speed. You can also change other operating environment settings, such as the date and time, background colors, and network configuration.

Install a new printer

When you install a new printer, you specify the type of printer you plan to use and add the printer driver software for that printer.

1 In the Control Panel Window, choose the Printers icon.

```
┌────────────────────────────────────────────────────────────────┐
│ ▬           Printers                                           │
│ ┌─ Default Printer ──────────────────────┐   ┌──────────────┐  │
│   HP LaserJet Series II on LPT2:          │   │    Close     │  │
│ └────────────────────────────────────────┘   └──────────────┘  │
│ ┌─ Installed Printers: ──────────────────┐   ┌──────────────┐  │
│   HP LaserJet III on LPT1:            ↑  │   │  Connect...  │  │
│   HP LaserJet Series II on LPT2:         │   └──────────────┘  │
│                                          │   ┌──────────────┐  │
│                                          │   │   Setup...   │  │
│                                       ↓  │   └──────────────┘  │
│                                          │   ┌──────────────┐  │
│   ┌────────────────────────────┐         │   │   Remove     │  │
│   │   Set As Default Printer   │         │   └──────────────┘  │
│   └────────────────────────────┘         │   ┌──────────────┐  │
│ └────────────────────────────────────────┘   │   Add >>     │  │
│ ⊠ Use Print Manager                           └──────────────┘  │
│                                               ┌──────────────┐  │
│                                               │    Help      │  │
│                                               └──────────────┘  │
└────────────────────────────────────────────────────────────────┘
```

Windows displays the Printers dialog box.

2 To install a new printer, choose the Add button.

The Printers dialog box expands, displaying a list of printers.

3 In the List Of Printers box, select the type of printer you want to install.

4 Choose the Install button.

You will see a message asking you to insert the disk that contains the printer driver software for the printer.

5 Insert the disk, and choose the OK button.

Choose a printer port

After you've installed a printer, you specify which printer port it's attached to.

1 Open the Printers dialog box (if it's not already open) by choosing the Printers icon in the Control Panel window.

2 In the Installed Printers box, select the printer for which you want to specify a printer port.

3 Choose the Connect button.

```
┌─────────────────────────────────────────────────┐
│ ─          Connect                                │
├─────────────────────────────────────────────────┤
│ HP LaserJet Series II              ┌──────────┐  │
│                                    │    OK    │  │
│ Ports:                             └──────────┘  │
│ ┌─────────────────────────────┐    ┌──────────┐  │
│ │LPT1:   Local Port         ▲ │    │  Cancel  │  │
│ │LPT2:   Local Port           │    └──────────┘  │
│ │LPT3:   Local Port Not Present│   ┌──────────┐  │
│ │COM1:   Local Port Not Present│   │ Settings.│  │
│ │COM2:   Local Port         ▼ │    └──────────┘  │
│ └─────────────────────────────┘    ┌──────────┐  │
│ ┌─Timeouts (seconds)──────────┐    │ Network. │  │
│ │ Device Not Selected:  ┌────┐│    └──────────┘  │
│ │                       │ 15 ││    ┌──────────┐  │
│ │ Transmission Retry:   ┌────┐│    │   Help   │  │
│ │                       │ 45 ││    └──────────┘  │
│ └─────────────────────────────┘                  │
│ ☒ Fast Printing Direct to Port                   │
└─────────────────────────────────────────────────┘
```

Windows displays the Connect dialog box.

4 Select the port to which you want to connect the printer.

5 Choose the OK button to connect the printer.

6 Choose the Close button to close the Printers dialog box.

Quit Control Panel

▶ In the upper-left corner of the Control Panel window, double-click the Control-menu box.

Changing Printer Settings

For more information, search Help for "Print Setup command" and "printing: forms/reports/ datasheets."

After you've set up your printer using Windows Control Panel, you can print a table, query, form, or report. You can also change printer settings from within Microsoft Access. For example, you can select a printer that's different from the default printer, or you can change the settings for paper orientation (portrait or landscape), paper size, or paper source (such as a specific tray or manual feed).

For forms and reports, Microsoft Access saves the options you specify in the Print Setup dialog box for the form or report. For other objects, the Print Setup options apply only until you close the object. The next time you open the object, Microsoft Access uses the current default Windows printing options.

To change printer settings

1 Open the table, query, form, or report. (Or for forms and reports, you can simply select the object in the Database window.)

2 From the File menu, choose Print Setup.

Windows displays the Print Setup dialog box.

3 Select the options you want to change. For information on the dialog box options, press F1.

4 Choose the OK button.

Solutions to Database Design Problems

This appendix includes solutions to the "One Step Further" exercises in Lesson 9, "Relating Tables."

Your solutions might look a little different from these, but the primary keys and relationships between the tables should be the same.

Which employee took this order?

To relate the Employees and Orders tables, you add an Employee ID field to the Orders table, and then you match the Employee ID field in the Employees table (the primary table) to the Employee ID field in the Orders table (the related table).

Primary key fields are shown in bold.

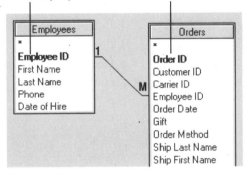

The number 1 indicates the "one" side of the relationship; the letter M indicates the "many" side.

What products appear on an order?

The Orders and Boxes tables are in a many-to-many relationship, so you must create a linking table between them. The linking table includes the primary key from the Orders table (Order ID) and the primary key from the Boxes table (Box ID). The combination of these two fields makes up the primary key for the linking table. A Quantity field in the linking table tells you how many of each box the customer ordered.

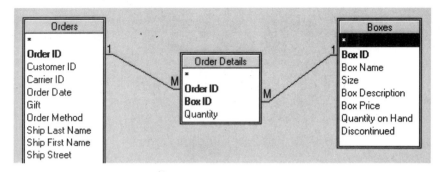

You create two relationships: a one-to-many relationship between the Orders table and the Order Details table and a one-to-many relationship between the Boxes table and the Order Details table. With these two relationships, you can find out both which boxes appear on a particular order and which orders include a particular box.

Which movie will we watch tonight?

The Movies and Actors tables have a many-to-many relationship: One movie can have more than one actor in it, and one actor can appear in more than one movie. To relate the two tables correctly, you need a linking table between them. The linking table includes the primary key of the Movies table (Movie ID) and the primary key of the Actors table (Actor ID). The combination of these two fields makes up the primary key for the linking table. You might want to include a Role field to tell you what role each actor played in each movie.

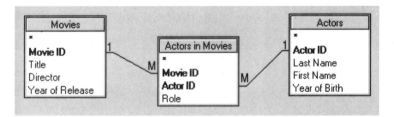

With the tables related as shown in the illustration, you can find out both which actors appear in a particular movie and which movies include a particular actor.

Using Expressions

No matter what type of work you're doing with Microsoft Access, you'll most likely need to use expressions. For example, say you want to calculate a subtotal on a report or design a query that asks for all products that cost $10. Or maybe you want to filter a form so that you see only the records for your sales region. In all these cases, you need to create an expression. This appendix provides guidelines on writing expressions and examples of common expressions.

What Are Expressions?

Expressions are formulas that calculate a value. For example, the following expression multiples the box price by 1.1 (which is the same as raising the price by 10%):

=[Box Price] * 1.1

An expression can include *identifiers*, *operators*, *functions*, *literal values*, and *constants*. The following expression contains most of these elements.

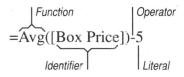

Identifiers   refer to a value in your database, such as the value of a field, control, or property. For example, [Order Date] refers to the value in the Order Date field.

Operators   specify an action (such as addition) to be performed on one or more elements of an expression. Operators include familiar arithmetic operators like +, –, *, and /, as well as other operators such as **And**, **Or**, and **Like**.

Functions   help you perform specialized calculations easily. For example, you can use the **Avg** function to find the average of values in a field or the **Sum** function to find the total of all values in a field.

Literals   are values that Microsoft Access uses exactly as you enter them. For example, the number 25 and the text value "San Francisco" are literals.

Constants   represent a value that doesn't change. For example, the constant **Null** always means a field that contains no characters or values.

Guidelines for Entering Expressions

Follow these general guidelines when you're typing an expression.

Element	How to enter	Example
Identifiers	Enclose field names and control names in brackets.	[Order Date] [Boxes].[Box Price]
	Use a . (dot) to separate the name of a table and a field in the table.	
Dates	Enclose in number signs (#).	#10-Oct-92# #10/10/92#
Text	Enclose in quotation marks.	"California" "British Columbia"
Numbers	Don't enter currency symbols or symbols for separating thousands.	8934.75 (not $8,934.75 or 8,934.75)

Note When you type an expression, Microsoft Access often inserts certain characters for you automatically after you press the ENTER key or move the focus. For example, Microsoft Access may insert brackets, number signs, or quotation marks. The examples in this appendix show how to type the entire expression rather than having Microsoft Access supply additional characters.

More on Identifiers

Identifiers refer to a value in your database, such as the value of a field, control, or property. Suppose you're designing a form, and you want to add a text box that multiplies the value in the Quantity control by the value in the Box Price control. You'd refer to these two controls by using an expression like this:

| Names of fields

=[Quantity]*[Box Price]

But what if you're designing a form and you want to create a calculated control that gets its values from a control on a different form? In this case, you'll have to use an identifier that gives a more detailed "address" for the control. Microsoft Access would need to know the type of object (a form), the name of the form, and the name of the control on the form. So your expression would contain an identifier with three parts separated by exclamation points (!):

| Type of object (form) | Name of control on form

=Forms![Boxes]![Box ID]

| Name of form

The Boxes form would have to be open for this expression to actually take the value from the Box ID control. For complete information on how to use identifiers, see Appendix C, "Expressions," in the *Microsoft Access User's Guide*. Or search Help for "expressions."

Using Expressions in Forms and Reports

You use expressions in forms and reports to get information that you cannot get directly from the tables in a database. For example, you can create expressions that calculate totals, add the values from two fields, or set a default value for a field.

Calculated Control Expression Examples

When you want a form or report to calculate a value, you can create a calculated control that gets its value from an expression. You add the control to your form or report, and then you type an expression directly in the control (frequently a text box) or in the ControlSource property box for the control.

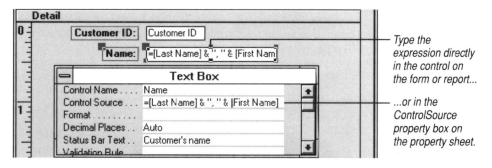

When you type expressions in calculated controls, be sure to include an equal sign (=) to the left of the expression. For example: =**[Salary]** * **2**

The following table shows some common expressions used for calculated controls.

Expression	Microsoft Access displays
=[Quantity] * [Box Price]	The product of the Quantity and Box Price field values.
=[First Name] & " " & [Last Name]	The values of the First Name and Last Name fields, separated by a space.

Expression	Microsoft Access displays
=[Bonbon Cost] * 1.5	The value in the Bonbon Cost field multiplied by 1.5 (adds 50 percent to the Bonbon Cost value).
=Date( )	Today's date.
=Page	The page number of the current page.
="Sales for " & [State/Province]	The text "Sales for " followed by the value in the State/Province field.
=[State/Province Total]/[Grand Total]	The value from the State/Province Total control divided by the value from the Grand Total control.
=Sum([Bonbon Cost])	The sum of the values in the Bonbon Cost field.
=[Orders Subform].Form![Order Subtotal]	The value from the Order Subtotal control on the Orders Subform. (You use this expression on the main form that contains the Orders Subform. To see how to use the expression, refer to the Subtotal control on the Orders form.)
=DatePart("yyyy", [Order Date])	Only the year portion of the date.

Validation Expression Examples

You can set validation rules for a field on a form to make sure that you enter the right type of data into the field. To specify a rule, you type an expression in the ValidationRule property box for the control.

Account Number:	unt Number
Expiration Date:	Expiration D Gift ☒

— *For this text box on a form...*

Text Box

Control Name	Expiration Date
Control Source . . .	Expiration Date
Format	mm/yy
Decimal Places . .	Auto
Status Bar Text . .	Credit card expiration d
Validation Rule . .	>=Date()
Validation Text . . .	Credit card has expired
Before Update	

— *...type a validation expression in the ValidationRule property box in the property sheet.*

The following table shows some typical validation expressions.

Expression	When you enter data, it must
>=Date( )	Be a date that's either today's date or some date in the future.
Between 10 And 100	Be a value between 10 and 100, inclusive.
"USA" Or "Canada"	Match USA or Canada.
Like "[A–Z]##"	Include one letter followed by two numbers (for example, B23).

Using Expressions in Queries and Filters

You use expressions in queries and filters to specify criteria. In queries, you can also use expressions to create fields that are based on a calculation. You don't have to include an equal sign to the left of a query or filter expression.

Criteria Expression Examples

When you're designing a query or filter, you use expressions as criteria. These criteria tell Microsoft Access which records you want to see. You enter criteria for a field into the Criteria cell for that field. For example, to find people with customer IDs greater than 100, you'd type the expression **>100** in the Criteria cell for the Customer ID field.

Field:	Customer ID	Last Name	First Name	
Sort:				
Show:	☒	☒	☒	
Criteria:	>100			
or:				

Type query criteria expressions in the Criteria cell in the Query window.

The following examples show some frequently used criteria expressions that you might use in a query based on the Orders table in the Sweet database.

Field	Criteria expression	Query finds orders
Customer ID	89	For the customer whose ID is 89.
Customer ID	>=60	For customers with IDs greater than or equal to 60.
Ship City	"Seattle" Or "New York"	For Seattle or New York.

Field	Criteria expression	Query finds orders
Ship City	In("Ann Arbor", "Albany")	For Ann Arbor or Albany.
Ship State/Province	Not "Ontario"	For all states and provinces except Ontario.
Ship Last Name	Like "Mc*"	For names beginning with "Mc".
Ship Last Name	Like "J*son"	For names beginning with "J" and ending in "son".
Carrier ID	Null	That have no value in the Carrier ID field.
Order Date	Between 1-Dec-92 And 15-Dec-92	Placed during the first 15 days of December 1992.
Ship Last Name	Like [Enter the first letter of the name] & "*" *(for parameter queries only)*	This expression prompts you for the first letter of the name. If you type **C**, the query returns a list of names starting with C.

Calculated Field Expression Examples

You can use expressions to create new query fields. You enter the expression into a Field cell in the QBE grid.

Type calculated field expressions in the Field cell in the Query window.

Field:	Reduced Cost: [Bonbon Cost]-0.15	Bonbon Name	
Sort:			
Show:	☒	☒	
Criteria:			
or:			

The following examples show some common calculated field expressions:

Name and expression	Microsoft Access displays
Sale Price: [Box Price] * 0.8	The values of the Box Price field multiplied by 0.8 (reduces the values by 20 percent).
Sale Price: CCur([Box Price] * 0.8)	The values of the Box Price field reduced by 20 percent and formatted as a currency value (for example, $2,345.50).
Extended Price: [Order Details].[Quantity]* [Boxes].[Box Price]	The product of the Quantity field in the Order Details table and the Box Price field in the Boxes table.

For More Information

Although this appendix shows examples of expressions in forms, reports, queries, and filters, you can also use expressions in tables, macros, and modules. You'll find extensive information on expressions in the Microsoft Access documentation.

For more information on	See
Expressions (general)	Appendix C, "Expressions," in the *Microsoft Access User's Guide*.
	Search Help for "expressions," "functions: reference," "operators: reference," "identifiers in expressions," and "constants."
Expressions in forms and reports	Chapter 11, "Using Expressions in Forms," and Chapter 20, "Using Expressions in Reports," in the *Microsoft Access User's Guide*.
	Search Help for "expressions: as property settings."
Expressions in queries and filters	Chapter 5, "Query Basics," Chapter 6, "Designing Select Queries," and Chapter 15, "Finding and Sorting Data," in the *Microsoft Access User's Guide*.
	Search Help for "expressions: in queries/filters."

Glossary

This glossary contains definitions of terms used in *Microsoft Access Step by Step*. For definitions of additional database terms, see the online glossary in Microsoft Access Help. (Click Glossary on the Help Table of Contents screen.)

AccessWizards　Microsoft Access tools that help you create forms and reports by asking you questions and then creating the form or report based on your answers.

Action　The basic building block of a macro. An action is a self-contained instruction that you can combine with other actions to automate tasks.

Action argument　Additional information needed for some actions. For example, for the OpenForm action you specify which form the action should open in the action argument box in the lower portion of the Macro window.

Action query　A query that changes or moves existing data. Append, delete, make-table, and update queries are all action queries. Refer also to "Select query."

Append query　An action query that adds the records in a query's dynaset to the end of an existing table.

Attached table　A table stored in a file outside the open database but from which Microsoft Access can access records. You can add, edit, and delete records in an attached table, but you can't modify its structure.

Bound control　A control that's tied to a specific field in the underlying table or query so that it can display data from the underlying field. Refer also to "Unbound control."

Bound object frame　An object frame that displays objects that are stored in a field in a table. In Form view and in reports you see a different object in the object frame for each record. Refer also to "Unbound object frame."

Calculated control　A control on a form or report that is tied to an expression rather than a field. A calculated control can combine text values from fields in the underlying table or query, or it can perform calculations on values from the fields. Refer also to "Calculated field."

Calculated field　A field defined in a query that displays the result of an expression rather than stored data. The value is recalculated each time a value in the expression changes. Refer also to "Calculated control."

Check box   A control that provides a graphical way to display Yes/No data. An X is displayed in the box when the check box is selected.

Clipboard   The temporary storage area used by Windows to store text, graphics, and other data. You transfer data onto the Clipboard using the Copy or Cut command and from the Clipboard using the Paste command.

Combo box   A control, similar to both a list box and a text box, in which you type a value or select a value from a list.

Command button   A control that runs a macro or calls an Access Basic function. A command button condenses related tasks into a single step. Command buttons are sometimes referred to as push buttons.

Constant   A constant represents a value that doesn't change. For example, the constant **Null** always means a field that contains no characters or values.

Control   An object on a form or report that displays data, performs an action, or decorates the form or report.

Control-menu box   The box in the upper-left corner of an application or window that contains a short horizontal line. You click the Control-menu box to open the **Control menu**, which contains commands to move, resize, and close the window. As a shortcut, you can double-click the Control-menu box to close a window or application.

Criteria   A set of limiting conditions, such as "Denmark" or > 3000. You can use criteria in creating queries or filters to show a specific set of records.

Cue Cards   An online coach that walks you through the most common Microsoft Access tasks as you work with your own data. (Choose Cue Cards from the Help menu.)

Data   The information stored in tables in a database. In Microsoft Access, data can be text, numbers, dates, and pictures or other OLE objects.

Data type   An attribute of a field that determines what kind of data it can hold.

Database   A collection of data related to a particular topic or purpose. A Microsoft Access database file can contain tables, queries, forms, reports, macros, and modules.

Database object buttons   Buttons in the Database window that you can click to display a list of objects of the same type. For example, you click the Form button to display a list of all the forms in your database.

Database objects   Tables, queries, forms, reports, macros, and modules.

Database window   The window that is displayed when you open a Microsoft Access database. It contains the Table, Query, Form, Report, Macro, and Module buttons, which you can click to display a list of all objects of that type in the database.

Datasheet view   A view that displays multiple records in a row-and-column format, enabling you to view many records at the same time. Datasheet view is available for tables, queries, and forms.

Delete query   An action query that deletes a set of records that match the criteria you specify.

Design view   A view you use to design tables, queries, forms, and reports.

Detail section   A section of a report or form used to display the records from the underlying table or query.

Drag and drop   The ability to drag an object onto another to perform an action. For example, in the Query window you can drag a field from the field list to the QBE grid to add the field to your query. To drag an object, position the pointer over the object, hold down the mouse button while you move the mouse, and then release the mouse button when the object is where you want it to be.

Dynaset   The set of records that results from running a query or applying a filter.

Embed   Inserting an object into a form or report either by creating the object using the Insert Object command or by inserting an existing OLE object using the Copy and Paste commands. Microsoft Access stores the object in your database file, and you can easily modify the object. If the object comes from another file, only the embedded object in your database is changed when you modify it. Refer also to "Link."

Expression   A formula that calculates a value. You can use expressions in forms, reports, tables, queries, and macros. For example, in queries you use expressions, such as >**100**, in criteria to specify which records Microsoft Access should retrieve.

External table   A table outside the open Microsoft Access database.

Field   A category of information, such as last name or address. On a form, a field is an area where you can enter data. A field is represented as a column in a datasheet.

Field list   A small window that lists all the fields in the underlying table or query. You use field lists in Design view of a form, report, or query and in the Filter window.

Field selector   A small box or bar at the top of a datasheet column that you can click to select an entire column.

Filter   A set of criteria you apply to records to show a subset of the records or to sort the records.

Filter grid   The grid in the lower portion of the Filter window. You use it to define the filter.

Foreign key   A field or fields in a related table that contain the values that match the values in the primary key field or fields in the primary table.

Form   A Microsoft Access database object on which you place controls for entering, displaying, and editing data in fields.

Form view   A view that displays the data one record at a time in fields on a form. Form view is convenient for entering and modifying data in a database.

FormWizard   A Microsoft Access tool that helps you create a form by asking you questions and then creating the form based on your answers.

Function   A routine that performs a specialized calculation. For example, you can use the **Avg** function to find the average of values in a field.

Group   A collection of similar records in a report.

Group footer   Text and/or graphics that appear at the bottom of a group in a report. For example, a group footer can display the total sales for the group.

Group header   Text and/or graphics that appear at the top of a group in a report. A group header typically displays the group name.

Import   A process by which Microsoft Access copies data from another source into your database.

Join   A database operation that associates data in two tables on the basis of matching values so that the combined data can be used in a query. A join works only for the query in which it was created. Refer also to "Relationship between tables."

Join line   A line between fields displayed in field lists in the Query window that indicates the matching fields in the underlying tables.

Label   A control that displays text that you use as a title for a form or report or to identify fields on a form or report.

Link   A connection between a source file and a destination file. A link inserts a copy of an object from the source file into the destination file while maintaining the connection between the two. When you make changes to a linked object, the changes are saved in the object's source file, not in your database file. Refer also to "Embed."

List box   A control that displays a list of values you can select from.

Macro   A Microsoft Access database object that contains an action or set of actions you can use to automate tasks.

Macro group   A collection of related macros that are stored together. A macro group is often referred to simply as a macro.

Make-table query   An action query that creates a new table from selected data in your tables.

Many-to-many relationship   A relationship between two tables in which one record in either the primary or related table can have many matching records in the other table. Refer also to "One-to-many relationship" and "One-to-one relationship."

Navigation buttons   The four arrows in the lower-left corner in Datasheet view, Form view, and Print Preview. Use these buttons to move to the first record (or page), the previous record (or page), the next record (or page), and the last record (or page).

Object buttons   See Database object buttons.

Object frame   A control used to add, edit, or view OLE objects. There are two types of object frames: bound object frames and unbound object frames. Refer also to the definitions for the two types of frames.

Object linking and embedding (OLE)   A protocol by which an object, such as a graph, in a source application or document can be linked to or embedded in a destination document, such as a form or report.

OLE object   Any piece of information created with an application for Windows that supports object linking and embedding (OLE). OLE objects include pictures, graphs, and sounds.

One-to-many relationship   A relationship between tables in which one record in the primary table can have many matching records in the related table. Refer also to "Many-to-many relationship" and "One-to-one relationship."

One-to-one relationship   A relationship between tables in which one record in the primary table can have only one matching record in the related table. Refer also to "Many-to-many relationship" and "One-to-many relationship."

Operator   A symbol or word, such as > and **Or**, that indicates an action to be performed on one or more elements of an expression. For example, the arithmetic operators +, -, *, and / indicate addition, subtraction, multiplication, and division.

Option group   A control used to present a set of choices. An option group can contain a set of check boxes, option buttons, or toggle buttons.

Page footer   Text and/or graphics that appear at the bottom of every page of a report. A page footer typically displays the page number.

Page header   Text and/or graphics that appear at the top of every page of a report. A page header typically displays a heading for each column of data.

Palette   A dialog box containing choices for color and other special effects that you use when designing a form or report.

Parameter query   A query that asks you to enter one or more parameters—or criteria—when you run the query. For example, a parameter query might ask you to enter a beginning and ending date or a city name.

Primary key   One or more fields whose value or values uniquely identify each record in a table.

Print Preview   A view that shows you how your form or report will look when it is printed.

Property   An attribute of a control, field, table, query, form, or report that you can set to define one of the object's characteristics (such as size, color, or position) or an aspect of its behavior (such as whether or not it is hidden).

Property sheet   A window in which you can view and modify the full set of properties for the selected object.

QBE (query by example)   A technique for designing queries. With graphical QBE, which Microsoft Access uses, you create queries visually by dragging the fields you want to include in the query from the upper portion of the Query window to the QBE grid in the lower portion of the window.

QBE grid   The grid that appears in the lower portion of the Query window. You use it to define a query.

Query   A Microsoft Access database object that represents the group of records you want to work with. You can think of a query as a request for a particular collection of data. Refer also to "Action query" and "Select query."

Record   A set of information that belongs together, such as all the information on one job application or one magazine subscription card.

Record number box   A small box that displays the current record number in the lower-left corner in Datasheet view of a table, query, or form and in Form view. To move to a specific record, type the record number in the box and press the ENTER key. There is a similar box in the lower-left corner of the Print Preview window that you use to move to a specific page in a form or report.

Record selector   A small box or bar on the left side in Datasheet view of a table, query, or form and in Form view that you can click to select an entire record.

Relationship between tables   The result of a database operation that associates data in two tables on the basis of matching values so that the combined data can be used in a new query, form, or report that contains the two tables. Refer also to "Join."

Report   A Microsoft Access database object that presents data formatted and organized according to your specifications.

Report footer   Text and/or graphics that appear once at the end of a report and typically contain summaries, such as grand totals.

Report header   Text and/or graphics that appear once at the beginning of a report and typically contain the report title, date, and company logo.

ReportWizard   A Microsoft Access tool that helps you create a report by asking you questions and then creating the report based on your answers.

Select query   A query that asks a question about the data stored in your tables and returns a dynaset in the form of a datasheet without changing the data. Refer also to "Action query."

Shortcut key   A function key, such as F5, or a key combination, such as CTRL+A, that you can press to carry out a menu command.

Sort order   The order in which records are displayed—either ascending (A-Z or 1-100) or descending (Z-A or 100-1).

Subform   A form contained within another form or report.

Table   A collection of data with the same subject or topic. A table stores data in records (rows) and fields (columns).

Tab order   The order in which the insertion point moves through fields when you tab from field to field in Form view.

Text box   A control that displays data from a field. A text box can display text, numbers, or dates, and you can use it to type in new data or change existing data.

Toolbar   A bar at the top of the Microsoft Access window containing a set of buttons that you can click to carry out common menu commands. The buttons displayed on the toolbar change depending on which window or view has the focus.

Toolbox   A box containing the set of tools you use in Design view to place controls on a form or report.

Update query   An action query that changes data in your tables according to the criteria you specify.

Unbound control   A control that is not connected to a field or expression. You can use an unbound control to display informational text, such as instructions about using your form, or graphics and pictures from other applications. Refer also to "Bound control."

Unbound object frame   A frame that displays an object that's part of the design of the form or report, such as a company logo. Refer also to "Bound object frame."

Underlying table or query   The table or query that contains the fields you want to display in a form, report, or query.

Validation   The process of checking whether entered data meets certain conditions or limitations.

Validation rule   A rule that sets limits or conditions on what can be entered in a particular field.

Value   An individual piece of data, such as a last name, an address, or an ID number.

Wildcard character   You can use wildcard characters, such as the asterisk (*) and the question mark (?) in searches using the Find and Replace commands and in query criteria and other expressions to include all records or other items that begin with specific characters or match a certain pattern. For more information on wildcard characters, search Help for "wildcard characters."

Zoom box   An expanded text box that you can use to enter expressions or text instead of using the small input area in a property sheet or in the QBE grid. You open the Zoom box by pressing SHIFT+F2.

Index